A FRACTURED MIND

A FRACTURED MIND

My Life with Multiple Personality Disorder

ROBERT B. OXNAM

NEW YORK

Library of Congress Cataloging-in-Publication Data

Oxnam, Robert B.
    A fractured mind : my life with multiple personality disorder / by Robert B. Oxnam.—1st ed.
        p. cm.
    ISBN 1-4013-0227-0
    1. Oxnam, Robert B.—Mental health. 2. Multiple personality—Patients—Biography. 3. Multiple personality—Treatment. I. Title.

RC569.5.M8O96 2005
616.85'236'0092–dc22
[B]

                                                                        2005040438

Hyperion books are available for special promotions and premiums. For details contact Michael Rentas, Assistant Director, Inventory Operations, Hyperion, 77 West 66th Street, 11th floor, New York, New York 10023, or call 212-456-0133.

FIRST EDITION

10   9   8   7   6   5   4   3   2   1

To my families
in the United States, India, and China

CONTENTS

———

ACKNOWLEDGMENTS

Although this book focuses more on my inner evolution than outer associations, I want to express my deepest gratitude to many people who shaped, guided, and even saved my often-bumpy life. All have been crucial to the story in one way or another, some knowingly, others unknowingly, but all showing a loving spirit.

For those who have read this book and made excellent suggestions, I am especially grateful. I have included others who have not read this book, even some who may not be aware of my inner story, but since they have had such a positive impact on me over the years, I hope they will not mind this expression of thanks.

Of course, none of them is responsible for the content in this book or the life it describes—that responsibility rests entirely with me (and with the other occupants of my inner self).

ACKNOWLEDGMENTS

- Jeffery Smith, remarkable psychiatrist, who has written the epilogue to this book and who has nurtured all of us inside so that we can better cope with those outside.

- Agnese Barolo, "midwife of the mind," who has brought single-minded dedication and love to a multiminded friend in need; and Gowher Rizvi, an inspiration to all who care about multicultural values and a multipolar world.

- Forrest Church, true brother-in-arms, without whom this book could not be imagined and the rest of my life would be unimaginable; and Carolyn Luce Buck for her loving heart and imaginative guidance.

- Wendy Strothman, editor and agent, and above all, a remarkable lady who nourished this book to completion and publication, with special thanks to Dan O'Connell for his gentle persistence and publicity expertise.

- Will Schwalbe and Leslie Wells—and the Hyperion family—who have treated me and my story with uncommon thoughtfulness and consummate professionalism.

- Musicians and music lovers who found the song inside us when we could not find it ourselves—Yasha Kofman, David Leisner, Ralph Jackson, Dorothea von Haeften, Arnold Steinhardt, Ted Mook, Lynne Rutkin, Aleksandra Vrebalov, Allesandro Benetello, Jenn Lee, Yo-Yo Ma, Yvonne Hicks, Nancy Garniez, Joan Farber.

- My extended Indian family, with special thanks to those who commented creatively about this book—Ben, Papa, Falgun, Shruti,

Anokhi, Antara, Mauli, Chitra, Vishrut, Reema, Anuradha, Abhijit, Julie, Preeya, Aloke, Sahil, Saptarshi, Parul, Maansi, Viren, Amita, Swati, Anaar, Josh, Nimish and Parul, and the two other "gringos," Gary and Michael.

- My adopted Chinese family—Gao Jun, Edith Wang, Chen Jing, Liu Hua, Yao Yuan.

- New York's most vibrant extended family—my brothers and sisters of the Central Park Dance Skaters Association—with special thanks to James, Tommy, Egal, Janice, Beth, Meredith, Agata, Lezley, Robin, Robert, Claude, Richard, and Eleanor.

- Blessed folks from China, Asia, Buddhist, RBF connections who have stayed by me in so many ways—Doug Murray and Peggy Blumenthal, Terry and Ellen Lautz, Jan Berris, Richard and Marty Bush, Harry and Roca Harding, Robert Kapp, John Major, David Lampton, Daisy Kwoh, Irv Drasnin and Zhao Xiaoyan, Jonathan Spence and Chin Annping, Bill McKeever, Berkley McKeever, Marty and Pamela Krasney, Yifa, Trish Rohrer, Karen Tse, Anna Shen, Cynthia and Lee Polsky, Dee Sherwood, Yuan Ming, Marty Garbus and Serena Tang, Patricia Lloyd, Colin Campbell, Stephen Heintz and Lise Stone, Steven and Barbara Rockefeller, Abby and George O'Neill, Priscilla Lewis, Michael Northrup, Bill McCalpin, Elizabeth McCormack, Russell Phillips, George Papamichael, Elaine Hutchinson, Roy Huffington, John Whitehead, Nick and Sheila Platt, Peter Stern and Margaret Johns, Phil and Mildred Talbot, Allen and Sally Wardwell, Marshall Bouton, Peter and Erika Aron, Gerald Hatherly, Gerald Curtis, Hugh Patrick, Carol Gluck, Peter Frost, Lynn Gumpert, Alan Helms, Linda Sweet, Barbara Haeger and Kelly Allen, Jane Pauley.

- Brilliant and gentle souls who helped light my path—Ralph and Audrey Mosher, Fred Mueller, Geoffrey Willoughby, Richard and Joan Barickman, Kathy Payne, Bill Sharp, Randy Nuckolls, Bill Starnes, Sevgin Eroglu, Sid and Mary Harris, Elizabeth Byerly, Dave Forquer, Fenwick Hus, Jan Hall, Michael O'Neill, Ronald Spencer, Theodore Lockwood, Helen and Leo Malonis, Richard Rosan.

- And my beloved wife—Vishakha N. Desai—whose strength, wisdom, courage, and heart have buoyed me—indeed, all of us—over these many years.

There is one other acknowledgment to loved ones whose names are intentionally absent from this list and this book. I am reminded of an old Chinese saying: "I have given you stones, and you have given me jade in return." For my failings and transgressions, I ask your forgiveness; for your love and understanding, you have my enduring gratitude. This book, above all, is written in that spirit and that hope.

A FRACTURED MIND

FRACTURED MIND, ONE HEART?

All my life, now more than sixty years, I've felt a kinship with Humpty-Dumpty, that hapless egg with human features who toppled from his perch. As a child, I often leafed through my English nursery rhyme book, staring at Humpty-Dumpty, proudly teetering on his wall, a fat little egg dressed as if going to some nineteenth-century London men's club, not a care in the world. There was only one illustration, a "before" portrait, leaving the reader to imagine Humpty-Dumpty's fate after he splatted on the busy roadway below. Perhaps the story was poking fun at pretentious English merchants. Maybe it was to remind us of the biblical verse "pride goeth before a fall."

What caught my attention was not the jolly "before" picture, but rather imagining the terrible aftermath of the fall, with a broken yolk, oozing whites, and eggshell fragments everywhere. It seemed impossible, but I wondered whether "all the King's horses and all the King's men" might find a way to put Humpty-Dumpty "back together again."

I'm quite serious. I thought long and hard about how it might be done. After all, I knew you didn't really need the yolk and the whites. I'd seen those "blown eggs" at Easter time. Wasn't there some way to glue the broken eggshell pieces together and bring Humpty back to life?

Today I understand why Humpty-Dumpty caught my attention so many years ago. Multiple personality disorder (MPD) might just be called the Humpty-Dumpty disease, but psychiatrists now call it dissociative identity disorder (DID). I didn't know that I had MPD until 1990, when a remarkable psychiatrist, Dr. Jeffery Smith, made the diagnosis. Since then, I have met with several other dissociation specialists, mainly as a talking case study of an MPD patient. But I want to emphasize that I am neither a specialist in MPD nor a psychiatrist of any kind. What I have learned about the disorder comes from my own experience, from a few books I've sampled since being diagnosed, and from the insights of Dr. Smith.

My name is Robert. I'm one of eleven personalities whom you'll meet in this book. At one time or another, all eleven personalities revealed themselves as part of one human being, officially called "Robert Bromley Oxnam." On the outside, "Robert B. Oxnam" has done reasonably well for himself as a specialist on China and Asia, a published writer of both fiction and nonfiction about China, former president of the Asia Society, professor of Asian history and contemporary affairs.

But that's not the point. I want to be very clear that this is not an autobiography of "Robert B. Oxnam." This book gives limited attention to what happened in the "outer world"—the world of professional life, family ties, of relationships, of successes and failures. We did not write it to reveal "who did what to whom." Instead, we wrote the book to convey our inner experiences with MPD—surprising discoveries, arduous therapy, and a lifetime of coping.

For those with MPD, these personal pronouns—*I* and *we*—get pretty confusing sometimes. Remember that I told you there were once eleven personalities. Now, I'm proud to say, we have whittled it down to three remaining personalities through a process of "integration." The three who remain—Robert, Bobby, and Wanda—made a joint decision to proceed with this book, and all three of us agreed to very clear rules about how it would be written.

Since I'm the most outspoken in the group, I get the job of "narrator," but don't think for a moment that either Bobby or Wanda is powerless. Quite the contrary, both are potent personalities, as you will discover. Indeed we agreed that, to portray accurately our inner divided reality, each of the eleven personalities would speak in his or her own voice.

So, in one sense, this book represents eleven autobiographies. But it also seeks to capture the constant inner monologues and dialogues that are common with multiple personality disorder. Life inside the world of MPD is filled with squabbles and power struggles, often over which individual personality will dominate on the outside. Since all of the personalities eventually communicated with Dr. Jeffery Smith, the book also reveals the enormous complexity of conducting therapy sessions with an MPD patient.

When Bobby and Wanda first pressured me to narrate this story, I was very reluctant. Imagine the daunting task of narrating the sixty-year history of eleven personalities to an outside world filled with people who have never experienced extreme dissociation. Wanda sought to persuade me with quietly passionate pleas: "None of the rest of us is a writer. It's a story that should be told. It's eleven personalities in search of one soul." But I think it was Bobby, our naughty imp, who sold me. "Robert, you're such a worrywart," Bobby said with a laugh. "It's not such a big deal. Think of it this way. You're the tour guide on the starship *Enterprise*—exploring the farthest reaches of *inner* space."

So, we—Bobby, Wanda, and Robert—all decided that this book would not focus primarily on the "outer world," which was really quite remote from many of us, but rather on our "inner world" of severe dissociation. We do not seek to destroy or protect reputations of anyone on the outside, living or dead, but rather to explore the inner MPD psyche that we have occupied.

But how can readers possibly believe this story? For a while, we all fretted about this issue. We vowed to tell the story as accurately as we could, letting each personality speak for himself or herself. We carefully corroborated our own recollections with the records and remembrances of Dr. Jeffery Smith in the long therapy process. We cross-checked our memories with several of those close enough to have witnessed our multiple personalities firsthand. Finally, we came to believe that we could do no more than that. The ultimate verdict on credibility will rest with you, the reader, after you have absorbed the story.

If this book raises more questions than it answers, then we will consider it a success, as long as the questions are more sophisticated by the end of the book than they were at the beginning. Indeed, it is our hope that you, the reader, will be asking questions throughout—not only about us and our story, but also about yourself and the society in which we all live.

Over the past seven years, I, Robert, have related shortened versions of this story, always on a confidential basis, to roughly a hundred people, either individually or in small groups. With few exceptions, the response has been riveted attention, people often nodding their heads affirmatively as I described various personalities or inner episodes.

When I have asked why they were reacting so strongly, the response was almost always the same. "I'm nodding because it's my story, too. Don't get me wrong. I don't have MPD. But I can really relate to different inner personae. Unlike people with MPD, I don't have memory blocks between those personae, but I act so differently with different people, in different places, at different times." One person elaborated: "When I have a difficult decision to make, I always convene an inner committee meeting. I allow all parts of me to air opinions; that way I know that all of me owns the decision."

I have come to think that a lot of people, possibly all people, have multiple personae. Everyone I know reports feeling differently and acting differently in different places and with different people. Many describe various "roles" or "masks," suggesting that my experience may be an extreme exaggeration of what is normal human behavior.

Probably the biggest difference between "normal multiplicity" and MPD is that most people recall what happens when they move through their array of personae. By contrast, MPD is characterized by rigid memory walls that prevent such recall until therapy begins to break down the barriers. While normal people have "multiple personae," they do not suffer from "multiple identities." In this sense, the new term, *dissociative identity disorder,* is more descriptive of what is commonly called "multiple personality disorder."

So, while acknowledging that my case is extremely rare, maybe the multiple framework is embedded in all human beings. If this unusual tale helps shed some light on what we often call "normal human behavior," then I (and we) will feel both gratified and, to be honest, somewhat vindicated.

For those who have experienced abuse and dissociation, I hope this story has some special resonance. For me, the hardest thing was not suffering severe trauma, but rather suffering a lifetime of consequences—finding out what actually happened, understanding the devastating impacts on my psyche, and, hardest of all, trying to rebuild my life based on hope, trust, and love. All of us inside reach out to all those on the outside who have confronted similar challenges in their own lives.

But we on the inside hardly have the last word on how those on the outside might find our MPD perspectives useful in their own lives. Unlike Dr. Smith, none of us is a professional psychiatrist, and all of us have been distracted from such outer issues. We have been much too busy trying to put Humpty-Dumpty back together again.

SECTION ONE

LIVING IN THE WORLD, HIDING IN A CASTLE

ONE

BOB: "I ALWAYS THOUGHT I WAS 'REAL.'"

O N A COLD, CLOUDY afternoon in March 1990, driving my black Honda through the spiderweb of highways north of New York City, I had no idea that this day would change my life forever. I was in a funk of a mood, dark and irritable, loathing the meeting with my psychiatrist that lay ahead. Seven months earlier, when I first met Dr. Jeffery Smith, I had real hope that he could cure my spiraling depression and anger. But now, after enduring extensive therapy sessions and a month in a rehabilitation clinic, I felt worse than ever. It was time to break from Dr. Smith.

But I realized that cutting off relations with Dr. Smith would be a challenge. He seemed like a genuinely concerned colleague, professional but approachable, a very hard man to dislike. Working from a simple office in an unpretentious modern building, he certainly was not the sort of shrink who siphons off patients' money to pay huge overhead. He dressed in a casually professional way—button-down shirt, plain tie, sport jacket—never offering an imposing image. And, unlike any other therapist I had encountered, he conducted our meetings in an easy but attentive style: listening carefully with sharply focused eyes, letting me talk without interrupting, then offering cogent insights rather than "psychobabble."

I resolved to come right to the point. "Hello," I said as coldly as possible, "we've got to talk."

"Yes, Bob," he said quietly, "what's on your mind?"

I shut my eyes for a moment, letting the raging frustration well up inside, then stared angrily at the psychiatrist. "Look, I've been religious about this recovery business. I go to AA meetings daily and to your sessions twice a week. I know it's good that I've stopped drinking. But every other aspect of my life feels the same as it did before. No, it's worse. I hate my life. I hate myself."

Suddenly I felt a slight warmth in my face, blinked my eyes a bit, and then stared at him.

"Bob, I'm afraid our time's up," Smith said in a matter-of-fact style.

"Time's up?" I exclaimed. "I just got here."

"No." He shook his head, glancing at his clock. "It's been fifty minutes. You don't remember anything?"

"I remember everything. I was just telling you that these sessions don't seem to be working for me."

Smith paused to choose his words very carefully. "Do you know a very angry boy named 'Tommy'?"

"No," I said in bewilderment, "except for my cousin Tommy whom I haven't seen in twenty years . . ."

"No." He stopped me short. "This Tommy's not your cousin. I spent this last fifty minutes talking with another Tommy. He's full of anger. And he's inside of you."

"You're kidding?"

"No, I'm not. Look. I want to take a little time to think over what happened today. And don't worry about this. I'll set up an emergency session with you tomorrow. We'll deal with it then."

ROBERT

This is Robert speaking. Today I'm the only personality who is strongly visible inside and outside. My own term for such an MPD role is *dominant personality*. Fifteen years ago, I rarely appeared on the outside, though I had considerable influence on the inside; back then, I was what one might call a "recessive personality." My passage from "recessive" to "dominant" is a key part of our story; be patient, you'll learn lots more about me later on.

Indeed, since you will meet all eleven personalities who once roamed about, it gets a bit complex in the first half of this book; but don't worry, you don't have to remember them all, and it gets sorted out in the last half of the book. You may be wondering—if not "Robert," who, then, was the dominant MPD personality back in the 1980s and earlier? His name was "Bob," and his dominance amounted to a long reign, from the early 1960s to the early 1990s. Since "Robert B. Oxnam" was born in 1942, you can see that "Bob" was in command from early to middle adulthood.

Although he was the dominant MPD personality for thirty years, Bob did not have a clue that he was afflicted by multiple personality disorder until 1990, the very last year of his dominance. That was the fateful moment when Bob first heard that he had an "angry boy named Tommy" inside of him. How, you might ask, can someone have MPD for half a lifetime without knowing it? And even if he didn't know it, didn't others around him spot it?

To outsiders, this is one of the most perplexing aspects of MPD. Multiple personality is an extreme disorder, and yet it can go undetected for decades, by the patient, by family and close friends, even by trained therapists. Part of the explanation is the very nature of the disorder itself: MPD thrives on secrecy because the dissociative individual is repressing a terrible inner secret. The MPD individual becomes so skilled in hiding from himself that he becomes a specialist, often unknowingly, in hiding from others. Part of the explanation is rooted in outside observers: MPD often manifests itself in other behaviors, frequently addiction and emotional outbursts, which are wrongly seen as the "real problem."

The fact of the matter is that Bob did not see himself as the dominant personality inside Robert B. Oxnam. Instead, he saw himself as a whole person. In his mind, Bob was merely a nickname for Bob Oxnam, Robert Oxnam, Dr. Robert B. Oxnam, PhD.

BOB

This feels so strange. It's the first time in more than a decade that I'm speaking directly to outsiders. I feel awkward and tongue-tied. I used to find it easy to speak in public; the bigger the audience, the better. I thrived on television work. I once hosted a TV series called *Asia: Half the Human Race.* You see, I was an Asia expert with a specialization on Chinese history and contemporary affairs. So when China news was hot, I was often a TV guest for the *Today* show with Jane Pauley, and . . .

Oh, sorry, I used to be quite a name-dropper, too. But I was making a point. I'm really nervous talking to you. I'm out of practice. And now Robert introduces me? I used to be the one who made introductions. I was making introductions before anyone ever heard of Robert.

In the old days, when I was outside and he was inside, Robert was constantly criticizing me. You can't believe what he said about me. He was really nasty. Let's see if I can remember. "Mr. Rolodex and Mr. Résumé." "Willing to suspend a mile of values to achieve an inch of ambition." Then later, in 1990, as you will discover, Robert changed his tune and began saying nice things.

Know why I'm really anxious? Want to guess who was the egg who took the "great fall"? You got it. I'm Bob, your Humpty-Dumpty. For the longest time, I saw myself as the whole egg. By the time I found out about MPD, the egg was splattered all over the sidewalk.

During much of my early life, from the 1950s to the 1970s, I was on a pretty good roll. It wasn't until the late 1970s, and even more in the 1980s, that the dark clouds moved in. Look, I'll try to give you a balanced picture, both the upside and the downside. Bottom line—though I didn't know it at the time—both sides were directly related to multiple personality disorder.

My memories of childhood are very hazy, though I always had a rather rosy view of my early years in the 1940s. During World War II, I lived with my mother and her parents in a modest, comfortable house in southern California. My memory bank contains a few shards from those very early years— an upright piano that my grandfather played, sunshine streaming into the backyard, hummingbirds darting around flowering plants, a gum tree that put sticky sap on your hands, a view of a white-capped mountain from the breakfast nook. My grandfather worked as a Con Edison lineman, and my grandmother was, among other things, an early Tupperware salesperson.

My mother always described my relationship with her parents as "warm and loving," but I remember them with a mixture of sun and clouds. Both my grandparents were into fishing, and it was fun to accompany them and watch them use home-tied lures to catch trout by the dozen. They taught me to fish, and though I was better at splashing in the stream, one time I did catch a pretty rainbow trout. I remember that my grandparents had a small house trailer in the driveway, a great place to find a safe cubbyhole when playing hide-and-seek or just hiding from adults.

But one day, my grandparents took me to a chicken farm and I remember with horror watching chickens run around with their heads cut off; my grand-mother had grabbed a chicken by the neck, killing it instantly with an expert ropelike snap of the wrist. I can't remember exactly when I started finding my grandparents' humor rather odd—my grandmother once said, "Wee, wee, wee . . . that's what the French say when they take a piss," only to be matched by my grandfather's question, "What's the longest thing on a giraffe? . . . Answer: it ain't his neck."

My father's side of the family couldn't have been more different. His fa-ther was Bishop G. Bromley Oxnam, the leader of the American Methodist Church and the first president of the World Council of Churches. Grand-daddy Oxnam was well known as a supporter of many liberal causes. He achieved national attention in the McCarthy era when he appeared before the House Un-American Activities Committee. After grueling testimony, he was cleared of any "Communist leanings," but in the minds of some American conservatives, he was always seen as the "Red bishop."

I told Granddaddy I thought it was "cool" that he was on the cover of *Time* magazine. His response stays with me—"Yes, Robbey, I suppose it's 'cool.' But you see *Time* magazine every week at your house. Who was on the cover of last week's *Time* magazine?" I couldn't remember. He just smiled knowingly. I had learned an important lesson about the fleeting importance of fame.

My dad was prominent in his own right as a university administrator—a dean at Syracuse University, vice president of Boston University, president of Pratt Institute, and finally president of Drew University. Although I often sensed he was frustrated that he didn't match fully Granddaddy's achieve-ments, Dad was always heroic in my eyes. He was my role model as a profes-sor and an intellectual leader; I desperately sought to follow his example. Dad also had a genial laugh and inner warmth that drew others to him; in my eyes, he was both a "hero" and very "real" at the same time.

Dad also had a wild side. One time, when my grandfather was proudly sitting at a homecoming football game at Depauw University, where he was president, his son buzzed the field in his biplane, causing the players to scatter for cover during a play. With that bizarre sense of humor, Dad was a hard man to dislike, even when he resorted to strict discipline, such as whipping me with a thick leather belt when I had been "sassy" or had "broken the rules."

In his early twenties, Dad went off to Hollywood and studied to be an actor. According to my mother's reports, he was "too studied" to be a good actor, but he had the looks, with a Clark Gable mustache and a Rudy Valentino dark complexion and flowing jet-black hair. It was there he met my mother, Dalys Houts, blond and beautiful (so it appears in her publicity photos).

They were married in 1939 and I arrived in 1942. In the late 1930s, my mother pursued her undergraduate degree (courtesy of support from my dad's grandmother) and my father began his graduate studies, both at the University of Southern California. It was the end of their acting careers and the beginning of a more successful life in the academic world.

Mom, who died in the summer of 2004 during the editing of this book, was a complicated lady who had her share of supporters and critics. By the end of her long life, especially in the thirty years after my father died in 1974, I think the supporters outweighed the critics (surely spearheaded by two true gentlemen who were by her side in the later years: her genteel second husband, Harry Jaecker, and later, the lovable Ralph McVain, both of whom predeceased her). At Heritage Village in Southbury, Connecticut, where she lived after Dad's death, Mom finally fulfilled her acting dream by starring in several amateur productions and in a one-woman show where she took on various roles as defined by their hats.

But it was her acting penchant that also prompted her critics; back when Dad was alive, she frequently described herself as "the first lady of Drew University" or as the "hostess with the mostest." For some in Dad's family as well, her posturing prompted irritation, almost as if there was a family feud between the Oxnam cosmopolitan clan and the Houtses' earthier roots.

I actually felt closest to my mother when she was too weak and too needy to resort to acting. When Dad died, she needed my help sorting out the finances and establishing her new widowed life in Connecticut. I was touched when she vowed to always eat in the dining room, setting another place just so that she could sense Dad's presence. In the 1990s, when she had a near-fatal illness, I rushed to her hospital bedside. She grasped my hands and said, "Thanks so much for being here. I love you." I was so happy to connect that I ran out to the drugstore and bought balloons and a stuffed animal as presents. Finally, she had shown the genuine mother–son love that I had longed for all my life.

Looking back on her life, I feel grateful for those loving moments, but also sorry for a mother who seemed so much better at promoting her "ideal family" than she was at dealing with her own feelings. Once, late in her life, after I was married, when I had pushed her hard on this "always acting" matter, she stood up and pointed to where she had been sitting. Her voice changed into a deep rasping, and she said, "I hate that person. I hate everything she does." Then, re-alizing that it was a very odd revelation, she quickly sat back down and pre-tended nothing had happened. My wife and I simply stared in astonishment.

Early on, I became aware that Mom and Dad had very high expectations for my success. When Mom talked with family or friends, she would often tell them, "There's Robbey. He reads books when other kids are playing. He's such a good student, you know." I sometimes thought that Mom, along with Dad, wanted me to prove something to my father's family—was it that their son might also be a superstar? After all, I had my father's first name, "Robert"— and "Bromley" was my grandfather's middle name that he always used. It wasn't that the pressure was overt, at least not most of the time, but rather that the notion of a high-achieving son was built into an understated WASP family ethic. Successes produced smiles and failures prompted frowns. That was enough for me. I bought into the system with unquestioning passion.

I was always obsessed with success, feeling fleeting glee when I achieved it, then on to the next challenge. But failure, even partial failure or even almost-success, filled me with searing guilt and self-loathing. The successes never stayed with me. I harbored agonizing memories of every single mistake or shortcoming. To this day, I can reconstruct those ghastly moments in perfect detail.

Throughout my life—beginning as a teenager and later as an adult—perceived failures prompted severe self-punishments. Hiding in an attic or a secluded forest, I would scream at myself: "You're stupid! A stupid idiot! I hate you!" I pummeled myself with clenched fists slamming against body and arms, and then hammered my forehead against a tree or a wall. For days, I would sit sullenly, recalling the terrible episode, often writing the words *You're stupid!* on a notepad or whatever scrap of paper was at hand.

So, given the inner penalties for failure, my outer pressure to succeed was pretty strong. An early test was the sport of target archery. Dad, worried that I was going to maim someone with my homemade bow and arrow, declared solemnly: "Boy, if you're going to use a weapon, let's use it right." A firearms instructor in the war who almost lost his life when another soldier accidentally discharged a sidearm in the barracks, Dad was adamant about doing things safely and methodically. So, after buying archery books and making a couple of lovely, if rather hefty, bows, he joined the Newton Archers just outside of Boston. Inventing his own modified military system of teaching archery "by the numbers," Dad became a very competent archer himself, and I, not yet a teenager, was his pupil. His approach to archery taught me many lessons: disciplined practice was the key to success (so I began practicing several hours a day); quality equipment was essential to quality performance (my father bought the very best bows and aluminum arrows); and success in competition made my father happy.

So between ages eleven and fifteen, I embarked on a short archery career, filled with enough victories to make both my parents and me very happy indeed. Within the junior archery ranks, I was club champion the first year, eastern regional champion the following year, and national American junior champion the following year. I recall with some pride the many victories, the medals and trophies, the growing list of national record scores. Mom, to my consternation, sent news releases of my archery achievements to both local and national papers, claiming that was her role as "head of public relations for the Newton Archers." So failure, such as my third-place finish at the Junior Nationals in 1956, is forever fixed in my memory. "You're terrible," I yelled, throwing open my archery tackle case, pulling out a handful of aluminum arrows, bending them into an unusable mess of spent metal.

Only later in life did I learn that failure can be the best teacher, but that lesson escaped me in my archery years. Once I lost a regional championship to a remarkable archer named Lloyd Corby who kept shooting in an awful thunderstorm. Ignoring the high winds and biting rain, he scored very well while those of us who sought shelter stared in amazement. When the storm abated, I was so stunned by his composure that I finished badly and lost the championship. How had he done it? "It's Zen," he explained later with a quiet smile.

I thought I understood the paradox that made Lloyd Corby a champion: his state of mind was everything; the weather was irrelevant; he achieved perfection by not seeking perfection at all. Sadly, it was a truth that did not sink into my soul for forty years. I persisted with my simple method: rigorous preparation yields success, and total preparation yields the highest success. I was not about to change it; it seemed foolish, and almost un-American, to give up such a treasured formula for a wild notion like Zen. Vince Lombardi of the Green Bay Packers was more my style: "Winning isn't just the goal. Winning is everything."

In 1957, after finally winning the national championship, I was flattered to be invited by the women's world champion to spend the summer at her rural Pennsylvania home so she could coach me for the Olympics. We knew that the International Olympic Committee was considering archery as an official sport in its meeting that very summer, so I had visions of making the team and competing in the Rome Olympics in 1960.

One day my coach approached me with a long face: "There's good news and bad news," she reported. "Archery was approved, but archery competitions won't occur until 1972. What will you do?" No way was I going to keep practicing eight hours a day for the intervening fifteen years, when I'd be an old man of thirty. At age fifteen, my archery career was over. To this day, I cannot bear to watch Olympic awards ceremonies on TV; it hurts too much to imagine how glorious that gold medal would have felt around my neck. Of course, not going to the Olympics did have one advantage: imagine my self-punishments if I had lost the biggest competition on earth!

So archery was over. The next battleground was the classroom. I had coasted through elementary and junior high school, usually getting stellar report cards, until one day in the eighth grade. The task was to produce a five-page paper on some aspect of twentieth-century American history. My draft paper produced a shocking result, a grade of C for "sloppy writing and almost no background reading": worse yet, we were required to enlist parental help in producing the final paper. I can still see my father's frown as he read my shamble of a paper, tightened eyes reflecting his agreement with my teacher, and his penetrating stare hurting worse than a whipping. On this occasion, there was no time for my self-abuse ritual; it was late Thursday, and the paper was due on Monday after a long holiday weekend.

For the next three days, under Dad's uncompromising scrunity, I had a tutorial on paper writing "by the numbers": a day in the library learning the card catalog system and how to take notes, a day at home discovering how to make an outline and write a first draft, another day at home absorbing how to edit, to make footnotes and a bibliography, and to prepare a perfect final copy. When it was all done, presented to the teacher in a neat green binder, I was delighted to discover that schoolwork was really archery by another name. The grade for "Admiral Mahan and the Modern American Navy" was A-plus; the wayward son was welcomed back into the fold with smiles all around.

My mother taught me another trick that had helped her produce an admirable record at the University of Southern California. "Take all your notes from class," she said, "organize them well, and type them into a finished copy. At exam time, you memorize the notes and the underlined parts of your books." So, after teaching myself to type, I became the only student at my high school, maybe in the whole United States, who had three-ring binders chock-full of typed notes. Even after I transferred to Poly Prep, a private school in Brooklyn, New York, my father's paper-writing method and my mother's system of memorizing typed notes worked wonders.

So, even before the term was invented, I was a *nerd* of the first order. At Williams College in the early 1960s, my secret system flourished, but, of course, it demanded huge amounts of time. My Williams day was nothing but classes, studying in a hidden carrel deep in the library, and occasional breaks for meals and a squash game for exercise. Social life was nonexistent; I had only a couple of dates in high school, and three dates in my first two years of college.

Late one night, a fellow student barged through my closed door, saw my meticulously typed notes, and observed, "Ox, you're one fucking obsessed nut." My immediate reaction was not anger—who could deny that he was right? But I felt guilty at being discovered in a clandestine act.

In my mind, my approach was a secret trick, a labor-intensive device to beat the academic system. For most of my life, I assumed that my academic achievements came solely from obsessive work, not from intellectual ability. I viewed myself as a successful fraud, a driven but "stupid" fellow, basking in grade-measured success, while keeping his memory-driven system top secret. Throughout life, I have been uncomfortable with praise because I feel it is not deserved.

In spite of my low intellectual self-image, Williams College prompted a newfound joy in the rich array of courses and readings. Williams was a teaching college par excellence and many of the professors in the English and History departments were brilliant. It was at Williams, under such great minds as Bob Waite, Dudley Bahlman, Russ Bostert, and Chris Breiseth, that I learned to think analytically and to write clearly. New worlds opened as I read Plato and Kant, Tillich and Éliade, Conrad and Sartre, and I started participating in class discussions and preparing less methodical and more imaginative papers.

From Williams I went directly to graduate school at Yale University in Asian studies. I suppose I was fated to keep plodding on the academic treadmill, but why pick Asian studies? Unfortunately, Williams College, like most liberal arts colleges of that day, offered little about countries across the Pacific, with the exception of Fred Greene's informative course on Asian politics. But I did read three nonassigned books about China and Japan. My only childhood exposure was hearing a few tales and seeing a few art objects brought back by my grandfather from trips to Japan, China, and India.

I just had a hunch that China, with its great history and remarkable cultural inheritance, might be a more positive force someday. That was a pretty radical thought at the time; most people still saw a malevolent "Red China" with harsh images from the Korean War and the Cold War. Oh yes, Dad also urged me to consider international studies. He told me a popular joke: "What's the difference between an optimist and a pessimist?" Answer: "Optimists study Russian. Pessimists study Chinese." My optimistic father was already learning Russian, so I—not a pessimist, but perhaps a more cautious optimist—picked Chinese.

The clincher was money: I got a terrific financial aid package from Yale Asian studies courtesy of the National Defense Education Act (NDEA), supporting studies about "critical countries" (that often meant enemy countries like China and the Soviet Union). By the way, it was the same "studying the enemy" argument that prevailed with my draft board to give me a student deferment during the Vietnam War. I will never forget the gruff chairman of the draft board asking me "one final question to see if you're a real Asia expert" before granting the deferment: "Was it chow mein or chop suey that was invented in China?" (I'm not kidding!) My correct answer—"Chow mein . . . because chop suey was created in America"—kept me out of the Vietnam conflict. I blessed my nerdish memory for trivia that fateful day.

My Yale experience from 1964 to 1969 was an eye-opening voyage into Chinese and Asian art, history, politics, and economics at a time when few graduate students were attracted to the field. The Chinese program was spearheaded by two exceptional scholars, Arthur and Mary Wright (Mary was a pioneer in modern Chinese history and the first female full professor at Yale). The Chinese-language department, created to train air-force officers in the Second World War, had a great array of linguists. My first Chinese teacher, the talented Daisy Kwoh, eventually became my assistant at the Asia Society and has been a close friend ever since. It was Daisy Kwoh who gave me a lovely Chinese name—An Xilong (安熙龙)—rich in meaning and historical allusion, always producing knowing nods from prominent Chinese.

Incidentally, my penchant for short-term memorization worked less well in the Chinese language: I could pass the examinations with ease, but I could not keep the vocabulary, especially the devilish written characters, in my head long enough to build a solid linguistic foundation. In good automaton tradition, I went from the first few words of Chinese-language study in the fall of 1964 to a doctorate in Qing dynasty history in the spring of 1969 (something of a speed record in a difficult field). My mentor was the brilliant Professor Jonathan Spence, who painstakingly guided me through a doctoral dissertation—*Policies and Factionalism in the Oboi Regency, 1661–1669*—demanding two years of research, all in classical documentary Chinese.

The rigors of scholarship never suited me at all. I enjoyed learning about Asian history and culture, but I never felt at home doing fastidious library research. Spence could make ancient Chinese records come alive with magical stories, but for me, it was more like dissecting old Yellow Pages. I just turned on my inner machine, conducted disembodied research, wore out Chinese-language sources and dictionaries, and spit out a doctoral thesis.

So why spend so many years pursuing something not in my heart? The honest answer is that I had to get that doctorate. I couldn't wait to receive the deep blue doctoral robe and hood that signified "Dr. Robert Oxnam." Like the Chinese scholar-officials who wore emblems to signify their status, I sought to project the image of "success" in every sense of the word.

For the next two decades, I sought to reap the rewards of all this academic preparation, to live the dream of success. But like the famous twin masks of Greek drama, one face radiated smiling confidence, but the other face, generally hidden from view, was contorted with rising pain.

Over time, the balance changed. The 1970s were filled with a good bit of sunny weather, allowing me to ignore dark clouds on my inner horizon. But in the 1980s, the few shafts of sunshine were obliterated by a violent series of inner storms. The big question of the 1970s—"So what's the next big professional challenge?"—was replaced by the big dilemma of the 1980s—"What's really wrong with me?

It all began so well. From Yale, I went directly to Trinity College in Hartford, Connecticut, as assistant professor teaching Asian history, feeling very much at home in the comfortable, almost nineteenth-century, Trinity academic environment. The department chairman, English history professor George Cooper, was very supportive and called me "Ox" in a paternally proud way. I bonded with several faculty members, especially of the younger generation, over lunches, coffee, and an occasional midday boccie game in the Quad.

Realizing that my knowledge of Asia was totally from books and courses, I felt a need to broaden my approaches in teaching. In addition to publishing my dissertation, which made the college and my parents happy, I also invented a radically new method for teaching about China, which raised some eyebrows among older faculty. *The Ch'ing Game,* as it was called in its published version, was a simulation of eighteenth-century China in which my undergraduates played different roles (emperor, magistrate, censor, gentry, etc.) over a daylong process that used the entire Trinity campus to replicate Beijing and various Chinese provinces. The game, brilliantly developed by my graduate students, was designed to enhance undergraduate interest in Chinese history and to prompt better papers as they prepared to play roles in the simulation. The Ch'ing Game not only worked wonders for teaching (many students still have vivid memories of Chinese history as a result), but it also attracted a lot of publicity in Hartford papers and the local TV station.

So, I became both a published scholar and an academic innovator. The result was rapid promotion—I was named associate professor of history with tenure after three years, and also assistant to Trinity's imaginative and affable president, Theodore Lockwood, for academic planning. At the same time, I pursued a variety of liberal causes, something that began at Yale, where I first spoke out against the Vietnam War in 1964 and later mobilized Asian scholars to protest against American involvement in that conflict. At Trinity, I was a faculty leader of the successful effort, in the wake of the Kent State massacre, to promote a campuswide strike of students and faculty with teach-ins as alternatives to regular classes.

In 1964, I married an attractive and caring lady who was very supportive of my academic life. She also pursued her interests in teaching English at private preparatory schools, which supplemented my limited college teaching salary. We had two children—a boy, born in 1969, and a girl, born in 1972. We had many happy times together, including our travels to Europe and our summers at the Oxnam grandparents' place on Lake Winnipesaukee in New

Hampshire. I thought of myself as a pretty good father who spent many hours with the children, carrying them on my back hiking or cross-country skiing, teaching them about wildlife and rocks, or just telling stories at bed-time. But there's no doubt that my former wife, having left her job while the kids were growing up, deserves the lion's share of credit for the fact that our children are loving and successful adults today.

Then, in 1974, came the awful news that Dad was afflicted with lung cancer, surely the result of a lifetime of heavy smoking. His decline was as-tonishingly rapid: he was diagnosed on May 1, and he was dead on July 19. I was with him when he died and will always hear his muted cry, "No, no," as he struggled to get his last breaths. Without Dad as my role model, my inner light seemed dimmed. Together we had planned a trip to China. The follow-ing year, when I finally got to China (tagging onto a delegation of American women), I buried a little envelope of Dad memorabilia under a rock in a Suzhou garden.

On the surface, Dad's death prompted me to pursue new avenues with feverish energy, perhaps trying to maintain his commitment to "making a difference." Dad knew that while I thrived on teaching Asian history, I found the isolated existence of the scholar stultifying and hated the very thought of writing another historical monograph. So I think he would have applauded when, in lieu of a sabbatical, I took on the responsibility of developing a na-tional public education initiative on China at New York's Asia Society in 1975. The China Council, as it was called, was a new institution, to draw to-gether a wide array of China specialists (not just academics, but also busi-nesspeople, journalists, educators, and former government officials) to develop national programs offering balanced, accurate portrayals of China.

It was a heady period for the China Council: right after the Nixon–Mao détente and before the Carter–Deng normalization. We were trying to coun-teract the long history of China lobbies (right-wing in the McCarthy tradi-tion of 1950s and 1960s and then left-wing among 1970s neo-Maoists).

I found it exciting to shape a new organization with a good purpose: setting up fifteen regional China Councils across the country, spearheading a variety of key studies about China, coediting two books on U.S.–China relations, and often briefing the national print and broadcast media on China. It was teaching at its best: bringing outstanding American experts on China to a truly national classroom. Oh yes, it was also fun to get phone calls from Walter Cronkite ("Can you be on the show tonight?") or from Tom Brokaw ("How do you pronounce *Deng*? Really? Like cow dung?").

Totally hidden from outsiders were mounting inner problems. At night, I was filled with anger and depression, and I began drinking myself to sleep with several slugs of scotch or bourbon. I visited a rather classic Freudian psychiatrist, replete with "uh-huh" responses and puffs on his pipe, who told me that he thought I had "problems with authority." Then he asked me, "When you told your story about your father's death, did you realize that you were smiling?" I was furious. How could he speak about Dad that way? In retrospect, I'm sure there was truth in his observation. After all, a great deal of my success-driven career had its roots in trying to emulate and please my father. But back then, it was a good excuse to stop seeing the psychiatrist.

Also in the late 1970s, I fell prey to another addiction, more prevalent among women than men. I didn't know the name at the time, but it was bulimia. When I was a child, I loved eating fatty foods and ice cream. By my archery years, I was a chunky little kid. Once, when photos of the archery team were planned, Mom prompted me to wear a girdle so that I wouldn't look so fat. But food was always plentiful at home, and I often stole extra food from the refrigerator (raw hot dogs were among my favorites). During the China Council years, I discovered the delight of having free business lunches where I could gorge myself and charge it to American Express. My weight soared to above 250 pounds, a lot even on a six-foot four-inch frame; although I lost a lot of it by virtue of an illness on a China trip, I never gave up the love of eating too much.

Then, one day in 1979, after I had moved to Washington, I got ill after feasting on a two-pound bag of peanuts and half gallon of vanilla ice cream. *Bang,* it suddenly dawned on me: I could eat whatever I wanted and not gain weight. And so began a pattern which I could not overcome until the late 1990s; it cost me dearly in energy loss, in enormous weight fluctuations, and in tooth decay (stomach acid rots teeth very quickly and forced me to wear a "partial" set of false teeth in my late forties). I was surprised that this method of weight control was not my invention, and astonished when a television friend told me that *bulimia* means "eats like a cow."

Perhaps because I fooled myself by ignoring these rising problems, the effect was to hide them from others as well. At least, there was no apparent impact on my professional career. Indeed, Phil Talbot, president of the Asia Society and a true old Asia hand, was grooming me as his successor. In 1979, I was named Asia Society vice president and director of its Washington Center, taking the China Council with me to the nation's capital. Thanks to a travel grant from the Ford Foundation to visit the whole Asia Pacific region and the enormous array of Asia-wide programs at the Washington Center, I made the quick transition from "China specialist" to "Asianist."

In 1981, at the age of thirty-eight, I was named president of the Asia Society, suddenly responsible for leading American public education about all the countries and cultures of the Asia Pacific region. I took over a multimillion-dollar operation, in a brand-new building on Park Avenue designed by Edward Barnes, continuing a legacy established by John and Blanchette Rockefeller. Looking rather splendid, I thought, in my new suits and ties, I set out to create a new array of programs on Asian arts, education, and contemporary affairs. I would take the energy of the China Council and inject it into the Asia Society as a whole.

Within a few months, it was clear I was in for a rude awakening. Several million dollars had to be raised for the new building and its higher operating costs. John Rockefeller 3rd, who had died in a car accident in the late 1970s, was no longer there to provide financial assistance. His widow, Blanchette, and her remarkable associate, Elizabeth McCormack, concerned about the situation, fashioned a devilish challenge grant forcing the Society to raise a lot of endowment money very quickly. And, to complicate matters further, Mayor Edward Koch decided to try to tax the Asia Society on the grounds that it was not an "educational institution" because it did not offer courses or grant degrees.

Overnight, it became apparent that my job priority was crisis management, not Asian expertise. And I knew that everyone was watching—was the young president up to the task? One supportive trustee gave me an appropriate gift for my headaches—a huge replica of a Bayer aspirin tablet. I thought long and hard about quitting, but I knew that would be professional suicide. And so, steeling myself, I resolved to confront the problems. It meant severe budget cuts—eliminating over twenty employees in a hundred-person staff (causing a huge internal uproar and an enormous decline in morale) and renting out space in our new building (forcing those who remained into much tighter quarters). Working day and night, we managed to raise the capital for the Rockefeller challenge grant, creating the first Asia Society endowment and, after three years, bringing balanced budgets for the remainder of my tenure. We joined forces with other embattled institutions to fight Mayor Koch's tax efforts in the courts and in the press; eventually he backed down when we made it clear that New York's cultural and educational not-for-profits brought billions of dollars to the city every year.

By 1984, the Asia Society had won its battles, but inwardly I felt I had lost the war. The job, once an exciting challenge, now seemed a hollow pursuit, filled with vexations, a demanding daily schedule, and lots of human problems. I stuck it out and initiated reforms—regional Asia Societies in the United States and Asia, a new K–12 education program, well-attended corporate conferences in Asia, pathbreaking studies on key U.S.–Asia relations issues, a staff and board that included many Asians and Asian-Americans.

But the fun was gone. Rather than driving the vehicle, I often felt that I was hanging on for the ride. My shiny self-image began to tarnish and corrode. Earlier flaws in the picture, which I had tried to discount, quickly turned into very serious problems. When I became angry, it often turned to a furious rage that prompted me to say terrible things and leave everyone around absolutely flabbergasted. In professional settings, I was able to keep my anger under control. But every few months, the anger would surge with family or close friends. A small provocation would throw me into a furious frenzy and screaming invectives. I would pace a room until the anger took a physical form and I broke something—a door, a piece of furniture, my glasses, or a clock. Then, as it slowly dawned on me that I was totally in the wrong, I went through a contrition ritual. I took full blame and promised that my rage would never happen again. But I could sense people shying away. A friend said that life around me was "like walking on eggshells."

On one occasion, I flew into a frenzy at the end of a three-day race on the boat of a very good friend whom I knew professionally. Since I was the most experienced skipper on board, I had stayed at the helm for much for the race, losing sleep trying to keep what was not a very competitive boat in contention. Toward the end of the race, he told me that my decisions had put us into a lull in the wind as other boats had caught a breeze and whisked them to the finish line. My anger was uncontrollable; I screamed at him for his insensitivity and incompetence, and then went into the cabin to sulk. An hour later, when I tried to apologize, he said he forgave me, but I knew that serious damage was done. I later heard that he still tells the story of the "boat race from hell."

I kept telling myself that the Asia Society was the culprit—look, this is a tough job, it's just stress, it would make anybody frustrated. Many people told me I looked tired, and warned me of burnout. I desperately wanted to show them I wasn't falling apart inside.

In spite of inner problems, I still saw myself doing professional work attentively and well. And when my political passions were engaged, I felt an old rush of energy fuel my activities and statements. My instinctive hatred for repression was reactivated in June 1989, when the Beijing government killed hundreds of protestors at Tiananmen Square. The fact that I had predicted this terrible outcome two weeks earlier did not make it any easier when I saw the awful images on television. I strongly condemned the Tiananmen massacre—in television interviews, in an address to some four hundred people who packed an auditorium at my twenty-fifth reunion at Williams College, and in comments for a thousand people at the Asia Society's annual dinner. At the same time, I also argued that we must remain engaged with China, not suspending most-favored-nation trading privileges, instead working to achieve human rights through tough negotiations on specific cases.

But inside, I was crumbling, falling apart with appalling speed. I seldom drank very much at the constant rounds of dinners and parties that the president of the Asia Society had to attend for "representational purposes" (that usually meant fund-raising in one way or another). But when I got home, I began knocking down drinks until I passed out. My consumption of alcohol eventually amounted to something between a third and a half a quart per night. I began buying extra bottles and hiding them so that those around me could not see how much was being consumed.

By the late 1980s, as things became worse, my wife and I agreed to a separation. I moved to a tiny New York City apartment where I embarked on an "addiction ritual" at least two or three nights a week. It required several specific ingredients—two packs of cigarettes, Polish sausage, a gallon of ice cream, a two-pound bag of peanuts, a bottle of scotch, and a pornographic movie on the VCR. As I think back on it, it all seems incredibly wacko, but then it felt like the right release at the end of a busy day. Somehow I managed, through huge intakes of caffeine during the day (both coffee itself and Djet Coke as well), to keep sufficient clarity to do my expected work.

People began telling me that I regularly talked to myself. Someone at work once asked me—"Did I hear you correctly? Did you say, 'Bob is so tired. He's just exhausted'? Are you talking about yourself?" I don't remember what I replied. I didn't remember saying anything in the first place.

But there was something else, a strange pattern that began long before, accelerating in the 1980s. There were blank spots in my memory where I could not recall anything that happened for blocks of time. Sometimes, when a luncheon appointment was canceled, I would go out at noon and come back at 3 P.M. with no knowledge of where I had been or what I had done. I returned tired, a bit sweaty, but I quickly showered and got back to work. Once, on a trip to Taiwan, a whole series of meetings was canceled because of a national holiday; I had zero memory of what I did for almost three days, but I do recall that, after that blank spot disappeared, I had a severe headache and what seemed to be cigarette burns on my arm.

Or there were selective memory blanks. When I was sailing, I found it impossible to respond intelligently when asked questions about China. Once someone asked me: "Bob, what's your take on human rights in China?" I deflected the question with an absolutely unrelated comment about a new sailboat device called the "quik vang." Luckily, sailors are fascinated by such technological innovations, and the conversation never returned to China. The scary fact of the matter was that, when I was on the boat or working on the boat, I honestly could not draw on my China or Asia expertise at all. I was simply a different person altogether.

I found myself living for the release of sailing. It was as if something just snapped as I left the office for the boat: work time had become playtime. But I worked just as obsessively on the boat as in the office. Though no boat is ever in perfect shape, my boat had to function perfectly. A broken knot meter could destroy a whole day for me as I sought, often unsuccessfully, to repair it. When I was on a boating vacation, I would count down the days remaining before returning to work like a man on death row facing execution.

Inevitably, the cluster of bizarre behaviors started to affect my work. By the late 1980s, I was calling in sick when I felt compelled to stay at the yacht yard. And in the winter months, I started figure skating for exercise and it quickly became a new obsession. One day, I apparently fainted in the men's room and hit my head. At the hospital, I was immediately assigned to intensive care and began a series of tests for three days (including an MRI and a spinal tap). My hospitalization coincided with the famous stock market crash of 1987 and, perhaps not coincidentally, with an Asia Society board meeting.

When they released me from the hospital, the doctor remarked: "We can't find anything wrong with you, nothing at all. It's not blood, not heart. You passed the stress test with flying colors. I think you had best see a psychiatrist." She must have seen the shock in my eyes. Luckily, she knew how to use humor to ease the tension. "Heard the one about the stock market crash? Who's better off—a yuppie or a pigeon? Answer: a pigeon—because a pigeon can still drop a deposit on a BMW."

Good joke, but the situation wasn't funny at all. Clearly, my skating episode was not just a fainting spell, but another of those strange blank spots. What the hell had really happened? Life was spinning totally out of control. I hated myself. I hated what I was doing. I hated life itself. Twice I tried to commit suicide; on both occasions, I was prevented by family or friends. Once I was stopped after I was overheard slamming the action shut on a Luger I had inherited from my father. Another time I was pulled from a car after I had returned, depressed and drunk, and left the engine running in a closed garage. To those who saved me, and who have suffered from witnessing almost suicides, I owe not only my life, but also lifelong apologies.

In late 1989, a family member, shocked and hurt by my out-of-control behaviors, finally summoned the strength to confront me and perform an "intervention." "I've talked to a doctor. He says it sounds like serious alcoholism. He says you must see a Dr. Jeffery Smith. And he says that your life depends on it. No questions. You've just got to do it."

· · ·

Dr. Smith, a balding fortyish fellow in a casual sport jacket, offered comforting, professional warmth behind his unruly desk. Initially, his soft voice relaxed me, but soon I was squirming before Dr. Smith's demanding litany of questions and his unblinking better-tell-the-truth look.

"I only drink at night. Well, just a few drinks, mainly to sleep. How much exactly? I suppose I go through a bottle in about a week. Well, more like three days. I drink until I crash. I drink coffee all day long to keep me sharp. I'm real careful with the alcohol—never at the office, not even social events. I can quit the alcohol—I've done it for several periods before, once for over six months.

"Inside I feel terrible. I feel like I'm a bad person. That's what I find myself muttering a lot—'I'm bad.' Then there are the weird times when I can't remember what happened for several hours in a day. Total blank spots. Or when I'm on the boat and someone asks about China and I can't think of anything about China, nothing at all.

"Oh yes, there are the angry explosions. Someone or something sets me off, always someone very close to me, and I just fly off. I often break things—it's usually a watch or a clock or my glasses. I don't hit people, but I scream and yell. It scares the hell out of everybody. Then I feel awful and try to apologize."

Dr. Smith never gave much of a reaction, neither a smile nor a frown, just his undivided attention, eyes occasionally tightening. When he was done with his questions, he took a long moment to scan the form on his clipboard and looked sharply at me. "I can't believe you're not in therapy. First off, you don't have a drinking problem. It's much worse: you're a class-A alcoholic. You've got every symptom of a really serious drinker—uncontrolled emotions, frequent blackouts, drinking only to get drunk, periods of proud abstinence before another fall."

I was dumbfounded. I tried to keep the inner trembling from showing. "It's really that serious?"

"So serious that I'm going to tell you what you have to do. You need to go to a rehabilitation center. I mean right now. You must stay there for a month, not just to dry out and begin to get healthy, but also to get a grip on your life. And then you are going to have to join an AA program to stay straight."

I rubbed my forehead in disbelief. "But I'm running a major institution. I've got a board meeting in two weeks. We're barely balancing the budget. Then I've got to go to Hong Kong, where we're opening a new center that I've been working on for years. I can't just take off for a month. What could I possibly say to the trustees?"

Smith stood up and looked down with a gentle firmness that tended to close options. "You can pretend it's just a little problem and continue for a while. But what you have is deadly. It will surely kill you, probably sooner than you think. It's also devastating to others—maybe you'll avoid killing someone with an automobile, but you're doing terrible psychological damage to those around you. You're not alone, you know. There are lots of so-called successful people who are classic alcoholics and no one really knows. Most of them don't have the guts to deal with their disease."

After Dr. Smith waited for it to settle in, he made it concrete. "I can make a call right now to a good friend, former alcoholic himself, now runs the famous Edgehill Center in Newport, Rhode Island. Maybe he can make room for you. What do you say?"

I closed my eyes, trembling inside as I pondered the consequences, then looked back at Dr. Smith, who hadn't moved an inch. "Okay"—I sighed— "make the call." Twenty minutes later, he called me back into the office. "It's all arranged. You are to arrive tonight before midnight."

I nodded with resignation. "One more thing," Dr. Smith added. "I want to see you when you get back. Not just for the alcoholism. You're a rather rare bird psychologically, you know. You're a male hysteric. You need treatment."

My mind was spinning as I drove back home. Had I done the right thing? Can I get out of it? No, I'd made the decision, now let's be organized. Got to call my office and my board chairman. No alternative but to be honest. What the hell is a male hysteric anyway? Oh damn, why me, why am I so bad?

Twelve hours later, I arrived at the rehabilitation clinic, totally drunk after consuming a third of a bottle of bourbon while putting away my sailboat for the winter. Edgehill Center was a complex of new brick buildings on a lovely estate overlooking dramatic Newport Harbor, which I knew so well from years of sailing into it. It never occurred to me that I'd see it this way: dressed in a hospital gown, stripped of all clothing, my belongings searched for alcohol, drugs, and weapons. I acknowledged what I had drunk that evening to the admitting nurse; she just nodded and muttered "typical." I walked out into the starry night, looked down at the twinkling lights of Newport, and began to cry until there were no more tears, just aching gasps.

I was assigned to a floor housing some twenty alcohol addicts, and the rugged process of rehabilitation began. Two professional therapists were attached to each unit, supplemented by other trained personnel who watched over us all at night. The group consisted of a crosscut of society: a teacher, a dentist, an investment banker, a few older students, a housewife, a retired man, a construction worker, an environmental code specialist, a carpenter. At age forty-seven, I was in the middle of the group ranging from late teens to late sixties.

The initial briefing was clear-cut—we would be kicked out of Edgehill for infractions such as drinking or drugs, leaving the walled property, acting in violent ways. We had a "serious disease" and we were to undergo the only process that would make us "recovering alcoholics" (one never says "recovered"). We learned the twelve-step program in elaborate detail and I began my sessions by saying "Hi, I'm Bob. I'm an alcoholic." The day consisted of rigorous group- and individual-therapy sessions from morning to night, interspersed with times for art therapy and physical exercise. Everything was controlled; one couldn't even get aspirin without going to the medical office, and caffeinated drinks were prohibited. Only smoking was allowed, but I decided to use the occasion to quit smoking as well as drinking.

At first, I was aloof from the group. I felt I didn't belong at Edgehill. I wasn't a regular drunk; I was a special drunk, a high-achiever drunk. I was like the famous people who came to Edgehill: the wife of a major politician, a world-renowned movie actor. When it came time for me to tell my history to the group, I decided to be honest and let it all hang out. It was the kiss of death. My various accomplishments didn't impress most colleagues at all; it just made me look like I was some elitist braggart. And my admissions of other disorders, especially bulimia, made me the source of special mockery. To some, I was seen as the most sick of all—I was called "Barfing Bob," in the words of one detractor. There was little way to express my frustration. One day, in art-therapy class, I made a clay sculpture of a seagull with out-stretched wings that looked a bit like Christ's arms on the cross. The art teacher said, "Hey, that's beautiful." I looked at the seagull, smashed it flat with my hand, and ran from the room.

I felt very alone and scared for the first two weeks, and then a change started to come over me. Okay, I thought, I've done what I have done. At least now I know my problem. I will be the best damned "recovering alcoholic" imaginable. I will put my life back on track. I will go back and honestly explain my problem. I've made a mess out of success. Now I'll make a success out of this mess.

So after a month in rehabilitation, I returned home with all the fervor and contrition of a true convert. It would be a new life, filled with honesty and purity. Yes, the problems were serious, but I was facing them directly. No, I wasn't "cured," but I knew that I had hit bottom. Surely, the worst was over.

I was totally wrong—much worse times lay ahead. The next year, 1990, would hold the greatest shock of all. It would hit me like a sledgehammer. But before that giant earthquake, I confronted a series of significant tremors. I was being warned, it seems, that the apparent afflictions—alcoholism, bulimia, rage, blank spots, suicidal tendencies—were not the "real problems." The real problems were deeper, so much deeper, than I could have ever imagined.

At an all-staff meeting, I informed the Asia Society of my alcohol addiction and treatment, summoning as much calm directness as I could. I will always remember the warmth of some of the longer-term staff members, especially building operations director George Papamichael and switchboard operator Elaine Hutchison, who gathered around and gave me hugs afterward. Then, with the full support of my board chairman, John Whitehead, I decided not to fly to Hong Kong; instead, he presided at the opening of the Hong Kong center, introduced Henry Kissinger and the other dignitaries, and fully represented the Asia Society. On the very night that the Hong Kong center was inaugurated, a dream I had worked so hard to realize, I was attending my first Alcoholics Anonymous meeting in White Plains. And for the next several months, I attended those AA meetings every night, "sharing" my story and concerns, receiving encouragement from other "recovering alcoholics," including my very caring "sponsor."

In spite of my efforts to show a resilient spirit, I could not escape a rising sense of inner foreboding. That dark mood was captured by the rise and fall of my first novel, *Cinnabar,* published in the same eventful year of 1989. *Cinnabar* was a mystery thriller featuring an unsuspecting Columbia University professor who inherits a mysterious red lacquer box from his dead wife that lures him into the swirling world of modern China, Hong Kong, and Taiwan.

It seemed like a good idea—a mental break from my rigorous professional life and yet another way to bring China alive in unconventional fashion—but, in retrospect, I have almost no memory of how the book emerged. All I remember is sitting down at the computer, over a few vacation periods and some long weekends, and transcribing what already seemed to be written. So *Cinnabar* was composed in a strange stupor, perhaps a prolonged series of my mysterious blank periods. At the time, it seemed odd, but not alarming.

Nothing prepared me for the bombshells when the book reached the market. The reviews were lukewarm to outright hostile. *Cinnabar* was an embarrassing bomb in spite of my best intentions. Shortly after enduring the difficult return from alcoholism rehabilitation, I was coping with a short-lived career as a thriller author. I stayed off the booze, but my depression was just like my pre-Edgehill days. I began smoking again. I began getting sick after meals again. I began experiencing the blank spots again. And the voices started crying out again: "You're stupid! You're bad! You're very bad!"

Deeply despondent, I started a new ritual, hiding in a remote corner of Grand Central Station at the beginning of my daily round-trip, watching the wriggling flood of salmonlike commuters, trying to make sense of my life. No, I'm not bad, I screamed silently, again and again. There's got to be a purpose, but what the hell is it? I breathed hard at first, and then more quietly and easily; my eyes fluttered in a dreamy state and my mind floated above the bustle and noise. I felt like a French medieval monk, properly punished for his sins, awaiting a sign of divine guidance. I wanted to be free of all these painful memories; I wanted release; I wanted rebirth. "Rebirth"? Ah, thought the monk, *renaissance!*

Renaissance was the very name I had selected for the thirty-eight-foot Sabre sloop that I purchased in 1989 to symbolize hopes for a new beginning. What about a long ocean voyage to let my soul rebuild itself? Together with a wonderful sailing friend, I mapped out an itinerary. We would sail the boat together to Newfoundland, spend some time exploring its southern coast, and I would bring it back to western Long Island Sound single-handed, a total trip of over two thousand miles. For me, it seemed the perfect project, fulfilling a lifetime dream at the time of nightmarish life changes. And so we threw ourselves into two months of preparations for a blue-water trip, marking our progress with endless checklists revised every few days.

As we set off at daybreak, *Renaissance* felt heavy with the couple of tons of additional weight, but she moved smoothly into the bright morning sun. Her blue hull cut gently into the tranquil waters of Long Island Sound; her shapely bow pointed due east toward the open Atlantic with the Canadian maritime provinces hundreds of miles over the horizon. We chatted for a bit and then settled into our separate thoughts, he looking ahead where we were going and I looking back where we had been. I huddled against the early-morning chill, zipped my fleece pullover up the neck, and tried to shake off the fatigue of many sleep-shortened nights in the final week of preparation. I was genuinely excited about the voyage and delighted that Dr. Smith had endorsed the trip in spite of initial worries about a hiatus from the ongoing alcohol rehabilitation program. But, as I watched my eight-ton boat leave a rolling blue-black stern wake, a cold cloud enveloped me, tempering the joyful departure with memories I desperately wanted to suppress.

For me, the Newfoundland venture was as much an escape as it was a glorious fulfillment. I was escaping a professional life that had become frustrating and running away from awful recollections of a novel I wished I had never published. Deeper down, I felt the harsh embrace of old and menacing patterns. The "great Newfoundland voyage" was possibly my most classic effort at seeking perfection. The boat had to be absolutely flawless in its preparation and in its sailing. And, come to think of it, I wonder whether I subconsciously picked "newfoundland" with discovery of a perfect new world in mind.

More ominously, even in the long hours of readying *Renaissance* for the trip, there were big blank spots in my memory. In the frenzy of predeparture list fulfillment, I made frequent trips to the local marine supplier with an excellent staff whom I'd known for years on a first-name basis. The whole process became routine—make a list, buy the supplies, charge it to my account, return to the boat—and it put me into a sort of robotic state of doing chores as fast as I could. Suddenly one day, two of the staff suddenly came downstairs, and one said, "We were watching you on an antitheft video. We saw you stuffing all those items in your sailing bag. I suppose you really meant to buy them." I was truly shocked: "Of course I'm going to buy them just as I always do," I protested as they escorted me quickly to the cashier's counter, where I gave them everything that I had in the bag and they tallied it up, just as I always had done.

But curiously, rather than being outraged at their treatment, I left the store feeling terribly guilty, cowering like a true criminal caught in the act. When I got home, I tried to tally what I had bought from the store over the past two months versus what I had actually paid in the monthly bills. Oh, my God, I had paid several hundred dollars less than what I estimated. Could it be? Was I stuffing everything in my large canvas bag and then only removing some items when it came time to pay? Was I stealing from a store which had treated me so well for so long? Why would I do such a thing?

Filled with visions of the police coming to my door, I called Dr. Smith for an emergency meeting. His calm voice quieted me immediately: "No, it's very unlikely that they will press charges. Yes, it does sound like you have been stealing from them, covering it by buying part of the items. Yes, severe stress together with a recent history of alcoholism is one explanation for such behavior with no recollection. But there are other possibilities that I want to explore later. No, don't try to explain it to the store now—what would you say anyway? Pay them later when it's a past issue.

"You know," Smith continued, "when I've asked you about dreams, you remember nothing, except dreams in which you feel suddenly 'caught' and 'very guilty.' I think we have a clue today."

I left Smith with some confidence I wasn't about to be arrested, but scared to death about what was actually happening during the blank memory periods. A few months later, I sent the store an envelope with cash, more than sufficient to cover their losses, and an unsigned note saying *to cover an overdue account.*

Now we were on the way to Newfoundland, a chance to forget the past and revel in the present. I rubbed my face to clear my head, bolted down a second Danish, darted below to the head, and immediately became sick, purging both my breakfast and an awful memory. It was not exactly an auspicious start for what I had called "the voyage to get my life back together." The pattern for the next seven weeks was already established in the first hour. It would be an incredible maritime experience, interspersed with ghostly recollections about the past and anxious ruminations about the future.

On one level, it was the trip of a lifetime. We managed to sail through a severe storm and navigate our way through Cape Breton and onward to Newfoundland. Dolphins followed us all the way, so close we could recognize them individually and see them almost as household pets. We sailed up the back of a sleeping humpback whale, twice the size of our boat, which just snorted, shot a spray of foul-smelling water, and sounded gently into the deep. We became friends with a family of "Newfies" (as Newfoundlanders call themselves), marveling at their hospitality and their strange dialect (I later learned that it is very close to what was spoken among the working class in England three centuries ago). We anchored in the long fjords of southern Newfoundland, with thousand-foot cliffs and cascading waterfalls, spotting only one other sailboat in six weeks. After my friend left, I single-handed the vessel back from Nova Scotia to New York, stopping in Halifax long enough to visit the cemetery containing bodies of many *Titanic* victims (I was a *Titanic* buff long before the famous, and often inaccurate, film was produced). And, with a little divine help, I was whisked back to Long Island Sound by a persistent easterly breeze (as opposed to the usual southwesterly air that would have made the trip take twice as long).

Sailing solo is a demanding experience, requiring enormous labor to keep the boat on course and out of danger. Essentially, you are the captain and the crew, working almost constantly, sleeping short two-hour naps, awakened by an alarm clock to make sure all is okay. At night, the radar was set with an alarm to indicate if any vessel or other object came within a sixteen-mile radius. Like most single-handed sailors, I heard strange noises at sea. At night, I would listen to the cries of whales, the whistle of the wind in the rigging, and even imaginary voices. I really thought I was being approached one night by a bunch of kids drinking beer in a small outboard, but that seems unlikely a hundred miles at sea. Odd happenings aside, I proved that I could single-hand happily and safely, and that was an accomplishment. Like the climbers of Everest, my only real justification is that I did it "because it's there."

Sailing at night, alone in the eerie cockpit red glow, I could keep the boat moving easily on course, but I fretted about what was "out there." The radar would spot vessels, but what about floating objects like the dangerous containers dropped from freighters? What about the dead whale reported over the coast-guard radio? (It would surely do huge damage to a sailboat surging along at over eight knots.) What else was out there? Every few minutes the sea around the boat lit up with long green flashes, frightening even after I realized they were my sweet dolphins streaking through the phosphors suspended in the seawater. I remembered a terrible scare a few years earlier when an idyllic sail from Montauk to Block Island was interrupted with an ear-piercing explosion of air and water behind the boat as a nuclear submarine surfaced barely a quarter mile off the stern. Could monsters of the deep, natural or man-made, suddenly consume *Renaissance*?

It dawned on me that what I really feared was not "out there" but rather "in here," deep inside myself. At night, the total darkness of the ocean and the inescapable quiet sitting forced me to confront feelings and memories. I no longer had my alcoholic anesthesia to block nighttime thoughts. I pondered stern phrases from my family: "be strong, boy . . . where there's a will, there's a way . . . take stock . . . honesty's the best policy . . . God helps those that help themselves . . . if not to your family, you owe it to yourself." It's true: we were solid WASPs long before the term was invented.

"What the hell's your problem?" I shouted into the darkness of the North Atlantic. "What's your *real* problem?" A few months back I was certain I'd found the explanation for why my successful cultivated self-image had been wrecked on the shoals. It was alcoholism, of course. I had learned through bitter experience that for addictive souls like me, alcohol destroys everything in its path.

I was living proof of the devastating impact of white-collar alcoholism. I had totally lost the sense of professional purpose, and had even screwed up my quest for an alternative career path. My anger and rages had done untold damage to friends and family. Now I was struggling successfully to refrain from drinking again, and knew that should be seen as a significant accomplishment. I recognized, from my rehabilitation experience and from a lot of reading, that the recovery process takes a lifetime and does not promise instant happiness. But the initial surge of feeling like a perfect recovering alcoholic had worn off months before. The glorious escape of Newfoundland was receding quickly in my stern wake; the dark reality of New York City loomed just over the bow.

I wanted everything to be just fine, all under control, but I had to acknowledge that I was still very sick, more sick than any other recovering alcholic I knew. The bulimia continued throughout the trip; I purposely got sick to my stomach at least once a day. The anger sometimes raged forth. Once, in port, I almost had a fistfight with a trawler captain who came so close to swiping the side of *Renaissance* that I pushed his boat off with all my might. I think

I called him a "fucking drunken idiot" and had to leave the wharf that night for fear of retaliation. No, I wasn't refreshed by the Newfoundland journey, but rather I was totally drained by what I now knew was a classic escape.

Coming ashore after almost two months at sea had its moments. The first night I awoke at two in the morning, the usual time to check my navigation, and when I looked out the window through sleepy eyes, I saw rocks and trees. I screamed out, "Oh, my God, we're going aground." For a few days, solid ground felt strange, my legs still poised for the rolling of the sea. Curiously, the unpredictable lurching of the subway train seemed more normal.

But the realities of returning to life as usual were much more chastening. As I walked from the Sixty-eighth Street subway stop to the Asia Society, my legs suddenly stopped working, as if held by some invisible giant, and I had to sit down for fifteen minutes before forcing myself to go on. As the weeks went on, it became a pattern, sitting down and mumbling to myself— "You've got to do it, keep moving." "No, I'm too tired. I'm just plain exhausted."—finally summoning enough willpower to make it to work. After a while, a ritual emerged as I would sit in a corner under some steps, staring blankly, muttering about myself in the third person: "Bob's too tired. He's exhausted. Bob's dying." Only once did someone notice me, a female student wearing a Hunter College sweatshirt, who must have thought I was a curiously overdressed homeless person: "Are you sick, sir? Anything I can do?" I quickly ran off, saying, "Oh, it's nothing, just a little tired."

Tired or not, I wasn't going to let it show in my work. The Asia Society Bob was like a tire, inflated and on a roll by day, deflated and immobile at night. There were meetings to chair, money to raise, events to attend, letters to write, calls to make. These I kept doing with some of the same zeal, and trying to feign the same energy, as when I had assumed the presidency a decade earlier.

But most nights were different. I returned to my recovery process without enthusiasm—daily AA meetings and twice-a-week sessions with Dr. Smith.

The whole thing seemed a predictable, boring routine. Smith tried to keep my spirits up with comments like "Look, recovery is no fun and yet you are sticking with it. Right now recovery is the most important thing in your life." He refused to prescribe drugs in spite of my insistence that I needed anti-depressants and sleeping pills. He argued that my history of addictions made many drugs too dangerous, and besides, he contended, "I think there's a lot more going on that you are resisting telling me."

I became prickly and defensive—"Resisting? What do you mean? I've told you everything. Alcohol, cigarettes, bulimia, rages, terrible fatigue, blank spots in my memory, inability to go to work, a sense of hopelessness." In the back of my head, as I listened to Dr. Smith's calm response—"I know it gets rough sometimes, just give it time"—I resolved to break with my psychiatrist at the next session.

A week later, I staggered out of Dr. Smith's office trying to comprehend his crazy assertion that he had just met with a very angry "Tommy" inside of me. "Don't worry about it." he had said, obviously trying to comfort me.

"Don't worry about it." I kept repeating his phrase incredulously to my-self as I sat in the car. "Are you kidding!?" I checked my watch—he was right—a full hour had lapsed since the appointment began. I glanced at the clock on the dashboard—it indicated precisely the same time as my watch.

What the hell happened in that hour? Oh come on, there's got to be a better explanation. This is just plain nuts! After years of peeling back my in-sides, finding problem after problem, now I'm told that there's someone else inside me? What's this, some kind of silly sci-fi movie? Was Smith out of his mind, a shrink gone bonkers?

I'd had blank spots in my memory before, but never with anyone else present. Would Smith toy with me, maybe make up a story to keep a dis-gruntled patient coming back? Yes, that's it. Dr. Smith had to be an utter quack, inventing stories to keep pathetic souls writing checks.

Late the evening Dr. Smith called: "Are you okay? Just don't worry. I have an explanation. You're coming tomorrow night. Right?" I didn't know what to say, but agreed to show up. He sounded both professional and comforting, not at all like someone pulling a scam.

Tommy, who was Tommy? Let me think, maybe someone at work? No, I didn't know anybody professionally by the name "Tommy." How about outside, maybe in the sailing community? No, not a soul named "Tommy."

TWO

TOMMY: "OF COURSE I'M ANGRY.
IT'S YOUR FAULT."

THE INTENSIVE THERAPY SESSIONS which began in mid-1990 took place in Dr. Smith's office in Scarsdale, New York, on the first floor of a nondescript apartment building. The office was relatively small, perhaps ten by fourteen feet, psychiatric books along one wall, a window with venetian blinds drawn on the opposite wall. Dr. Smith sat in a chair and generally listened intently, making more frequent interventions than in Bob's earlier experience with a therapist. Bob sat across from Dr. Smith in a comfortable chair next to an end table with a lamp and a box of Kleenex, presumably for those emotional moments. There was a couch available, but it was never used in this therapy process.

BOB

I dressed carefully for my evening appointment—a smart sweater, button-down open-necked shirt, crisp khaki pants, loafers—conveying a casual and composed look. Relax, I told myself, there's got to be some kind of rational explanation for this "Tommy" foolishness. Of course it's Smith's error. Stay calm and help Smith see his mistake.

Dr. Smith greeted me with his usual quiet warmth, explaining that this Scarsdale office was for his private patients, often those with conditions that went beyond the scope of his other office at the Cortland Center, specializing in alcohol and drug addictions. I was already getting nervous.

Then he leaned forward in his chair. "I want to explain what happened when you were in my office yesterday. Please let me tell it all without interruptions. And then I'll explain what I think it's all about." I inhaled deeply and silently vowed to shut up.

Smith began by relating what I remembered: that I had voiced my frustrations with these therapy meetings, that I sounded ready to break off treatment, and that my eyes started to flutter. "Suddenly you seemed to change altogether. You huddled in the corner of the chair. Your face was tightened and your eyes were sharp and angry. Your hands tensed up like claws ready to strike out."

Smith stopped for a moment, making sure that I was really understanding. He seemed utterly sincere in his report. He was trying to take me back to what he recalled from yesterday's session.

After the pause, Smith continued with his recollection. "At that point, I said: 'What's going on? What's happening here?' You spoke like an angry adolescent boy." Tommy

TOMMY

"I don't like you. I hate you!" I was really mad. And I was on that stupid chair, in that stupid office. I said it and I meant it.

Then that dumb shrink, he starts walking over to me, like he's going to do huggy-shrink junk. He was making me feel stuck in this corner.

"Don't you come near me," I shouted. "Don't you dare touch me." I would have hit him. He knew I was going to hit him if he came closer. I could see the worry in his eyes.

"Okay," the shrink said. "I'll just stay here. No closer. I promise." He said it with that super-quiet shrink talk. But I knew he was really scared.

When I get mad, I don't say much. But I can scare people. For a long time, I stared at him without blinking. When I'm mad, I'm like a mean dog. I tried to kill him with my eyes. My mouth was angry and my teeth felt like I could bite him. I made those hissy noises like a snake. He was trying to stare me down. But I wouldn't give up. One inch closer and I would have jumped at him. I kept him from moving at all. Every once in a while, I suddenly said it again: "I hate you!"

Ha, I said to myself, now look who's boss. The shrink was staring at me, afraid to move closer, but not wanting to be chicken and quit. He couldn't stay there forever. He had to do something. So finally, he said, "What's your name?"

Ha, I thought, I forced him to do something. I surprised him by stopping my angry look. I surprised him even more with a little smile. You know, one of those fake smiles, the kind that make people nervous.

"My name? Take a guess," I said quickly.

"Is it Bob?"

Oh, my God, this shrink is really dumb. How could he possibly think I'm Bob? He's got so much to learn. So I sat up on the chair and just looked at him for a while. "I'm not Bob." I laughed at him. "How could you take me for Bob? Bob's old. Bob's tired. I think Bob's dying."

"If you're not Bob, who are you?"

"You really don't know?"

"No."

"I'm Tommy."

"Tommy, is there anything else you want to tell me?"

"No, except that I hate you." Was there "something else" to tell him? What a jerk! There was everything else to tell him. But how can you tell someone something when they don't know anything to begin with? So we go back to staring. But this time, it's not worth looking angry. I just give him this "you're an idiot" look. I keep shaking my head, looking at the ceiling from time to time, making him feel like he was nobody. It went on forever. Then finally, he looks at his watch and says, "Time's up."

BOB

After Smith had finished his story, he said, "Bob, you don't remember any of this?"

I just held my head in my hands. I was in utter shock. I wanted to find a way to deny what Dr. Smith had said. I had zero memory of the episode. But the psychiatrist spoke with such quiet conviction and in such detail that it would have seemed absurd to jump up and scream, "Liar, you're making it up." I just sat there shaking my head. I remembered, when I went into a rage, what Smith had said about Tommy—the sharp eyes, the clenched teeth, the fingers like claws—that's just what happened at those moments, just before I snapped.

"Want to know what I think?" Smith asked. I looked up. "I think you have a case of multiple personality. You've heard of it?" I just kept shaking my head. "No?" he said. "Never heard of multiple personality?"

"Yes. Of course I've heard of it. Everybody has. I saw *Three Faces of Eve.* But I'm not like that. I'm not a misfit. I've been able to do lots of things in life."

"I know you've done lots. Not everyone with MPD is dysfunctional."

"What's the *D* for?"

"*D* is for 'disorder.' Multiple personality disorder."

"How's it possible? I mean, how could it be? You really think I have this thing, this MPD? Isn't there some other explanation?"

"I've thought a lot about what happened yesterday. This morning I mentioned this case to another professional colleague on a confidential basis. He agrees. Besides, I have dealt with other similar cases. It all fits."

"Other similar cases?" I raised my eyebrows. "I thought multiple personality was very rare."

"It *is* relatively rare. Maybe one case in ten thousand people. But there is a significant overlap of MPD with those who have severe addiction problems with alcohol or other toxic substances. I have been working with a multiple personality patient for several years and belong to a professional association concerned with dissociative problems."

"So if I have this multiple thing, you could treat my problem?"

"I could try. And if you wish, I will try. But I can also recommend several other people who specialize in this field. It's important that you are totally comfortable with your therapist. Look, I know this whole thing is like a bombshell. I don't want you to reach any quick decisions. Just try to relax and live with it over the weekend. How about we have another session on Tuesday night? Meanwhile, my private beeper number is on this slip of paper. Feel free to call me if you need to talk. Whenever."

I spent the weekend in quiet shock. I didn't tell anyone about the

"Tommy" episode or about Smith's diagnosis of MPD. Instead, I did what I always did, trying to cure anxiety on the water. I tinkered on *Renaissance,* transforming her from a long-distance cruiser to a performance handicap racer for the fall season.

I could no longer find reasons to deny Smith's account. The multiple personality business seemed bizarre, but in one respect it made some sense. Maybe that's what happened in the blank periods? Maybe the rages were actually mini–blank periods? Maybe the stealing thing was some kind of anger? Maybe this Tommy guy was the explanation? If we could somehow just cope with Tommy, then maybe . . . Quit it, Bob, I admonished myself, you're way out of your league. Just keep draining the damned water tank. Talk with Smith on Tuesday.

On Monday, I found a spare hour to buy several books dealing with dissociation and multiple personality disorder, including the classic best-seller *Sybil,* which I'd never read. I have never been a casual reader, but when focused on a project, I can read huge amounts of material in a relatively short time. This time the project had an inescapable fascination: trying to figure out what was wrong with me. After selectively sampling the various psychiatric treatises, I devoured *Sybil* in about six hours. Page after page, I found details that dovetailed perfectly with my own story. Of course I had only one "alter" (as the psychiatric books called a separate personality). But the way Dr. Smith described Tommy, even the way he had emerged in the office, sounded just like Sybil's pattern. And so much of Sybil herself hit home with me: meticulous organization, quest for perfection, obsession with time, self-abuse, always feeling she was "bad," limited memory of childhood, deep desire for creative outlets, and sudden rages. I was moving rapidly from skeptic to outright believer.

On Tuesday evening, like an overzealous graduate student trying to impress a professor, I told Dr. Smith about all my reading and how it had confirmed his findings. He shook his head and told me that the worst thing I could do was to become my own psychiatrist. He wasn't at all surprised that I had found many similarities in my readings. But he also warned me that dissociation specialists were in a young field, and that the number of cases was still relatively small.

Dr. Smith confirmed that the goal of MPD therapy was to achieve "integration," the unifying of alters into a single, cohesive whole with a single set of values and a unified memory bank. He also said that it was a long and difficult process, both for the patient and the therapist, probing more and more deeply into past experiences. In every case he knew about, MPD was caused by terrifying childhood traumatic experiences which prompted the mind to fracture, some parts absorbing the pain, other parts surviving by separating themselves from it, eventually coming to live quite separate lives with separate experiences and separate memories. He noted that everyone wants to forget what's painful, and that MPD was "the ultimate survival mechanism of intelligent children faced with unbearable memories." In short, the therapy would probably take "years of work" with initial meetings scheduled two or three times a week. Before an MPD patient can "come together," he concluded, he must revisit the original traumatic experiences and thus get to the difficult source of his predicament.

"But I don't have bad memories of growing up. In fact, I don't remember much. I have mainly warm memories and, oh yes, there were a few bad moments. Isn't that usual? Are you really telling me that I'm just wrong?"

"I'm not trying to tell you anything. What you find in therapy will be your own memories. I'm saying you have a serious problem at the far end of dissociation. The good news is that it's not like certain other disorders, manic depression for instance, which are related to genetic predisposition. MPD comes from the outside, from terrible things done by other people. That's what causes someone to split into multiple parts, sometimes into lots of alters. I've heard of cases with over fifty alters."

"Are you saying there might be more personalities? You know, more than Tommy?"

"I don't know. Maybe I should talk with Tommy again. Could I talk with Tommy?"

I didn't get a chance to answer. A sudden warm dizziness came over me, my eyes seem to roll into my head, and I could feel a tightening in my face and hands.

TOMMY

I just knew that Smith guy, the shrink, would be back. He wants more. Ha, I thought, give him just a little more. He needs me. Give him just a little bit. It's a fun game. It's called "torture the dummy."

"Tommy?" Smith said. "Tommy, is that you?"

I rolled my eyes. "Who do you think it is? You were just talking to Bob. Couldn't be Bob. Of course it's me."

"I just wanted to be sure. How are you, Tommy?"

I'd been watching. I wasn't weak like old Bob. No way the dumb shrink was going to get control over me. I knew exactly what to say. "How am I? I'm mad." I growled at the shrink, trying to cut him up with my eyes. "I'm mad at you. I hate you!"

"I'm not mad at you, Tommy. I don't hate you. Why do you hate me?"

"Why should I tell you?"

"Do you hate Bob, too?"

I wasn't expecting that one. "No, I don't hate Bob. I feel sorry for him. He's working so hard that he's killing himself. But, of course, he's got no choice."

"No choice? How come?"

God, can you imagine being so stupid? If he didn't know why Bob had "no choice," he wasn't worth talking to. Besides, now he was asking too many questions. I didn't like that. So I crawled back into the chair, made my fists like a tiger, and hissed at the shrink. Then I just began staring. I didn't care how long it would take. He wouldn't get anything else out of me.

I knew he'd give up first. After a while, the shrink smiled a little. "Tommy, you know I don't hate you. In fact, I think I like you."

"Doesn't matter. I don't care. I still hate you."

"Why?"

"I won't tell you. Quit asking stupid questions."

"Okay, Tommy. Nothing more about this hate business. How about another question? Can you tell me where you live?"

Now that one surprised me. He was still an idiot. But even jerks sometimes get lucky. I could answer that one and still stay mad at him at the same time. Besides, since he didn't know anything, he was going to be surprised. So now I'd be talking and he'd be listening.

"Sure I'll tell you," I said. "I live in a Castle." *Tommy lives in Castle a abstract Angry boy.*

"A Castle? Really?"

As I suspected, the shrink was totally ignorant. So I told him all about the Castle. He listened very carefully, like he was taking notes in his head. I could see he really wanted to know this information, but I knew he wanted something more. No way he was going to get that.

I told him the truth. The Castle was Middle Ages–style, standing on a large hill. It was made of gray stones and topped with long walkways and towers at the corners. In front of the Castle was a drawbridge spanning a river leading down to a massive lake with a towering mountain range on the other side. Above the drawbridge was a high bell tower, featuring a large clock with golden hands and Roman numerals and flags fluttering on top.

"So that's where I live. Of course that's where Bob lives, too."

"Really?"

It did no harm in telling the shrink that Bob was always on the outside, pacing up and down the front walkway, sometimes taking quick rests in a bedroom just off the walkway, never going inside the Castle. "Bob is constantly moving. He scrunches up his face when he scribbles notes on a pad. He smiles only when he talks to people down below."

"And you, Tommy? Where in the Castle do you live?"

"In a tiny room, just behind the walkway. Just enough for me and a bed. It has a wooden door that opens to the inside of the Castle."

"Do you ever go through that door?"

"Not often. But when I do, everyone's scared."

"Why are they scared?"

"If you can't figure it out, then I'm not telling you."

"Okay, but what about the inside of the Castle? Are there other rooms?"

"God, it's a Castle! Of course there are other rooms!" I told him it was big inside, but very dark because of the small windows. The large living area contained a stone fireplace, a leather easy chair and an ottoman, an oil lamp on a heavy end table covered with stacks of leather-bound books. Halfway up the stone wall on the right side looking forward was a beam-supported walkway protected by a wrought-iron railing. The walkway, linked to the main floor by a spiral staircase, also led out to the front of the Castle. Along the inner walkway were several oak doors opening to a series of small bedrooms.

At the back of the living room were two massive doors to the Castle library. I told the shrink, "Of course no one dares go in there." The shrink wanted to ask why, but I cut him off with an angry look. I told him about the dungeon in the basement. The key to the dungeon was on an end table right next to the big leather chair. I grinned. "Of course there's also a secret passageway from my bedroom to the dungeon."

The shrink knew not to ask the obvious question. I just gave a little shake of my head. Now I had him trained. He was frustrated. Then he tried a trick. He decided to ask a giant question.

"Tommy, only one last question. Do others live inside the Castle? You know, besides you and Bob."

"Of course," I said, sounding like I was going to tell everything. "Of course others live in the Castle."

"Who?"

"You said 'one last question.' I answered it. Who lives inside? It's for me to know, and you to find out. Now it's time for me to go."

BOB

Smith raised his hands to indicate that I now knew all that he knew. "Bob, you haven't overheard any of this with Tommy?" I shook my head. He paused to let me speak, but my dazed mind didn't have a clue what to say.

"Okay," Smith continued, "this much is clear. This is undeniably multiple personality disorder. Tommy may hate me, but he's being very helpful in leading us into the inner parts of you. I have no doubt that there are others, but no idea how many. The Castle is an organizing structure; many with MPD have something like it, perhaps a house, a garden, or a maze."

Smith hesitated. "I really don't want to go any further with this work until you've made a decision about your therapist. You see, any therapist has to keep track of various personalities, often serving as the only common memory among them and thus the link between what's happening inside and the patient himself."

My head was swimming in a strange zone between utter shock and a desire to finally get at my core problem. In a curious way, I also felt a rising relief at

Smith's rendition of Tommy's story. Finally, there was an explanation of what might *really* be the core problem. There was a chance of pushing beyond the sense of treading water with alcoholism recovery. Smith had said the problem was not genetic but rather could be addressed with difficult psychiatric work. Although Tommy's tale seemed zany, to say the least, it offered a little hope that it might open ways to make me whole.

I started to sob uncontrollably. For the first time but hardly the last, I screamed: "Damn it! Why can't I be real? Why can't I be like normal people? Fuck this stupid life!"

Smith said nothing, just pointed out the box of Kleenex on the end table. I wiped off my eyes and nose and took a deep breath. Don't lose it, Bob, I counseled myself. All right, there was no question in my mind about one thing. "Okay, I'm ready to go ahead with you as my therapist. And you don't need to give me other names. I want to work with you. You know me and my situation. I like working with you."

"I want you to be absolutely sure. This may take a long time, many months, possibly years. There are other good therapists . . ."

"I'm absolutely sure."

"Okay, then, we'll begin with sessions three times a week. I've got a full schedule, so I'll have to stretch with sessions in the later evening. You must make this your highest priority. I assure you I will give it the same degree of attention. I would advise you not to tell others at this point. I know from experience, they just won't understand. Got it?"

"Yes."

"Oh, one last thing. You've made a big decision today. It's a decision to live life a better way. Terrible as MPD might seem, it's a disorder that has a cure called 'integration.' That's a lot more than many doctors can say to their patients. But never forget that there's another danger."

"What's that?"

"You're still a recovering alcoholic. Coping with MPD is no excuse for slipping back into drinking. In fact, if you were to start drinking again, it would be almost impossible to deal with multiple personalities. You're a fighter and you've got to give this everything you've got. You're literally fighting for your life." *gud cheun, 8 t, conportional adnisor & supportive.*

THREE

~~*#3*~~

~~YOUNG BOB:~~ "I WHISTLE,

AND THE BIRDS SING BACK."

ONE NIGHT, JUST A few weeks into intensive therapy, Dr. Smith was perplexed. "Tommy, is that you?" Up until now, Tommy had always appeared as a cowering hyena, tail between his legs but always ready to strike back. But today the image was radically different: open face, calm eyes, gentle smile, relaxed hands lying open in his lap. Had the hyena transformed overnight into a pensive fawn? "Tommy?"

The young ~~teenage boy rocked his head~~ shyly and momentarily hid his face with a delicate movement of his hands. Finally, he spoke haltingly in a soft child's voice devoid of any cynicism. *Young Bob #3*

YOUNG BOB #3.

"I'm not Tommy."

I could see Dr. Smith waiting. He wanted me to say more.

"I'm Young Bob."

Dr. Smith waited again.

"Not like the Bob you know. I don't do all his stuff. You know—talking and writing stuff. I mainly just sit. And sometimes," I said with a little smile, "I play the flute."

#3.
hears
sings

"Nice to meet you, Young Bob. I like the flute a lot."

"Well, it's not a shiny flute. It's made out of wood. Just a few holes. And I'm not very good at it. I just make little noises. Like birds singing."

"That's nice. Bob once told me that up at the lake, in New Hampshire, he used to sing to the birds early in the mornings?"

I shook my head. "That's not right. He didn't do it. When the old people said they liked it, he just smiled and maybe thought he did it in his sleep. I think it's kind of funny."

"So what do you do now?"

"I don't do anything now. I just sit on the top of the Castle walls. Play my flute. Kind of watch what's going on."

"Did you know I talked to Tommy?"

I didn't like his question. It made me nervous. "I know you talked. Everybody knows. But I promise I didn't hear what you said. Everybody's scared of Tommy."

"Why?"

Tommy #2
angry
harmful

"Well. Tommy's mostly quiet. But when he gets mad, he screams at people and he breaks things. He hurts them with words. On the outside, he doesn't hit people. But inside the Castle . . ."

Tommy's could be
mean to inside
to others.

"Yes, what happens inside?"

I was scared to say it out loud. I whispered so no one else could hear. "I can't see inside the Castle. But I can hear. When Tommy's mad, someone else always screams, sometimes lots of screams. I think Tommy's meanest inside."

"I understand," Dr. Smith said, but I could tell he really didn't understand. I gave him my little smiley look, like I hoped he'd change the subject. He understood. "So, tell me," he said quietly, "why don't you do anything now?"

"I used to think I'd get to do lots of things. You know, like music and maybe reading. Not boring school stuff. I wanted to do things on my own. But I don't think the older people liked me."

"I like you. Why wouldn't they like you?"

"I heard them talking one day. They said the singing to the birds was 'cute.' But what they really liked was doing things. Not just sitting on a rock."

"Doing things? Like what things?"

"You know, like archery or reading or sailing. But I get good ideas by doing nothing. I mean nothing you can see on the outside . . . Know what?"

"What?"

"I think they liked Robbey best. I had to get out of Robbey's way."

"Robbey? Wasn't that just Bob's nickname when he was a kid?"

I just shook my head and smiled. I never met Dr. Smith again.

BOB

"So what does that mean?" I asked, after hearing Smith's account of Young Bob. "And who's Robbey?"

"Slow down," Smith admonished. "We're just beginning. We have to build trust. Young Bob's such a smart and sweet kid. Maybe Tommy might be better than we think. And Robbey? He'll probably emerge in his own good time."

"You're making them sound like real people. They're just stick figures. Little bits of me."

"Right there"—Smith waved a finger at me—"that's the problem in doing your own reading. Alters must be seen as real persons. They have their own unique experiences, abilities, memories. Alters have enormous differences—in voices, demeanor, literacy levels, even heart rates. Most of all, they have their own identities and their own feelings. Deny that 'realness' and MPD therapy can't work."

I paused to absorb it all. "But then . . . who am 'I'? Am I just whoever's talking at the time? Or am I just a collection of people who don't know one another?" I was feeling like a stranded traveler, trapped in some remote village whose residents I had never met and who were all viewing me with curiosity and suspicion.

Dr. Smith gave an understanding smile. "Look, I know it's confusing. In a literal sense, the alters are all part of you. I mean, all part of Robert B. Oxnam. And, of course, if we can do what we want to—achieve integration—then it's all solved. Then there's just one person. That doesn't mean getting rid of the alters, but rather assimilating them into one whole individual who has the skills and the memories of all the alters. For the meantime, it seems you're the dominant personality and you're the one who mainly deals with outsiders. So you can say 'I,' even though you mean 'I, Bob,' and know that there are at least two others."

"Dominant personality? Can that change? Can someone else take over?"

"Not unusual at all. Sometimes there are power struggles, just like in politics or business."

"And then the 'I' shifts to someone else?"

"It can happen that way. But we're way ahead of ourselves. Right now I'm intrigued by how you've managed to be successful in spite of this disorder. I know you think you're a bad person. That's the MPD guilt trip. But you've got a lot of accomplishments to your credit. Next time, can we talk about that?"

Next time was three weeks later. In between, I had to take a whirlwind trip to Southeast Asia, with public presentations in Hong Kong; Bali; Indonesia; and Canberra, Australia. Given the intensity of my therapy sessions, I was worried about this trip. In spite of fatigue and worry, this was one of my very best voyages to Asia. I spoke enthusiastically to the several hundred leaders who attended the annual dinner of the new center in Hong Kong (the program was clearly on a roll and represented a giant step for the Asia Society).

Over a thousand businesspeople attended the Society's first corporate conference in Asia—it was in Bali. In my opening remarks, I illustrated the problem of American ignorance of Asia by citing my informal poll of a few New York City taxicab drivers: "Do you know where Indonesia is?" I asked them. My favorite response came from a gruff fellow who said: "Can't you see it's raining? When it's raining, I don't go beyond the city limits."

In Canberra, I participated in the Society's annual Williamsburg Conference of Asian and American leaders. Cyrus Vance, former secretary of state and cochair of the conference, asked me to summarize the three-day meeting before we adjourned. When my ten-minute summary was completed, Vance warmly tapped me on the back and said, "Nice job, Bob."

A compliment from someone I admired as much as Secretary Vance was a great lift, enough so that I forgot my notes and had to run back to the conference room to retrieve them. A page fell out when I picked up the legal pad. On it was a little floor plan of a castle that I only vaguely recall having drawn during the meeting. *Bob* was written on the front walkway, *Young Bob* on the front wall, *Tommy* in a little room just behind the front inner wall, and the question *Robbey?* loomed just to the side of the Castle.

THE CASTLE IS REAL,
THE WORLD IS NOT

#4 → Researcher, intellectual.

ROBBEY: "I'M THE SECRET WEAPON.

KEEP IT A SECRET."

IT WAS NOW THE late fall of 1990. Bob had already endured several months of intensive therapy (two, and sometimes three, sessions a week). Shortly after his return from Asia, the pace of therapy suddenly increased. The Castle, once sparsely populated as far as Dr. Smith and Bob knew, suddenly was filled with newly emerged personalities and lots of noise.

At the very first session after Bob's return, Dr. Smith confronted a very different personality. The new figure was supremely self-confident—arms folded, a smug smile, his sharp eyes scrutinizing the psychiatrist. He was clearly not the shy Young Bob and not the angry adolescent Tommy. This was a tough-minded adult, skilled in the world of negotiating, looking something like a dealer in the diamond district. ✦ Robbey #4

ROBBEY

"You figure it out, Smitty. You're a sharp guy."

I could see that the psychiatrist didn't want to make a mistake. "Let's see, I haven't met you before. Right?"

"A-plus so far, Smitty."

"Well, I only know one name I haven't met. Are you Robbey?"

"Top of the class. I'm not surprised. I've been watching you. You pretend to be mild-mannered. You're the Clark Kent of shrinks. Okay, Smitty, want to cut a deal?"

"Depends on what it is."

"Here's the deal. You want to know how a nutcase can be such a success. If I tell you the answer, can Bob take off three days from work next week? He's got the time. He needs the rest."

"Okay. It's a deal. If Bob keeps his therapy sessions."

"Tough bargainer. Okay, it's a deal. Get out your pad. Tell me if I'm going too fast."

This was going to be fun. I had never told the story, but it was already written in my head. I barely stopped for breath. It's true, I told him—I, Robbey, was the "favorite" of Mom and Dad, at least from the end of grade school until freshman year of college. Why? The answer was easy. "I was the best at lots of things—the fastest note taker, the speediest memorizer, the quickest paper writer. You gave me a job and it was always done well and on time."

I told Smith I could work day and night for long stretches. Besides, I let him know about my "mental clock." High school students were always amazed that I knew the time in my own head. How? It was easy. I just listened for the bells on the Castle tower, ringing every fifteen minutes, and the rest was easy.

 # #5 Clock
maker.

"I'll bet you never heard of Lawrence," I said casually to Smith, who shook his head. "He's inside, too. He runs a little antiques store specializing *# 6* in antique clocks. He keeps the Castle clock running on time." Not until much later did Dr. Smith meet Lawrence, whom he described as "quiet and shy, but quite professional about his clock expertise." Lawrence was the most minor of our personalities and Dr. Smith only encountered him once.

"But," Smith wondered, "who gave you the jobs? Who was in charge?"

"Simple," I replied. "Sometimes it was a teacher. Or an archery coach. And very often it was Dad or Mom."

"But didn't you get tired?"

"Sure. When a job was done, I crashed. Often for days at a time." I told him about my small bedroom, right above the Castle's living quarters, reachable either by the spiral staircase from the living room or by the door from the Castle's guard walkway. "It was like a medieval scholar's cell"—illuminated by suspended oil lamps, containing a desk and chair and a small straw bed, filled with towering stacks of books and papers. I stuffed papers around the door so as to avoid being distracted by whatever else was happening in the Castle. The adjoining bedroom was never occupied; it was cluttered with boxes of "finished projects."

"So, not so complicated, eh?" I grinned at my quick summary. "Success is a matter of planning and hard work. That's what I do." *Robbey #4.*

"So tell me," Smith asked, "how come it's not you, but rather Bob, who is dominant today?"

My smile faded. "I got fired. Well, not really fired. I got demoted."

I explained what happened in September 1961 at Williams College. When making plans for sophomore year, I included one course in public speaking. The professor gave his "how to be a good public speaker" tips in the first two weeks, then began having students deliver short speeches in each class, followed by critiques from the professor and other classmates.

"I just panicked. I had never talked in public. I did the research, not the talking. I thought the course was going to tell us *about* public speaking, not force us to *do* it. I was scared to death to talk. And so, after I learned all the tricks on speaking, I dropped the course. Dad was upset when I told him. "You've got to be a good speaker. It's very important. Like your grandfather. He's a great speaker."

"I didn't cry—I never cry—but I was very sad. That's just when someone else emerged in the Castle. Someone who could do things in public. You know, speaking, meetings, teaching, television."

"Was it Bob?"

"Exactly. He became number one. Thank God, Dad still used the names Robbey or Rob. But Bob was suddenly in charge."

"So what did you do?"

"What did I do?! I did the same things I always did. The new boss was Bob. I did whatever he needed. Notes, the best typed notes in history. Memorization, thousands of Chinese characters. Dissertation research. Teaching outlines. Speeches. Whatever Bob wanted, he got it. It's the same way today."

"But now he's exhausted."

"Smitty," I said with genuine fear, "I'm worried sick about Bob. He's burned out. He just doesn't seem to care anymore. I'm glad you're giving him permission to take the days off next week. But that's not enough."

"Robbey"—Smith looked me in the eyes—"maybe we can work together to help Bob out. I'll need all the help you can give me. Is it a deal?"

"It's a deal." I nodded with a smile. I could tell that Smith didn't like me much. But I didn't care. This was business—a lot was at stake—he needed me and I needed him.

BOB

As always, I was totally unaware of what happened with other personalities. Smith took the final ten minutes to brief me about his conversation with Robbey. "I think this is highly important," he said as I was leaving.

Highly important? It was the most astonishing insight I'd ever had into myself. It explained the workaholic part of the success story. It also told me why I felt like I was a fraud. The true spadework was being done by Robbey, and not by me. Robbey had revealed why it was not until 1961, my sophomore year in college, that I ever became involved in classroom discussions, and not until senior year and then in graduate school that I ever gave a speech.

I, Bob, literally was born in that year of 1961 with the task of developing all of the professional skills necessary for adult success, but relieved of all the obligations of doing the dirty work of content research. I could devote myself to learning how to speak in public, conduct meetings, engage in quick analysis, write smoothly, do television interviews. I was grooming myself to become a leader. Robbey was already the most fanatically loyal lieutenant one could ever imagine. It was the ultimate symbiotic relationship, right inside me, and I never knew about it.

I'm sure what I did next must sound a little crazy. But then again, everything that was happening back then seemed to be scenes from an episode of *The Twilight Zone*. That night in bed, I tried to send unspoken thoughts to Robbey. *I can't believe what you have done. You've been our secret weapon. You deserve a huge amount of the credit. And instead, you got demoted. I'm really sorry. All I can say is—endless thanks.*

I didn't hear anything back. I just felt a warm, inner smile. Tears came down my face. My God, it had worked. I had touched a secret inner part of myself, a personality whose existence I had never known. After years of rising and often baffling afflictions, and a few months of bizarre revelations of multiple personalities, I suddenly felt a little whiff of hope.

You know, I said silently to Robbey. *I'm going to need your help, more than ever. I've totally lost my way. Help me. Help Dr. Smith. Please?*

I didn't hear anything. But I felt an inner response. *You got it. It's a deal.*

At that moment, I realized the truth in an earlier Smith comment. Robbey was not some abstract "alter"; he was a very real personality on his own and a crucial part of a composite human being. Although I did not fully recognize it at the time, that unspoken moment—communicating with Robbey—was a major step toward the far-distant goal of integration. The best psychiatrist, and surely Smith was just that, could only point the way, but the challenge of putting the pieces back together would rest primarily with me and whoever else was inside.

FIVE

#6 - the feather

ROBERT: "VALUES COUNT MOST.

BUT WHO'S LISTENING?"

Now I know this chapter might feel a little weird since you've been *Robert now french* hearing from me, Robert, since the beginning. But remember, I was *person, y* sort of a late bloomer in the MPD therapy process. I was a "recessive person- *wrote* ality" (active only on the inside, not visible on the outside) until the early *the book* 1990s. *Bob by g*

The fact of the matter is that you know next to nothing about me. As of *Wanda* very late 1990, neither Dr. Smith nor Bob had any knowledge that I even existed. I was lodged very deeply in the Castle—plopped on my easy chair, surrounded by books—and had never emerged on the outside. All that changed one night in Dr. Smith's Scarsdale office. Dr. Smith's first clue was my dress and demeanor.

I came out of the closet—literally—making my appearance without Bob even knowing it. I recall dressing much more carefully than usual for that appointment, seeking to convey a thoughtful but casually "professorial" impression. So I donned a blue button-down shirt, a floppy gray sweater, clean but well-worn dungarees, and old leather boat shoes. I glanced in the mirror. Yes, I thought, he would see the "real me" inside of Bob—a fairly relaxed middle-aged guy with dark brown hair streaked with gray. Of course, he'd catch a few signs of aging—some furrows in my face and a slight slouch, perhaps making my six-foot-four height not as imposing. At the very least, I hoped he would know I was most comfortable in casual dress and just hated suits and ties. Actually, this dressing ritual seemed to calm my nervous anticipation of meeting Dr. Smith for the first time.

It was a little amusing, watching Smith try to figure out who was sitting in the chair that night. It wasn't that I was trying to be coy, but rather that I was fascinated by his eyes, looking me up and down and then right at my face, searching for clues. I had listened, of course, to months of therapy sessions, but it was different sitting on the hot seat myself.

Smith scrutinized me carefully, trying to get a hunch about my identity. "I hope I'm not insulting you," the psychiatrist said carefully, "but I'm just not sure who you are. Too old to be Young Bob, too calm to be Tommy, too relaxed to be Robbey. I'm just going to take a guess. I think you're someone else. Am I right?"

"Quite right," I replied. "It must be hard to keep us all straight in your mind."

"You bet it is," Smith agreed, shaking his head. "So many different looks and trying to stay on top of so many conversations."

"I know exactly how you feel," I replied with genuine empathy. "It's tough inside the Castle, too. For instance, I know about all the conversations you've had—Bob, Tommy, Young Bob, Robbey—the whole lot. But inside the Castle, don't get the idea I know all of what's going on. It's a beehive, buzzing with thoughts, feelings, memories, conversations, secrets."

"Excuse me," Smith interjected. "it's nice talking with you. But . . ."

"Oh, my goodness." I slapped my forehead for such forgetfulness. "I haven't introduced myself. How rude. My name is Robert. I have the name given at birth."

"So you're the original one? The first personality? The adult who emerged from the original baby?"

I rubbed my head. It was something that always confused me. "I'm not really sure. Those first few years are pretty hazy in my memory. Of course there's a way to find out. But I'd never dare do it."

"How? Can you help me find out what happened way back?"

I crossed my arms, staring at Dr. Smith with a look of mild chastisement. "Do I have to tell a psychiatrist to be patient? Frankly, what you seek is a long way off right now. And let me tell you"—I leaned forward in my chair and spoke softly—"it's dangerous. Make a mistake and you'll never get the right answers. You could make it lots worse for those of us inside the Castle."

"I understand," Dr. Smith said solemnly. "Can I count on your help?"

"Look, I'll do what I can," I replied. "But I'm not Robbey. I'm not going to make a deal. I'll tell you what I think will help, but only when I think it will help."

"Can I ask how many personalities there are altogether?"

I began counting on my fingers. "Let's see. Right now, you mean? It changes sometimes, you know. Right now there are eleven of us."

"Eleven!? And I've only met four—Tommy, Young Bob, Robbey, and you, Robert. Right?"

"Wrong. You've left out one. You left out Bob. Even though he appears on the outside, we see him as part of the Castle structure, walking on the outer ramparts. So you're not even halfway, huh?"

Smith shook his head. "It's not just numbers. The trick is to find out how you interact. And why some don't interact at all. For instance, it was a huge breakthrough to figure out the Bob–Robbey connection. Now, how about you and Bob?"

"Bob and me?" I sighed. "Now, that's not a happy story."

"How so?"

"Well, unlike Robbey, I don't have much direct access to Bob. Let me tell you something about the Castle. You see, Robbey's study is just a few steps along the iron-railed walkway to the outer walls, where Bob uses the research in his public life. They have the perfect direct connection. It's much harder for me. My chair is right in the middle of the Castle; it's a pain to trek across the big stone floor, climb up the damned spiral staircase, and wait for a break in the Robbey–Bob action. Usually Bob is too busy to absorb other thoughts. I never know what's going to sink in. And, of course, Bob has never even known that I exist. Not until you tell him after this conversation."

"Sure sounds frustrating."

"Frustrating? It's infuriating. I've got lots of good ideas, but so little gets through. That's been going on for decades. And in the last ten years, it's gotten so much worse. Right now it's awful."

"So what do you do?"

"Not much for me *to* do." I rubbed my temples, trying to ease the pain. "I'm just a frustrated dabbler." I gave Smith the short story of my "roller-coaster life": moments of satisfaction but long troughs of frustration. "I'm a values guy. I'm happiest when there's a big cause." I told Smith about anti–Vietnam War activities, the China Council heyday, speaking out against the Tiananmen massacre.

"But what about the Asia Society?"

"The Asia Society presidency?" I said with a sneer. "I would run it totally differently from Bob. I'd make it much harder-hitting on human rights, authoritarian systems, government corruption. Of course Bob did some good things—like studies on tricky issues such as Korea and the Philippines. But fund-raising is the main job—and Bob often pulls his punches rather than offend some potential donor." I looked at Smith earnestly. "In my mind, it's too much about smiles, too little about conscience. Without strong values, it's just constant work, and Bob burned out. I can only say, 'I told you so.' "

"But why haven't you taken action yourself?"

"Take action? I've been too busy to take action. I haven't told you everything. My life is filled with other responsibilities. Besides, I've told you how hard it is to get access to Bob."

Dr. Smith held his ground. He put his finger to his lips and stared at me with a "cut it out" look.

"Okay, you're right. I'll be honest. I can take strong stands on big issues. But when it comes to turning ideas into action, I'm a bit of a wimp. I'm a teacher by nature. But I'm not really an activist."

"So what do you really do these days?"

"You mean besides reading and scratching out some ideas? Well, I've been playing the classical guitar for the past couple of years. I practice three or four hours a day. And take lessons twice a week from a great Russian concert guitarist, Yasha Kofman."

"That's great. Sounds like you're serious about it."

"I'm serious about everything I do. I heard Andrés Segovia back in the 1950s—just loved the sound and the depth—finally decided to do it myself. But there's a deeper reason for trying to play music." I told Smith my "brainstorm": What would happen if we tried to draw everyone together in the Castle around a single instrument? I had even taken the trouble of diagramming the Castle residents as sections of an orchestra, assigning myself the role of "conductor."

"So you must be getting good at the guitar by now?"

"No. I've done everything by the book. Fantastic teacher, superb guitars, constant practice. And the result? Even on my best days, I'm quite a mediocre guitarist. On my worst days, I sound pretty much like a beginner. And in front of people, I'm awful." My lips tightened and I shook my head.

"Know what I proved? I proved that you've got to be 'together' to play music well."

"You sure you aren't just being hard on yourself?"

"No. I'm just being honest. But I'm not going to quit playing music. Maybe I'll get better as we sort all this stuff out." I was really stubborn about the guitar playing, partly because it was the only time that I got to emerge on the outside in those years. Bob would say, "I think I'll play some music," then disappear; I would temporarily be the outside personality, but only while the guitar was in my hands.

Actually, by the end of this first meeting with Dr. Smith, I was pretty annoyed with him. After all, I thought he'd be so happy to meet me. I took him deeper inside the Castle than anyone had before. Besides, I thought I was closer in style to Dr. Smith than anyone else was. I sensed we had similar values, and like me, he was committed to helping people. I saw us both as conscience people in casual packages. God, wasn't he tired of Bob, always decked out in suits and tuxedos, killing himself on the achievement treadmill? Surely Dr. Smith must have wanted a kindred spirit inside the Castle. Here I was, just waiting for discovery.

"Well, time to go," I announced, hoping to provoke a warm farewell.

"Nice to meet you, Robert," he replied. "Hope we can meet again before long."

Damn, I thought, that's just what he said to everybody else. Was he even listening to me? So I gave him a sullen look and just faded away.

BOB

When Smith told me Robert's story, I lost it. "Are you telling me that this Robert jerk is taking potshots at me from within? That's unbelievable.

It's one thing to have ivory-tower types making nasty comments from the outside, but to have one inside me? Damn, let Robert try to raise money for a ten-million-dollar annual budget and cope with a bunch of bickering staff, trustees, and donors at the same time. Given that, I think I've done a lot to keep the values flag flying."

I expected Dr. Smith to back me up. Surely he understood the challenges of running an institution. But the psychiatrist just smiled as if trying to stay in the neutral zone. Later he explained that it was potentially destructive for a therapist to lean to one side or the other in such a classic instance of bickering MPD personalities.

"Bob, I really wish you could find a way to resolve these differences. You've told me that you've lost heart in your work. Robert has all the heart you could want. And yes, he's got the teacher's dilemma of putting things into action. You really know how to make institutions work. Imagine if you were working together, as one."

"Sounds like a formula for constant fighting."

Smith knew he was pushing hard, but he also knew that MPD therapy required a more assertive style at times. "Come on, Bob, look at it as a business issue. Why not work out a deal? Robbey—your super-researcher—could be a key part of the deal. I think he'd like that notion."

"Sure. But who's the loser? How many times have deals ended up with one party winning big-time and the other losing his shirt? I've worked too hard to roll over dead."

"I'm not talking about death. When alters merge, no one 'dies.' We are talking about a big step toward integration. And that's a step toward a better life, not toward death."

I listened, but I saw Smith observing my clenched fists. "I appreciate what you're trying to do. But look. I've just heard about this Professor Robert guy. I'm not about to jump into bed with him."

"You're already in bed with him. Every night."

Smith's words rolled over and over in my mind for the next two days. One thing I was finding about MPD therapy is that it inhibited any semblance of peaceful sleep. The control I exerted during the day, keeping everything seemingly normal at all costs, fell apart in the nighttime hours. Logical patterns of thought broke down entirely. My head was filled with babbling sounds, stray ideas, crazy noises. Oddly enough, I found I couldn't sleep until I gave up trying to control anything at all; it was almost like trying to be drunk when I was stone sober. And even more strangely, I couldn't sleep until the image of some little animal—a deer, a mouse, a seal—came into my head. I figured the animals were sort of adult teddy bears I was conjuring up to soothe my nerves.

When I told Smith about it, he immediately wondered "whether Robert has any answers for Bob."

As soon as he said it, I felt a "switch" happening. My eyes fluttered, as if going into a hypnotic state. I didn't fight it. It was becoming a familiar sensation.

ROBERT

"After all those nasty comments," Robert said sharply, "why should I do anything for Bob? He's been ignoring me for years."

"It's not for Bob," Smith replied, "it's for me. I really need your help. I need some answers."

"You want to know about the sleep thing?"

"Please. Tell me about it."

"I can do better than that. When it comes to sleeping, it's not my department. You've got to meet somebody else." As soon as I said the words, I was a little angry with myself. I was trying to show Smith that I had a lot of influence inside the Castle. But it was a tricky strategy. I was worried about Smith's next discovery.

"Who should I meet?" Smith asked anxiously.

Damn my big mouth. Now I had to make way for another personality. "Okay, Dr. Smith," I said anxiously. "I'm trusting you here. Let me warn you. Don't believe everything you hear."

SIX

BOBBY: "WHY AM I A PRISONER?

'CAUSE I'M BAD."

D<small>R. SMITH WAS CONFRONTED</small> by what seemed a strangely fretful young boy who squirmed uneasily. His hands fidgeted with his pants and then wriggled around the arms of the chair. His head kept bouncing around and his eyes never engaged Dr. Smith. His mouth made funny shapes, sometimes a little smile, sometimes a quizzical look of wonderment, sometimes a sad pout.

After a minute or two, Dr. Smith broke into the boy's gyrations. "I wonder. Who are you?"

BOBBY

the prisoner.

"Bobby. I'm Bobby." It was funny talking to Smith. I'd heard him for a long time. But I'd never spoken to anyone before, you know, not to anyone outside the Castle. I didn't speak very loud. I was sure others were trying to listen.

"Nice to meet you, Bobby. I'm Dr. Smith."

"I know. I know. I know. But I just can't believe . . ."

"Believe what?"

"You know . . . You know that, uh, Robert . . . that Robert let you see me. This is the first time anyone's come to see me in here."

"In where?"

"In this place. It's the dungeon, you know. It's a prison. I've been here for a long time. I think it's been about fifty years."

"Fifty years!" Smith was really surprised. "Why? Why are you in prison?"

I began rocking back and forth. "It's because . . . It's because . . . It's because I'm bad. I'm very bad. So they put me here. I don't think I'll ever get out."

"Who do you mean by 'they'? I mean, who put you here?"

"It's not important. I deserved it. I'm bad. I'm so bad."

"Is the door to the dungeon locked? Who keeps the key?"

"Of course it's locked. And . . . you didn't know? Robert keeps the key."

"Robert?! The nice professor? He keeps you under lock and key?"

"Robert's smart. He knows how bad I am. That's why he does it."

"What did you do that was so bad?"

"What did I do?! Everything I do is bad."

"What do you mean 'everything'? Can you give me an example?"

I felt like I was tied up with ropes all over my body. I was wiggling, like, you know, to get free. Then I stopped and smiled. "Guess what? I've got animals!

Lots of animals! Right down here in the dungeon. They're my friends. Of course Robert thinks it's silly to have animals. He says they're 'imaginary animals.' He says I make them up. I know it's bad to make them up. But I do it anyway."

"I don't think it's silly at all."

I began bouncing on the chair. "It's silly. But do you want to hear about one of the animals?"

"Sure."

"Well, one of them is called Nester. He's a desert mouse. Nester the Desert Mouse. I spell it *N-E-S-T-E-R.* Robert says that's wrong. It's supposed to be 'Nestor.' I'm kind of stupid and can't spell very well. You know, I can't really read or write. But I don't care. I like it my way. You know, Nester."

"Tell me about Nester."

"Well, Nester lives in a big desert. He's a cool mouse. He dresses up. He's got shiny boots. And an old blue army coat, you know the kind with gold buttons and white inside. And he's got one of those old funny hats like French soldiers used to wear—it's got holes for his ears. And he carries this wooden sword that has silver paint so it looks real."

"What does Nester do?"

"Well, when those camel caravans come along the desert at night, Nester waits behind a big sand dune. Sometimes there are hundreds of camels. Lots of them with big bags of grain. Just when the first camel comes by, that's when Nester jumps out, hands in the air, waving his shiny sword. He shouts in his biggest voice: 'I'm Nester the Desert Mouse.' All the camels jump because they're scared. Camels are scared of mice, you know. And when they jump, some of the bags of grain fall on the sand, splitting open. The camels make these big snorting noises. Then the whole caravan goes running off into the night. Nester laughs and laughs."

Smith chuckled. "It is funny."

"But then guess what happens? All of the other desert mice come running out and they eat up the grain. They eat and eat until they're so fat and happy.

Then they sing songs about Nester and he rides on their shoulders. They love Nester the Desert Mouse!"

I smiled for a second. Then I got kind of nervous. I started wiggling around. "I know it's a stupid story. It's silly. It's not real. I just made it up."

"What's silly about it? It's funny. And I really like Nester. You tell the story very well."

"Really?"

"Really! Honest."

"I've got lots of other animals. Like the Mentally Retarded Fawn who just bangs his head against trees and makes the other deer laugh at him. And the Harp Seal who's always worried that the men are going to spear him, but his mother takes care of him so it doesn't happen. And Ragamuffin, he's a Saint Bernard puppy, who runs up little snowbanks with one of those kegs of brandy around his neck, pretending he's rescuing somebody. Ragamuffin's my very favorite. There are lots of others, too. They live right down under the dungeon stairs. I can talk to them whenever I want to."

Smith gave me a nice smile. Not like a mean smile. "Know what else?" I asked. "I've got one special power. I play with my animals late at night and early in the morning. No one in the whole Castle can sleep until I sleep. And everyone gets up when I get up."

I gave Dr. Smith my "so there" look. You know, the look where you sort of rock your head back and forth. And then, I just left.

BOB

"Bob? Are you there, Bob?" I hear Smith call out softly as if rousing someone from sleep. "Bob, I think I've got the reason for your insomnia problem."

A few weeks earlier, I would have reacted in disbelief. Now I heard Bobby's story with rapt fascination. One part of me absorbed it as a colorful narrative, a vivid introduction to a hidden part of myself. I couldn't help wanting to cuddle sad little Bobby just as he found solace in his animals. Another part of me was leaping ahead and trying to figure out the significance of Bobby. Smith was right: I wanted to be the psychiatrist as much as the patient. What did Bobby represent? And why did he see himself as so bad?

"Damn it, Robert!" I shouted. "How can you lock up a sweet kid for so long? How can you make him feel so bad?"

ROBERT

As soon as I heard my name, I was there. I had to defend myself. "Just like Bob," I said sharply, "coming to conclusions without enough evidence. He just doesn't understand. Bobby *is* bad. Do you think I like locking him up? It's for his own good. It's for all of our good."

I could see that Smith was upset. "I don't understand," he said. "What do you mean 'for his own good'?"

I spoke as calmly as I could. Smith had to understand my position. "Yes, he's been a prisoner for a long time. But I've got a heart. I let him out from time to time. And every time he comes back, he's done it again. Time after time, he always does something bad!"

"What do you mean 'bad'?"

I threw up my hands in exasperation. "Let me count the ways. He's the one who started smoking. He's the one who drank like a fish. He's the one who eats too much and throws up. He's the one who loves to play with himself looking at girlie magazines. He's an addict, and no one can control him."

"I didn't know this. But sounds like maybe he became an addict because you're trying to control him too much. Isn't it possible that he does all these things as a release?"

"That's just what I thought," I replied. "It took lots of control on his part to stop drinking. I told him that I was proud of him, and that he deserved a reward. He loves to do things outside. Incidentally, that's why China questions can't be answered while sailing—it's Bobby who's at the helm. In any case, when Bobby asked, I said the Newfoundland trip was okay if he didn't drink."

"I think I was the one who said that," Smith interjected.

"Well, anyway, I agreed right away. It was a stupid idea anyway."

"Why was it stupid?"

"Because all the other addictions came back with a vengeance—smoking, bulimia. And besides"—I paused for emphasis—"who do you think stole those things from the marine store?"

"Bobby?"

"You see what I mean? It was a stupid idea to let him out for such a long time! I don't blame you. I blame myself."

BOB

When Dr. Smith told me Robert's explanation, I was truly speechless. Little Bobby with his imaginary animals a hardened addict? A thief? How could it possibly be? I actually felt a pang of sympathy for Robert. He wanted to be a loving father to Bobby, but had to cope with a chronic delinquent instead.

For me, the discovery of Bobby created a serious moral quandary. Of course "normal people" might have such antisocial instincts, but they are usually restrained by an integrated moral structure as they become adults. If only I had known all these things, I was sure I could have kept such behaviors under check.

Of one thing I was sure—I wasn't going to use MPD as an excuse. Terrible acts had taken place on my watch. However this therapy worked out, I was going to try to make amends for past behaviors and try to prevent them from happening again. That was the AA code and now it applied to everything. It was one thing to have bad things happen inside, but Bobby's actions affected others.

SEVEN

ONE CASTLE AND TWO KNIGHTS

IT ALL HAPPENED WITH stunning speed in the years of 1990 and 1991. Dr. Smith and Bob were left reeling just trying to keep track of ever-emerging new personalities. As late as February 1990, Bob felt that he was a "whole person," not afflicted by any dissociative disorder whatever and recovering from his alcohol addiction. A few months later, Bob had been diagnosed with multiple personality disorder, informed that his inner architecture was a castle, and introduced to a series of inner personalities—Tommy, Young Bob, Robbey, Bobby, and Robert. Bob had no idea where the MPD therapy would lead him, but he was already aware that other "undiscovered" personalities were waiting in the wings.

For Bob, of course, the experience was new and bewildering. He was discovering us for the first time, learning that we had all been active during what he saw as "his life." He encountered each of us sequentially as

Dr. Smith laid the groundwork and welcomed each new arrival with compassionate understanding. For Bob, these were moments of stunned surprise—premiere performances, week after week, in the stage setting of Dr. Smith's office. Of course, since Bob was not actually present at the performances, it was more like hearing Dr. Smith's critical reviews just after the curtain closed.

But for the rest of us, we all knew about Bob from way back and we all knew about one another. He was like a king preening and parading outside the walls, but the hard work was all being done within the Castle itself. The Castle had been there for a half century, not only housing several inner personalities, but also bubbling with activity. Just as each personality had a history, so, too, the Castle had a history. For Dr. Smith, now that he'd had a glimpse of the Castle and its occupants, the challenge was to become a historical sleuth.

Dr. Smith, as well as Bob, also had the challenge of coping with a very confusing present. Look at it this way. Until a few months earlier, Bob was outside and we were inside; we knew about him, we influenced him, but he knew nothing of us. Now both Smith and Bob were poking into a world they had just discovered. That changed everything. Not only were they making discoveries about us, but also we were suddenly relating to them, and to one another, in very different ways. Like Winnie-the-Pooh, Bob had stuck his paw into a beehive; he would soon find that beehives often offer more stings than honey.

BOB

Looking back on 1991, the last year of my life as I had known it, I will always wonder what would have happened without Dr. Smith's discovery of MPD. Would I have just "burned out" and collapsed? Would I have been institutionalized for a variety of self-destructive behaviors? Would I have finally, "successfully," committed suicide?

As it turned out, there was a much more intriguing alternative, possible only in the strange world of multiple personality disorder. My alternative fate manifested itself in that strange MPD zone where inside and outside personalities interact. Having recently discovered some astonishing things about myself, including that my brain was organized into a castle, I was about to take a guided tour inside this strange medieval structure.

Let me tell you the tale of 1991. It requires a little name-dropping, but you already know that is one of my sins. I hope you'll forgive me. My connection to the senior President and Mrs. Bush went back to 1975 when I met them at the liaison office (later the embassy) of the United States in Beijing; they hosted a lovely evening and screened *Citizen Kane* for the entertainment-starved diplomatic community. In the late 1990s, I was privileged to accompany George and Barbara Bush on a three-day trip to Beijing and Hong Kong. I found them delightful company. I cherished the hours of conversation with Barbara Bush about the challenges of writing, and with President Bush about China-related issues, particularly about Taiwan. I was moved by the fact that President Bush frequently said that "if I could choose only one global issue to help resolve since leaving the White House, I would pick the China–Taiwan relationship." Upon returning home, I was astonished to find President Bush's handwritten note thanking me for sending him one of my books on China: *I haven't read your book yet, but that's because Barbara insists on reading it first.*

In November 1991, President Bush was the featured speaker at the Asia Society's annual dinner, the biggest fund-raising event of our year. Unless you've done it, it is difficult to comprehend the challenges of organizing a special activity in honor of a sitting president of the United States. From mid-September, when John Whitehead, former deputy secretary of state and chairman of the Asia Society, worked his miracle of securing the president as our speaker, until November 12, when the dinner occurred, the advance planning was my number one priority (as well as that of my indefatigable executive vice president, Marshall Bouton). No one had to tell me that a great deal was riding on this presidential dinner. If the event came off well, it would considerably enhance the Society's reputation as a truly significant institution in both American and Asian eyes. Not inconsequentially, the evening might net over $1 million for the Society's hard-pressed budget of $10 million at the time. If the dinner came off badly, it would be remembered as a major glitch in the Society's history and surely in my tenure as its president.

Of course no one knew that the fall of 1991 was the worst possible time in my personal life. The event demanded the most integrated planning. But could the least-integrated figure imaginable handle the job? I vowed two things: the evening would be as successful as I could possibly make it, and I would not make the Bush dinner an excuse to delay my rigorous therapy for multiple personality disorder.

I repeatedly asked Dr. Smith whether I was up to such responsibilities. He said that I had proven, time and again, that my pride would shine through when needed. Besides, it was clear, though Dr. Smith did not say it, that if I were to be forced to step down suddenly because of deep inner problems, it might be devastating to any future hopes of integration.

In fact, there was no stopping the MPD therapy process anyway. By this point, in the latter half of 1991, it had been well over a year since Tommy first manifested himself in Smith's office. Not only were the visits to Dr. Smith a routine, but also I was increasingly aware of enormous activity inside the Castle. Although I could not yet discern clearly who was talking or what was being said, I could feel waves of emotion clearly coming from personalities deep within.

I began to surmise who was most active at any time. It was surely Robbey when there was a great pressure to compile to-do lists, making sure that nothing was overlooked in the Bush preparations. Perhaps the gnawing concern that we were fawning over a Republican president was the biting voice of Robert, but I always squelched it with an unstated rejoinder that "this isn't about a political party, but about the presidency as an institution." Late in the afternoon, when meetings became dull routine, I heard someone saying, "This is boring . . . blah, blah, blah. Got to get out of here." Was it Bobby? And being in Grand Central Station often prompted me to sit in a corner and observe the chaos as quietly as possible. Maybe it was Young Bob seeking solitude?

I found myself in a strange twilight zone between managing a demanding outer professional world and beginning to comprehend the influences of various parts of my MPD Castle. Curiously, I began to adapt to an existence of bouncing between sharply defined outer challenges and partially understood thoughts and moods. Although I knew my disorder was serious and rare, I also began to wonder if I wasn't experiencing something of the everyday life of "normal people." Don't most people experience waves of thoughts and feelings that often affect outer behaviors? It reminded me of bickering married couples.

"Why do you always give me that look when I mention your mother?"

"What look?"

"That 'there goes Betty meddling again' look?"

"That's just your projection. I don't have a look like that."

"See, you're not even aware of it."

Is it possible that unconscious or semiconscious "conversations" also occur among different mental parts of integrated persons? I wondered—do I have an extreme form of normal human thought and behavior in which my various internal parts are more discrete, with separate names, personalities, and memories? Aren't the required skills of MPD therapy—learning to listen to voices in your own head and to shape more healthy behaviors based on these conversations—really at the heart of any psychological therapy?

At first, the MPD meetings in Dr. Smith's office had been a "safe place" in which individual personalities manifested themselves. Smith was the trusted confidant of various personalities and then operated as a switchboard operator relaying the information to others inside the Castle. But as time went on, Smith seemed to become a social secretary, who could put the right people together, introduce them, and tell them what they needed to work out on their own.

It was almost as if Dr. Smith were saying: "Bob, this is Robert. I can't believe you've never met because you've been in the same circles for a long time. On the surface, I know you're probably not going to get along very well. You have very different values and personalities. But I've got a hunch you might get along better than you think. Anyway, you've got to cooperate somehow because you share a big problem. What are you going to do about Bobby?" Of course Dr. Smith was far too subtle to express it so boldly, but that was the effect.

At some point in the fall of 1991, the cumbersome therapy conversations (Robert talks, Smith relays it to me; I talk, Smith relays it back to Robert) diminished in importance. They were replaced by a strange new kind of direct conversation between me and Robert. Neither of us spoke directly with conventional words. Instead, ideas and emotions were conveyed in instantaneously transmitted packages, not unlike the file transfer process in the "explore" section of a Microsoft computer program. I would suddenly be startled with an incoming "mental e-mail" during some staff meeting, over lunch, or while reading on the commuter train. The messages came as jolts and, like the intrusive e-mail process, seemed to demand immediate attention. On one channel, I would continue whatever I was doing, but on another channel, I was able to formulate a response and shoot it back.

On more than one occasion, "Robert messages" intruded while I was giving a lecture, and a series of communications were exchanged without causing a break in the speaking. Apparently, from the applause and the generous post-lecture comments, the internal e-mail process had no negative impact on the speech. Curiously, however, in those cases, I have no recollection of the lecturing at all after I receive the first "You've Got Mail" impulse. One time, I was a bit dumbfounded when one person told me after a lecture—"loved that last joke; perfect way to end"—and I didn't have a clue as to what the joke was.

Many of these Robert–Bob exchanges focused on coping with the wayward Bobby. Try to imagine all of this as rapid-fire e-mail.

"So finally, something got through?" Robert's haughty tone was unmistakable. "I'm not just a spacey academic? So how would you have handled Bobby? Now do you see it wasn't so dumb to keep him grounded?"

"Look. I'm sorry," I replied. "But just because I was wrong on this one, it doesn't mean all your ideas are right. You think you could run something like this dinner for the president?"

"I wouldn't try running anything for *this* president."

"Robert, screw you! This isn't going anywhere. I want to talk about Bobby. How did he ever get that way?"

"You don't know?"

"Know what?"

"It's your fault. You never had time for Bobby."

"My fault?! That's crazy. I didn't even know of Bobby's existence until recently."

"Bob, that's too easy. It's still your fault. Ask Smith about it."

I was furious about Robert's accusation. And yet I felt guilty that somehow he might be right.

When I told Dr. Smith about the strange conversations and the uncomfortable feelings of anger and guilt, he thought quietly for a moment and then spoke carefully. "Bob, I know this isn't easy for you. But I'm afraid I understand exactly what Robert means. He's saying you were in charge, and you set the absolute priority as success at work."

"Okay, that's true, but I left lots of time for play."

"But, Bob"—Smith spoke firmly—"it was mainly success-driven play. Archery championships. Bicycle racing. Sailboat racing. It was play by your rules—very competitive rules. Come now, Bob, you didn't leave much time for good old-fashioned fun."

"So none of that really appealed to Bobby?"

"I don't know Bobby well enough to answer that. But my guess is no. Even with the sailing, I'll bet he liked the cruising rather than racing. I see Bobby as a much more freewheeling spirit. For all his shenanigans, I think Bobby's pretty special. I think he's the spark inside you. He seems like someone who enjoys playing for the fun of it, not for winning some competition. I sense he's got a deeply creative streak. He's got 'soul.'"

"But he's a delinquent kid. I'm supposed to accommodate a little criminal inside me?"

"You're missing my point. Yes, he's developed some bad habits, but that's the way of neglected children. It often happens when parents are too caught up in their work. Especially those who make work out of their play."

"But—"

"But nothing. Bob, I know it's tough to remember. Let me say it again— in therapy, alters must be thought about as separate personalities. But the goal of integration demands that we think about all personalities as part of a whole. The deep truth is that Bobby is a very significant piece of you. And you've ignored him altogether."

"But why? Why would I do such a thing?"

"I don't know the whole answer. But I believe I've got a significant chunk of it. I feel you're ready for this." Smith watched me carefully as I sat motionless, waiting for the shoe to drop. "I think a big part of the problem was how you related to your family, especially the role models of your father and grandfather, often underscored by your mother's ambitions for you. You sensed, often accurately, that they wanted you to be the perfect child, the perfect athlete, the perfect student, the perfect professional. And that's just what you sought to do. It brought lots of successes—but also an internal disaster. You made success your number one priority to the exclusion of almost everything else. And you squelched the Bobby inside almost entirely."

I was speechless. An icy anger rose up inside me. But his words also rang through me like reverberations through a steel bar. It seemed senseless even to speak. I was frozen with rage. It was the fury of confronting a cold, inescapable truth.

"I know what you're feeling," Smith said consolingly. "But don't feel so guilty. You were shouldering a collective weight—your grandfather's fame, your father's frustrations, your mother's ambitions. It all fell on you."

Smith paused, waiting for me to relax a bit, then continued. "But why, I wonder, did you buy into this success obsession so completely? Not just as a child but as an adult? Why didn't you cut free? Perhaps become a little rebellious, like so many others in the 1960s?"

I sat in stunned silence. The words didn't come forth. I just shook my head sadly and made a little empty gesture with my hands. I didn't begin to know why. It never had even occurred to me to ask myself such a question. I had done what I did because I hadn't ever considered that there should be another way.

"Look, Bob, we're after understanding, not blame," Smith said with comforting clarity. "You weren't born a success junkie. It's not because you're inherently bad. Trust me, there's a deeper reason. And we know where to find it."

"Where?"

"Hidden in your Castle someplace. I don't know the answer right now. But I'm going to need a lot of help to get there. Help from you and everybody else who lives inside."

"I don't want to make excuses," I replied. "But this isn't an easy time for me. I'm working flat out. It's not exactly easy to engage in full-time therapy."

"Look, Bob," Smith continued. "I know you've got a lot on your plate these days. But you've got another high priority. You and Robert have to deal with each other. Bobby's an important issue. Besides, you say you're burned out. Robert has energy, but has no way to use it. If you stay permanent enemies, everyone's a loser. This negotiation between the two of you is crucial to how you live the rest of your life."

EIGHT

THE GREAT MERGER: BOB'S FALL
AND ROBERT'S RISE

UNLIKE BOB, I, ROBERT, was just a voyeur when it came to the frenetic preparations for the Bush dinner. To me, it was pure puffery, lots of people pretending it was a big deal. I found the internal Castle drama much more interesting—everyone inside was riveted on the flow of conversations between Bob and me. Would there be more arguments or was there a new alliance in the making? In Castle history, the last alliance had occurred in 1961, with Bob's emergence as dominant personality and Robbey as his devoted ally. But no one in the Castle realized that Dr. Smith had even bigger plans in mind—instead of an alliance, he was thinking about a merger, a radical reshaping of the entire MPD structure.

It began with me wondering . . . had I misjudged Bob? Was he actually

*Robert &
Bob talking
directly*

capable of accepting criticism? Perhaps even capable of a tad of self-criticism? Maybe it was time to talk with Bob directly.

"Not bad," I said to Bob. "I thought you'd go nuts with Smith's comments. You know, about Dad and success, and about your responsibility for Bobby's behavior. You stayed cool. So I mean it, I'm impressed."

"Thanks. It still hurts like hell. But there's truth in much of what Smith said. It's really got me thinking about lots of things."

"Like what?"

"The hardest thing of all has been to realize that I'm only one of a whole group of personalities. I always thought it was all about me. I mean that when I said 'I,' it meant the whole thing, the whole 'me.' Damn, this is confusing to say, but do you know what I mean?"

"I know exactly."

"Okay, given that, I was so relieved to hear Smith say that MPD personalities don't die. Instead, they can merge their abilities and memories into other personalities. Until I heard that, I really thought I was dying. If I've got it right, there is a huge option for me, a giant decision."

"Which is?"

"Well, even if I'm not dying, it's certain this whole leadership business has burned me out. I've decided it will soon be time for me to step down as president of the Asia Society."

"Bob, that's a huge decision."

"There's more. When I think about it, I really can't imagine taking over another institution. I've just lost the fire for running things."

"And so what will you do?"

"I think the time's come for me to step aside. I mean inside the Castle. I thought maybe you, Robert, might take over."

"What? Me? I've never run anything. I wouldn't be good at it."

"Come on, Robert, just give it some thought."

"Honest. I can't imagine a life on the outside."

BOB

When Dr. Smith heard about this exchange, a warm smile crossed his face. "Bob, I'm so proud of you for thinking this way. It shows enormous strength. In my book, this is 'success' at its best."

"Thanks, that really means a lot." I had thought long and hard about stepping down from the Asia Society. And I didn't really have a clue about what I would do next. In an ironic way, finding out about MPD came as a relief in this process. My burnout was total, and so I avoided a post–Asia Society life of sputtering about trying to light wet coals. Maybe it sounds bonkers to someone who does not have this disorder, but MPD gave me a chance to pass on my skills and memory bank without the responsibility of doing new jobs. It wasn't like dying. It was more like planned reincarnation.

Smith allowed me a moment to reflect, then became remarkably businesslike. He explained it would be best if both Robert and I were quite meticulous about planning for "coming together." He observed that we were both adults, the only full adults he had met in the Castle. We should think of having an unwritten contract. "What conditions," he asked in a lawyerlike voice, "would you set for a merger?"

Although the question took me by surprise, I found that I had already thought out the answer pretty carefully. I gave Smith the following list.

never plan, coming together.

Bob: I hoped my name would still be used in professional dealings for several years to come, partly to avoid confusion, partly as a legacy of previous accomplishments.

Robbey: I wanted Robbey to be included in the "deal" and to work under the direction of Robert. I could not imagine any activity being fully successful without Robbey as the secret source of organization and research.

Abilities: I wanted to be sure that my various skills in administration, public speaking, human relations, long-range planning, and writing would all be incorporated into the new dominant personality.

From my perspective, the whole discussion had an eerie sense of professionalism about it. After all, we were discussing the end of my life as I had known it. The "I" that was Bob was about to pass to another part of the Castle that housed all of us. Robert would become the new "I." Pretty heady stuff by anyone's standards. I longed for a ceremony of some sort.

Dr. Smith broke in with a question. "If those are your conditions, do you mind if I speak to Robert?"

ROBERT

My head was swimming as I listened to Bob and Dr. Smith. "This is crazy!" I implored Smith. "It's all going too fast! I'm not a leader. I've spent a lifetime criticizing but not an hour leading. How the hell am I supposed to take over?"

"Relax! It's not as big a deal as you're making it." Smith spoke convincingly, but I sensed he was trying to sell me on the idea. "Bob has offered a pretty good deal, I think. You'll have all his skills. And Robbey is a terrific source of help. What stands in the way?"

"I've never done anything like this. I wouldn't be able to accept it unless . . ."

"Unless what? Tell me."

"Well, let me think. I've just got so many worries."

"You tell me your 'worries.' I'll just make them into 'conditions.' Okay?"

Name: I agreed that the name Bob could be used for most professional work, but that Robert might be increasingly used for personal friends and perhaps someday for all activities.

Leadership: I insisted that a date be set for stepping down from the Asia Society in the next year or so. And I wanted to be given full rein in determining new professional jobs.

Lifestyle: I was clear that it had to be my own private life as well. That meant I would be in charge of living arrangements, friendships, private time, and avocations.

"If Bob agrees to all this," Smith asked, "are you ready to take on this new challenge?"

"I really think I'm a bad choice," I said honestly. "No way I can do this on my own."

"You're not on your own. You've got all of Bob and all of those inside the Castle. And you've got me. I'll be with you throughout."

"Do you promise?" I waited until Dr. Smith nodded vigorously. "Okay," I said with the biggest sigh in my life. "I guess I'm ready."

BOB

For once, I was genuinely impressed with Robert. He'd had the guts to accept a challenge. He cut a pretty tough deal. And he only whined a little.

"Bob . . ." Smith interrupted my train of thought. "Do you accept Robert's conditions? Do you accept the deal?"

I pondered for a bit. What was I missing? I could think of only one possible hitch. "Okay, I agree. But there's one last issue. How can I be sure that Robert will keep to his bargain? I've got to know it will stick."

"It will be kept exactly as you both agreed," Smith said unequivocally. "For one thing, I will make sure that happens. But even more, if Robert reneges, it will surely activate a very common MPD phenomenon."

"What's that?"

"It's called 'regression.' But from your point of view, that's too negative a term. Quite simply, he reneges, you reappear. You would come back as Bob. Probably with a vengeance."

"You sure about that? Are you saying there's an escape clause?"

"That's just what I am saying. I'm absolutely sure. I promise you." Smith suddenly spoke with uncommon vigor. "Bob, this is a tremendously positive step. It's crucial to everyone in the Castle. If it doesn't work, there will be nothing but misery. That's why it's in everyone's interest to make sure the agreement sticks."

"Dr. Smith, just give me a second." Thank God, Smith didn't say anything. He just looked at me and let me sort out my thoughts. I suppose on one level it was like agreeing to my own execution. But it didn't feel that way. It felt more like a business deal. Yes, that was it—I was the tired old executive, taking early retirement but remaining on the board. Besides, I would still have veto power if the new boss rejected my legacy.

"Okay," I said finally, sucking in a deep breath. "I'm ready."

"Bob, it's been a pleasure talking with you over these two years." Dr. Smith's kind look had a strong tinge of emotion. "I'm really proud of you. Good-bye."

"Dr. Smith," I said, chills running up my spine. "I deeply appreciate your work. My eternal thanks. And I know this is the right decision." It was hard getting out the next word. I hesitated for the longest time. It seemed so final. But I knew it was right. Finally, I took a deep breath and said it. "Good-bye."

ROBERT *now become the dominate personality, the name Bob still appear as professional name*

"Robert?" Smith asked me. "Robert, are you there?"

"Yes," I replied, too stunned to say much. "I heard it all. Every single word. I'm overwhelmed. I didn't know that Bob had that kind of courage."

"Look. I think you're both showing courage here. It's a win-win merger. Don't sell yourself short."

"It's going to be strange without Bob on the outside."

"Frankly," Dr. Smith said with a soft shake of his head, "I'm amazed that he survived as long as he did. Incredible willpower. You're fortunate to have inherited his strengths."

"Dr. Smith, I'm really scared. You know that movie *The Candidate*? I feel like Robert Redford after he was elected senator. Remember, he asks his campaign manager, 'What do I do next?'"

Smith laughed, then looked at me comfortingly. "Not to worry. Just don't try too hard. Remember, you're not doing this on your own. Bob is now part of you. As is Robbey. You've experienced a partial integration. I'm proud of everyone involved. Including you."

"But what about Bob's work? The big dinner?"

"Just let it happen. Weigh in only if you're sure it's in all your interests. Outside people will still call you Bob, although they may spot some differences in demeanor. The big events will be done with the usual professional skill. Don't try too hard."

"And the long-term changes? The ones we agreed about?"

"They will happen in their own good time. You will reshape things—I'm sure mainly for the better. You'll make your mistakes, but I'm sure you'll learn from them. The real challenges will be measured in months and years, not in days and weeks. And, assuming you're willing, I'll be here to help as needed."

"Willing? I can't imagine doing this without you. I've never been outside, you know. The closest I ever got was when I tried to get Bob's attention at the door leading to the Castle walkway."

"Welcome to the outside world. Not such a bad place. And, above all, don't forget the most important thing."

"What's that?"

"Don't even think about reneging on your deal with Bob. I hate to think of the consequences."

For all the worry about taking over from Bob, the actual transition was remarkably uneventful. I, Robert, found it easy to follow Smith's advice and just let the job routine happen. When it came to running meetings, making calls, reaching decisions, I just turned everything over to the "Bob factor" inside me. Actually, I had witnessed all of this frenzied office activity before at a distance, but now it swirled around me. I had a new appreciation for the weighty pressures on Bob's schedule and his ability to make sensible decisions at high speed. It was a curious way to learn about administration—literally watching myself at work like a curious apprentice viewing an experienced craftsman.

One thing amazed me. The interaction of "real people" in an office had significant similarities to the interaction of "Castle people." Activities happened quickly and so much was expressed in little phrases, often without words at all. Thumbs up: "Got it, Bob. Good call." A quick circle of a finger at the head to indicate craziness: "Careful, remember he can fly off the handle." Firm slap on the desk: "When I say no, I mean no." And in a meeting, only one person talked, but silent interactions went on all the time.

Two people shared a look that said, "When is he going to shut up?" One person took notes while others were doodling; someone drew up a shopping list; one guy in the corner snorted disapproval of the speaker. It was just like inside the Castle. Late in the day, a senior figure came in and asked about budget projections; the Bob-inside-me gave a quick numerical guesstimate, and the man smiled: "Don't know why we even talk; we're always on the same wavelength."

So the initial fear of "doing Bob's job" quickly vanished, but my emergence as the dominant personality did bring some changes. For me, the Asia Society was only part of my life, albeit a significant part, where I felt an obligation to do things well, but my mind worked on other tracks. Since I did not feel Bob's persistent exhaustion, I also had no need to collapse and regroup on the daily commute.

When I met with Bob's assistant, a very perceptive lady named Daisy Kwoh, she clearly caught a glimpse of the transformation: "Mr. An," she said in Chinese (Bob always spoke Chinese when talking to her), "you seem different, more rested, more calm. Is something good happening to you?"

I smiled and nodded. "Yes, Miss Kwoh," I said, "things are changing for the better."

"I'm so glad," she replied. "I was so worried. Now I know my prayers are being answered." It seemed curiously natural that I could suddenly speak Chinese, just as if I'd had some new software added to the computer.

Perhaps, oddly, my merger with Bob and Robbey was making me more relaxed about implementing the radical changes in my part of "the deal." And so I concentrated my energies on what seemed the two highest priorities: "letting" the Bob-part-of-me focus on the annual dinner while I gave new attention to working with Bobby. I found that the new composite me had also inherited Bob's ability to work on multiple channels at the same time. It was a skill that was not required when I could focus single-mindedly on my activities inside the Castle.

Four days before the Bush dinner, I attended a security meeting with representatives from the Secret Service, NYPD, White House staff, JFK Airport security, and Waldorf senior staff. It was a tricky meeting, not only for all who were concerned about a presidential event, but also for me, since it was now "my dinner." I was stunned that Bobby selected this very moment to initiate a rapid-fire exchange of messages with me. In the past, we had never really communicated in a conventional sense; instead, I let him out when the pressure seemed to demand some freedom, kept him under control when I feared he might do something untoward, and directed anger at him when he misbehaved. Now I discovered that although Bobby "spoke" in his own inimitable style, the communications were handled very much like my earlier "e-mails" with Bob.

"This is cool," Bobby suddenly broke in. "It's like a movie. Look at the 'top-secret' charts and stuff. Secret Service guys. No one knows which car has the president. Dum-de-dum-dum . . . who stole the president?"

"Bobby, is that you?"

"Hee, hee, hee. It's me. I want to be a Secret Service guy."

"Please, Bobby, shut up. This is really important. I'm happy to talk to you. Just not right now."

"But I want to talk right now."

"All these years, we never really talked. Why now?"

"Because I know you're different now. Now you're together. You and Bob and Robbey."

"How do you know that?"

"I hear lots of things. Right through my keyhole."

"Okay, it's true. But I don't think it really makes a lot of difference for you. At least not right away."

"But I want it to be different. Want to hear about my animals? I've got a good one—he's a Mentally Retarded Fawn."

"Please, please, please! Not right now. Later. Okay?"

"You never want to hear my stories. Well, I'm going to tell Dr. Smith a secret. You'll be sorry."

"What secret?"

"About what happens sometimes late at night. You know: Tommy. You can hear it, can't you? I cry and scream."

"Of course I hear it. It wakes everyone up. It's just your nightmares."

"That's not true. It's not bad dreams. Tommy hurts me."

"You're just making that up."

"I am not. You won't listen. You never listen. I'm telling Dr. Smith."

Now this was the sort of crisis that I had never considered when I became—oh, this is hard to say—the "dominant personality." Since Bob did not know the inner workings of the Castle, he would only occasionally have to say "I'm sorry" for something that bubbled up into his outer domain. By contrast, I was taking a lot of inner baggage to the outer realm; I didn't know everything, but I knew a lot of darker Castle secrets. In the old days, I could carp about Bob's lack of values, but it was easy to look the other way when bad things happened inside the Castle. Now I was suddenly confronted with taking responsibility, not only for Bob's world but also for my own world. Things I had chosen to ignore within the Castle were about to come home to haunt me.

Smith smiled when I described how well the internal merger was working at the Asia Society. "But," he asked, "how's Bobby taking it?"

Damn, I thought, how did he know the vulnerable point? I told him about my exchange with Bobby, causing him to smile until he heard about Bobby's screams.

"Do you really know why he screams?"

I answered quickly. "It's just his nightmares."

"Really?" Smith queried, looking at my leg shake nervously.

"He's just a kid. He makes up things."

"Mind if I talk to Bobby?

What else could I say? "No, I guess not."

BOBBY

I didn't want to talk to Dr. Smith. I wanted to be a bunny rabbit hopping around the room. I wanted to tell stories. I wouldn't even look at Dr. Smith.

"Bobby, do you have something to tell me?"

"I guess so. You know I can hear a lot of what you and Robert say. And I was happy about the thing with Robert and Bob and Robbey. But now I don't know."

"Know what, Bobby?"

"I don't know if Robert's going to be nicer to me. He's pretending he doesn't know what happens. You know, sometimes late at night."

"What happens, Bobby?"

I stopped jumping. I just sat on the chair. Dr. Smith thought I was looking at the ceiling. But I wasn't. I was looking up and to the right side. That's where the danger always came from. I talked in a tiny whisper. Smith pulled his chair closer to me. "I'm scared to tell you. It happens after I've been bad. You know, like stealing things or looking at girlie magazines. Even after things I didn't do. Like when Bob messed up some talk. I can never sleep those nights. I know it's going to happen."

"What's that?"

"I can hear Tommy walking down the stairs. You know he has a secret way to get here without going by anybody. He comes in and stares at me. And then . . ."

I started to cry. Then I started screaming. Dr. Smith put his arms around me. "Tell me, Bobby. It's important that I know."

Tommy punishes Bobby.

"Tommy hits me with his hands. He bangs my head against the walls. Sometimes he scratches my face."

"I'm so sorry, Bobby."

"And sometimes . . ." I was still crying. "Sometimes, he takes away my food. Once for five days. And also twice he burned my arms."

"Oh, Bobby"—Smith cradled me—"that's terrible."

"And he yells at me. He shouts, 'You're so bad. You're always bad. You're a bad boy.' I think I hate his yelling as much as anything."

"Doesn't anybody try to stop it?"

"No one stops it. Only Robert could stop it. I think he knows what happens. But he says it's only bad dreams. That's not true. That's not true!"

ROBERT

"Robert," Dr. Smith asked firmly when Bobby disappeared in tears. "You heard that. What do you say?"

"You can't believe a thing he says," I snapped back.

"Robert! He didn't just make this up. Look, I know about the self-abuse from much earlier talks with Bob. Now we know how it's happening. And I know you know it's happening. You just turn a deaf ear."

A shudder went through me as I absorbed Smith's retort. Yes, it was true. I had surmised what was happening. Yes, I thought it was Tommy doing it. No, I wasn't exactly sure what Tommy did. But yes, I thought Bobby deserved punishment for being bad. And yes, it was a lot easier to look the other way when Tommy did it. I knew something else as well—I knew why Tommy did it. And just as I guessed, Smith didn't want to talk to me. He wanted to go directly to the source of self-abuse.

Tommy self-abuse alter.

"Tommy," Smith said sharply, "I'd like to talk to you."

TOMMY

"So what?" I said, making my hands like claws and snarling at that stupid shrink. "I did all those things and more. And I'll keep doing it until Bobby behaves. He's bad. He must be punished."

"So who gave you the right to be violent?"

"I'm not violent. I'm just doing my job. When Bobby's bad, he knows it's wrong. And he knows that punishment must happen. That's just the way it is."

"And who decides he's bad?"

"I really hate you." I hissed at him. "You think you're so smart. And you're so stupid."

Smith said it again. "Who decides he's bad?"

" 'Who decides he's bad?' You really want to know? I'll make sure you find out the answer. Very soon. And I guarantee one thing."

"What's that?"

"You'll be very sorry you asked!"

ROBERT

Tommy was right. Everyone inside was already sensing the awful times to come. Smith was probing dangerous territory. He was unleashing the darker forces in the Castle.

But I was determined not to let the impending internal turbulence undercut the Bush dinner. For a half century, there had been an unwritten, but unbreakable rule. When something outside required total concentration, nothing inside was allowed to get in the way. That was Bob's rule, and no one dared violate the memory of his former dominance.

As I stood before the mirror in my office bathroom at the Asia Society, it was both a familiar and strange image that looked back at me. I saw myself dressed in Bob's black-tie battle dress, ready for the challenge of what was not just another annual dinner. *Don't worry, Bob,* I said silently, *it's still your dinner. I won't screw it up.* But I also saw my own smile, a warmer smile than Bob's, albeit with some fretting lines around the eyes, foretelling the last of "Bob's annual dinners."

In my hand was the blue file folder Robbey had prepared with essential information. It contained my welcoming remarks, copies of John Whitehead's remarks, a just-released copy of President Bush's speech, a complete minute-by-minute scenario of the evening events, a copy of the annual dinner official program, and a list of all key contributors to the event. Just before John Whitehead and I greeted President Bush at a side entrance of the Waldorf, the chief of the Secret Service detachment put small pins on our lapels, indicating highest security clearance. It was eerie being in the "secure package" all evening—like being in a fish tank, swimming at your own pace, everyone else running around, trying to get the best glimpse of the king fish.

Suddenly, just as President Bush arrived, I felt inner vibrations, like a ringing cell phone. I knew there was an incoming Bobby message. *Communis*

"The president's not happy. He's sad."

"Of course he's happy. He's smiling. Please, not now!"

"Just look at his face. He's not happy. He's making a hurt smile. Who hurt him?"

"Okay, I see. But we can't talk now. I mean it. We'll talk later. Good-bye!"

I stared at President Bush. Bobby was right. Now I could see it, too. It was obvious if you looked behind the politician's well-practiced warm demeanor. A dark cloud seemed to envelop him. What was it? Not anything specific, except that his eyes seemed to lack a sharp focus and his body seemed to move as if on automatic. I had missed it entirely, but Bobby spotted it right away. Bobby couldn't have known it, but we were watching a politician who knew his presidency was in jeopardy. The Asia Society dinner was almost exactly a year from the day when Bush fell from office in a landslide decision for Arkansas governor Bill Clinton.

I felt a twinge of sadness for President Bush that night. It surely wasn't anything that changed my strong opposition to many of his more conservative policies and appointments. Instead, it came from some other force inside me. Part of me knew too well what it meant to be driving flat-out for success only to find out that the tank was running dry. That part of me also knew what it meant to struggle through each day, to put on the happy face in public, to be too tired for the "vision thing," and to try so hard that the result felt fake. That night I felt a sharp twinge of sadness for Bob.

Since President Bush was unable to stay for the dinner itself, the "secure package" was quickly escorted to the stage of the Waldorf Ballroom to hear his address. The president was greeted with a thunderous standing ovation; he waved his hands in the traditional politician's greeting and then gestured for everyone to sit down. I stood up, put both hands on the lectern, and paused to let the applause subside. As I took a couple of deep breaths, the scared-to-death feeling seeped away, replaced by an enlivened sense of calm energy, fueled by over a thousand people silently waiting. I heard Dr. Smith's words: "Just let it happen." And so I welcomed the president and greeted the throng at candlelit tables around the ballroom and in the three balcony tiers up above. No wonder Bob had found this such a public high; it was like being Maria Callas at La Scala.

I took my seat with a sigh of relief and John Whitehead graciously introduced President Bush.

Bobby whispered: "That plastic reading machine is really cool. See, he can read the big letters on both sides of him. The people can't see anything. It's really cool."

"I know. It's called a teleprompter. Hush now."

"See those guys way up there in the back? Right next to the spotlights. They're Secret Service. They've got guns. I saw it on TV. They shoot if someone tries to hurt the president."

"That's right. But no one's going to hurt the president. Now quiet, I'm listening."

"You're not listening. You're bored. This is boring."

"Okay, I'm not listening. I'm thinking about what I have to say later."

President Bush finished his speech, received an Asia Society plaque, and the "secure package" was whisked off to the Waldorf exit, where John and I waved good-bye. That was that; my relieved sigh was audible. "Nervous-making, isn't it?" John Whitehead remarked in the elevator back to the ballroom. I just said, "Whew!" John didn't know the half of it.

Actually, for those of us inside the Castle, the high point of the event was after dinner and well after the president had departed. Robbey did me proud: my five-minute presentation on major developments at the Asia Society, replete with neat statistics about attendance and impact, brought several rounds of applause. Bobby loved the huge percussive sounds made by the Japanese *taiko* drummer, stripped to the waist, playing on a giant six-foot drum. "That's *not* boring. That's cool."

SECTION THREE

BLACK CASTLE
ON THE HILL

NINE

#8 ~~WITCH:~~ "YOU'LL REGRET
THE DAY YOU MET ME."

A FEW NIGHTS LATER, Dr. Smith did not seem at all surprised that things had gone so smoothly at the Asia Society dinner. "I told you. All those abilities are inside you. Now, Robert, we have some work to do."

Actually, I was feeling pretty comfortable, not only at the Asia Society but also in the therapy process. With Dr. Smith as negotiator, we had made Castle history: after fifty years of fracturing, one new personality after another, we had reversed the process through a tripartite merger of Bob and Robbey into me, Robert. Not only was I handling my own "partial integration" pretty well professionally, but I could also engage in the conversations with Dr. Smith more knowledgeably than Bob. After all, I was now an outer figure with a clearer awareness of an inner life. I thought that perhaps, if I could keep the lid on internally, we might all be embarking upon a more healthy future. So, there was just a hint of cautious optimism in my smile to the psychiatrist.

That hopeful mood was dashed about five minutes into our session. "I hope you're not forgetting our last meeting," Dr. Smith counseled, a little chill in his voice. "Remember, Bobby cried terribly. He said you knew that Tommy was abusing him and did nothing. Then we spoke to Tommy. When I asked him why he hurt Bobby, Tommy said that he was operating on orders. And when I asked whose orders, he told me I'd be sorry that I ever asked. Do you remember all of this, Robert?"

"Yes," I acknowledged, hanging my head.

"And what do you say?"

I never got a chance to speak. Dr. Smith had never met the ominous figure who suddenly appeared. Her face was contorted into a horrible grimace with spiteful eyes; the mouth was open and teeth clenched together; the neck veins bulged out. One trembling finger jabbed toward Dr. Smith as if pointing out a criminal in a lineup. Coal-black eyes seemed to blame the psychiatrist for awful deeds. Then the figure began to laugh with the raspy cackle of an old woman.

WITCH

"Tommy hates you. But I don't hate you. I like you . . . You don't know how much I like you. You're my best friend."

"Who are you?"

"I watch you all the time. You do such good work. You make people happy. Happy people always become sad. You do such good work. Good work for me."

"Who are you?"

"Pushy, aren't you? Everyone in the Castle knows me. I don't live with them. I look down on them. I live in the other Castle. You've never heard of the other Castle? It's known as the Black Castle on the Hill."

"WHO ARE YOU?"

"I don't really have a name. But down there"—I pointed down to the left—". . . down there, they call me 'The Witch.' Suits me, don't you think? I scare everybody."

"You don't scare me."

"You're too stupid to be scared. Just what I want. It's perfect. You make them happy. Soon they'll be sad. Maybe even bad. Don't worry, I'll be back."

ROBERT

The Witch's words—"Don't worry, I'll be back"—sent a tremor through the Castle. Of course everyone inside knew about the Witch; I had known of her as far back as I could remember. We lived in mortal fear of those days, every few months, when she would suddenly appear in all her fury. The Castle would be sent into a frenzy of anger, invective, hatred, pain, and screams. We always whispered her name or, more often, just gestured to the right and trembled as we said: "You-know-who is out today."

Worse yet, you never knew when the Witch would silently exit her hilltop perch in the Black Castle. From our Castle, looking forward, the Witch's Black Castle loomed on a forbidding rocky spire above us and to the right. We always looked up when we were afraid—was the Witch coming again? But, of course, we never saw anything. The Black Castle was perpetually shrouded in fog, day and night, and neither sun nor moon revealed more than its ominous outline.

I felt personally responsible for causing the Witch to return after she had been dormant for several months. After all, I didn't have Bob's excuse; he'd never known about the Witch, although he often had to cope with her devastating damage. Not only had I always known of the Witch and her reign of terror, but also it was my sense of guilt over Bobby's pain that caused me to point the finger at Tommy. In my defense, I never anticipated that Tommy would get so furious at Dr. Smith that he would do the unthinkable. That little idiot, Tommy, he took Smith right to the Black Castle and the Witch herself!

When I told Dr. Smith about my worries about reactivating the Witch, I was flabbergasted at his response. He seemed aloof, very professional, and, worst of all, optimistic. "I know the Witch alarms you. There's a lot of internal history here. It's a delicate area, so I'll try to be sensitive. But try to remember, I'm not inside your Castle, nor am I inside the Witch's Black Castle. I'm on the outside trying to figure out what's going on."

"Look," I said in an almost insulting tone, "I don't think you understand. It was my fault. I should have told you about Tommy's punishment of Bobby earlier. I apologize. But you rushed ahead—talked to Tommy, found out who was really at work, and got her really mad. You've unlocked the worst part of the Castle. All hell's bound to break loose. It always does. And now, damn it, I'm in charge."

"Robert, let's get something clear," Smith replied sharply. "You're in charge of yourself. I mean, you're now the dominant figure in the Castle. But as long as you want me to do it, I'm in charge of your MPD therapy. And here's where we have go in different ways, at least temporarily. You see the Witch through the eyes of fear. But I see the Witch through the eyes of hope. Think about it from my perspective. Maybe the Witch has a crucial explanation for what we don't know."

"What's that?"

"How can someone so apparently successful live a life full of such self-loathing and self-abuse?"

"And you think that . . . 'you-know-who' can help resolve the question?"

"You bet I do. Think about it. The Witch thrives on fear and hatred. By contrast, you, along with Robbey and Bob, have formed a powerful merger to do very good things. I find Bobby caught in between, a wonderful kid and a naughty boy. I don't yet understand why everybody seems so sure that Bobby's always bad. Nor can I explain why Tommy seems to feel so justified in being a cruel bully."

"I know why Tommy does what he does." My words jumped out without thinking. Smith waited for me to finish. Should I tell him? I didn't know all that much about the Witch, but I did know one important thing. Besides, I felt terrible about standing idly by when Tommy hurt Bobby. "Okay," I whispered. "I'll tell you. Remember how Robbey only worked when he got an assignment from Bob? Well, Tommy only beats up Bobby on orders from you-know-who."

"So it's the Witch who determines when Bobby is bad and how he should be punished. Robert, I want to talk to the Witch."

"Oh, my God," I whispered. "Please be careful. Don't tell her that I let you know." Not until Smith promised did my eyes flutter as I made room for her frightening presence.

WITCH

"Back so soon?" I sneered. "Why should such a wise doctor come to silly old me?"

"I want to know why you pretend to be so mean. I'll bet you're really pretty nice underneath all that huffing and puffing."

I was furious. What a terrible accusation. And others were listening. "I'm not nice," I shouted back. "I've never been nice. You're the nice kind. I live on so-called nice people. You just watch."

"I do watch. Very carefully. I see a very good actress scaring everybody. Underneath, I see someone else. But there's one thing I can't understand . . ."

"You're spreading lies about me. You're making me very mad." But I was just a little intrigued by Smith's implied question. "So what, my super-nice doctor, don't you understand?"

"I don't understand why it's you who gives orders to Tommy to hurt Bobby."

"Who told you that? I want to know? Who?"

"Ha. I just guessed. I pretended that I knew. You fell for an old trick."

I glared at the psychiatrist, almost ready to hit him, then I backed off. "So we're playing games now, are we?"

"This isn't a game. I'm talking about a serious question. Why do you do it? Why make Tommy hurt Bobby?"

"Because Bobby's bad. I must make it known and I must make him pay."

"Who gave you the right to do that?"

"It's not a right!" I shrieked. "It's a responsibility. It's my job."

"So you just appointed yourself? So you know everything? You see everything?"

"No," I said, yelling more loudly. "I didn't appoint myself. It was a job given to me. A long time ago. I have to punish Bobby. It's just that way. I don't know everything. Only Eyes knows everything—"

I stopped short in horror. Damn, I'd done it again. That sneaky psychiatrist tricked me into revealing something else. There was nothing else to do. I gave a laugh, pretending nothing had happened. Then I disappeared in a flash.

TEN

EYES: "KNOWS ALL BUT CANNOT SPEAK."

[handwritten annotation: #9 anomaly — can, write, can't talk. sees all]

"SO, ROBERT," SMITH ASKED at the outset of the next session, "who is Eyes?" Smith spoke with the confidence of a private investigator hot on the trail. He seemed oblivious to the danger: now that the Witch loomed over the Castle, did he want to unlock another, more dangerous personality? Smith repeated himself more forcefully: "Who is Eyes?"

"Eyes?! I can't believe you found out about Eyes. Eyes lives up there, in a high tower of the Black Castle. She knows everything. Absolutely everything. She has always been there, always watching. She can see through fog and through walls. And she hears everything, too."

"Really?" Smith asked. "Robert, I need to talk with Eyes. Right away."

"Talk with her?" I laughed. "Eyes can't talk and she can't write. She only sees and hears. She doesn't meet anybody. Not even inside the Castle. Not even you-know-who."

"So you mean there's no way to find out what she knows? I can't communicate at all?"

"That's right." I thought seriously before going on. "But maybe there's one way. But damn, it would put me right in the middle. . . . Maybe I could . . ."

"Could what?"

"You see, it's this way. Every once in a while, some of us down in the Castle get help from Eyes. You know, when there's a big problem we can't solve. If we think hard about the problem and look right at Eyes, she sometimes helps find the answer."

"How can Eyes help if she can't communicate?"

"It's a strange way. If she wants to help—and that's a big *if*—then she just tells us without words where the answer can be found in the Castle."

"Robert. The answers to these questions are very important to me, but even more important to you. I really need your help in getting to Eyes."

"What questions?"

"Where does the anger come from? Why such self-hatred? Why such rage? What happened during childhood?"

"I'll try. I can't promise anything."

I tried to sound casual about this whole matter. In fact, I was churning inside. These weren't idle questions. The answers would unlock a whole chain of mysteries inside the Castle: about the Witch's frightening appearances, about Tommy's terrible punishments, about Bobby's perpetual badness. I had never dared venture to answer these questions myself. Such questions took you right to the heart of the Black Castle. The consequences of being caught by you-know-who were huge.

I spent a weekend pretending to tinker on the boat, but really fretting about what to do. Smith was pushing me hard.

Where could I go for advice? Inside myself? Since the merger, I had easy access to both Bob and Robbey since they were, in fact, part of me. But Bob was useless here. He'd never heard of the Witch or the Black Castle. And Robbey? He'd spent his whole life as a back-office guy, intentionally ignoring what was going on elsewhere in the Castle. Bobby? What could a little rebellious kid tell me at a moment like this? Young Bob? He was literally out of it since he'd never been inside the Castle walls. Tommy? Are you kidding— talk to the Witch's chief henchman?

Slowly, it became apparent. There was an inescapable, chilling truth. It all depended on me, Robert, to make a decision affecting everyone inside the Castle. But I hesitated. After all, if this went badly, it surely would unleash a chain of terrible events that would hurt us all. The Witch would be furious, Bobby would be blamed, Tommy would torture Bobby, and the Castle would echo with screams and be disrupted for days on end. I was now the outside guy, entrusted with leadership, and that required some inner stability. How could I possibly risk all those in the Castle?

I felt totally alone. I was being pressured to go where I had never gone— into forbidden parts of the Castle. My whole life had been spent in an easy chair, quite literally, never asking questions that must not be asked, never looking where I should not look. I certainly never sought to be a leader. Why stir up a hornet's nest?

My initial instinct was to do nothing, make no effort to contact Eyes. After all, would a commander risk all the troops for one foolhardy act? *Yes, that's the right decision,* I said to myself, *do nothing at all.* Whew, now I could relax. I'd weighed the odds and made a tough choice. Smith would be disappointed, but the others would be safe, at least for now.

Back I went to cleaning the winches on the boat; it was the perfect job, since, when properly greased, the winches made a soft whirring sound, telling you all was well with the world. But one of the winches didn't whir; instead it made a *whir, click-click, whir* sound; all was not completely well with the world. Why was Smith so damned insistent about my talking to Eyes anyway? Why couldn't he leave well enough alone?

Okay, Robert, face it. He talked to me because I'm now the dominant one. No, maybe it's even more than that. Maybe he's testing me, trying to see whether I have real leadership potential. Oh God, it suddenly hit me. Dr. Smith was asking me to use my inside influence to do something beyond all the other personalities. He wanted me to help solve the riddle of why we had multiple personalities in the first place.

So this was my time to choose. Would I pick the short-term safe alternative? Or would I take a giant risk that might help us all? For the longest time, I sat immobile in my boat's cockpit. Finally, I inhaled deeply and made my choice. I would trust Smith. I would try to contact Eyes.

That night in bed, after Bobby was asleep and the Castle was quiet, I stayed totally still but opened my eyes. I drew in my breath, turned my head slowly to the right, focused my eyes sharply upward, being careful to aim my gaze at the back of the Black Castle. Curiously, at just that moment, the fog lifted, and for the first time, the image of the Black Castle was crystal clear. My eyes were like a laser beam on a rifle; I would have one shot and it couldn't miss the target. I recalled each of Smith's questions—why the anger, self-hatred, rage, abuse?—and imagined all of them neatly packaged in a single bullet. I tried to breathe slowly and regularly, but my heart was pounding. Please let this work. Please let it get to Eyes. Please don't let it miss the mark. Whoosh—I sent the message.

Now all I could do was wait and see if Eyes would reply. Two days passed—I could barely concentrate at work—it was looking bad. I began projecting. Maybe Eyes had received the message but refused to answer. I was going to look weak to Dr. Smith. Or maybe worse, the Witch had intercepted the message. She was biding her time. Soon all hell would break loose—screaming, pain, anger, revenge, chaos. Everybody inside would hate me forever.

Still fretting, I couldn't sleep on Sunday night, less than a day before my appointment with Dr. Smith. In the early-morning hours, I suddenly felt a little tingling inside me. I wasn't sure whether it was heat or light, but I was sure that Eyes had responded.

I shut my own eyes and scanned the Castle. Where was the tingling coming from? It wasn't at all obvious. I had to scour the whole interior of the Castle. It was a dead-serious version of the old "hot-cold" game. Nothing was coming up "warmer"—not my living quarters, not Bobby's dungeon, not Tommy's garret, not Robbey's study, not Bob's walkway, not Young Bob's wall. Then I slowly stood up from the armchair I always occupied in the Castle. It was coming from behind me. I carefully turned around. I could feel it right in front of me. Eyes was pointing directly to the huge wooden doors of the Library.

ELEVEN

#10: aulmut matured woman-

LIBRARIAN: "YOU WANT THE ARCHIVES? I WANT A FAVOR."

I'D NEVER BEEN INSIDE the Library. Nobody had ever been inside the Library. We all knew the doors were bolted shut from the inside. When we said "The Library," we were really speaking of the rear of the Castle. Most of the time, we faced forward, toward the front of the Castle, or sideways, to interact among ourselves. We never looked backward. *murmur*

I stared at the Library entrance with its great dark oak doors and its black wrought-iron hinges. A pulsing glow of white light illuminated the two black iron rings that acted as door pulls. As I crept closer, a warm breath of energy seemed to draw me along, beckoning my hands to open the door. Brushing aside cobwebs and rust, I grasped the two black rings, feeling an energy pulse run through my arms and body. Astonishingly, the doors creaked open as I pulled.

Flickering oil lamps illuminated the large room, whose walls were lined with dark brown wooden bookcases. Remarkably, the Library seemed to be in active use. Leather-bound books were everywhere, not just crammed in the shelves but also stacked on the sliding ladder and on the well-worn rugs. Slowly, as my eyes became accustomed to the dim light, I could see the heavy wooden desk, dead center in the room, supporting rickety towers of piled books.

"Hello." It was a quiet call, the dark voice of a mature woman. "Hello, I'm right here." Where was the voice coming from? "Right in front of you." I heard a little rustling of paper. Aha, she was seated at the desk, hidden by the books.

I had never met the Librarian before. But Dr. Smith had encountered her once. He told me of her strange visit one night.

"Hello, good doctor," the Librarian had said to Smith.

"Hello," Smith replied. How odd, he thought, out of the blue, a new personality with a female voice. "And what's your name?"

The woman brushed back her hair with an affected motion. "I don't have a name," she said softly. "I'm not known by who I am, but rather by what I do. I'm the Librarian."

"It's nice to meet you. Can you tell me about your work at the Library?"

"It's a very busy job, you know," she said, sitting up prim and proper. "I keep track of every book in card files. Each entry is perfect. The rules require it."

"So who takes out books from the Library?"

"Takes out books? No one takes out books." On the surface, she seemed shocked that Dr. Smith was uninformed. But there was a teasing quality to her voice, almost as if she were toying with his ignorance. "I'm a little surprised, good doctor, that you didn't know this."

"But if no one is taking out books, why are you so busy?"

"Oh, my goodness. It's the donations. New material is coming all the time. I can barely keep up." She touched her fingers to her forehead, as if feigning a headache, then sensuously ran both hands through her hair. Bending her wrists, she carefully checked her fingernails and then softly stroked one hand with the other.

"I don't have much time for myself, dear doctor," she said. "But I do like to look presentable. It takes so much time on my nails and my hair. Tell me, good doctor, do you like my hair? Do you think I'm pretty?"

Dr. Smith said that he smiled (I would guess it was an awkward smile). Before he could reply, the Librarian suddenly vanished. Dr. Smith had wanted to ask the obvious question: How do we get into the Library? With the Librarian gone, I remember Dr. Smith asking me the same question. I told him flatly that there was no way; no one went inside, the doors were bolted.

And yet here I was, inside the forbidden Library, talking with a Librarian I had never met. Stranger still, I could not see her face, concealed by the mountains of books on her desk. Indeed, I would never see her face. But her voice was unforgettable. She spoke in dark, sultry tones. Her words emerged slowly. Each syllable seemed to be tasted with her tongue and licked with a little dose of syrup.

"Hello," I said, giving up trying to see the Librarian behind her books. "Do you know who I am?"

"Of course." She laughed. "I keep the records, after all. You've got stacks of records here. You're Robert."

"And do you know why I'm here?"

"Naturally," she replied. She paused, took a deep breath, and softly exhaled, a breath that seemed to be infused with jasmine incense. "You want to know what happened in childhood. You want the *Baby Book*."

"The *Baby Book*?"

"Of course—the childhood archives," she replied with a hint of a teasing laugh. "It's the story of Baby. Baby was the firstborn, you know. Before anyone, there was Baby."

"Yes, that's it. That's what we need. The *Baby Book*. Could I have it? Please?"

For a moment, nothing happened. Then two of the stacks of books parted, making a canyonlike opening. Her hands pushed a large leather-bound book through the opening. As I reached out with both hands, she kept both of her hands on the volume, firmly resisting my pull.

"Please," I pleaded. "It's important that I see this."

"I know." Again she laughed. "I know how much you want it. But it's not quite that simple." She laughed yet again. Her laughter rose and fell, like a high-pitched carillon. "You want something. But so do I."

We both kept our hands on the book. Her jasmine breath embraced both of us. We never saw each other, never touched each other, but we were drawn into a moment of raw sensuality. It seemed that every sense was captured: undulating sound, pure white light, musty library smell, tingling skin, salty-sweet taste. I cannot describe what transpired—was it energy from Eyes or from the Librarian? Whatever it was, it was unforgettable.

Then, in an instant, I was back in my familiar easy chair. I looked back at the Library. Its doors were firmly closed, as always, no sign of an entry. There was no book in my hands. But there was a smile on my face. It was all an indelible memory. I had been to the Library. I had experienced surreal delights with the Librarian. And the *Baby Book* was totally etched in my mind, waiting for me to open it. And as soon as I thought of its possible contents, my smile faded with a shudder.

TWELVE

#11 - and last after unexperienced trauma ises

BABY'S TERROR

IT IS DIFFICULT TO describe the array of emotions encircling me when I visited Dr. Smith for the next session. At first, I felt both exhilarated and frightened. It was a strange high to get closer to a deeply embedded truth inside me, almost as if I were Dr. Smith's partner rather than his patient. Besides, my experience with the Librarian left a tingling sense of excitement. I didn't confess the encounter to Smith at the time. Why not? you ask. Well, I've got this little prudish streak. I couldn't imagine saying, "Dr. Smith, the best sex I ever had was in my own head, fooling around with a Librarian." I feared his retort might be: "Get a life, Robert. Get a life."

The other feeling was raw fear. At first, I feared retribution from the Witch. Although she never targeted me personally, I feared the Witch would unleash Tommy's abusive behaviors, whether aimed physically at Bobby or emotionally toward outsiders. And yet nothing happened, and that told me a great deal. It meant that huge secrets could be kept inside the Castle, that they could be kept even from the most malevolent forces. Eyes and the Librarian, the two custodians of truth, seemed beyond the Witch's reach.

I felt strangely empowered, as the only personality who had ever explored so deeply into the secret recesses of the Castle. I had redefined "dominant personality" in terms of inner knowledge rather than outer power. And I had done so without the presence of Dr. Smith.

But as I drove through a dark night to Smith's office, I was visited by an even deeper sense of fear. For two days, I had access to the *Baby Book* in my mind. But I had not dared open it, not even for a peek. I knew it was my own internal nuclear device; I had no temptation to play with the fuse on my own. If there was going to be an explosion, Dr. Smith had to be at my side.

When I sat in the chair opposite Dr. Smith, I just stared at him for a long while. I didn't tell him the details about agonizing over whether to contact Eyes, finding my way into the Library, extracting the book from the Librarian. Instead, I gave him a quick recounting and cut to the chase. "Dr. Smith," I said finally with a foreboding sigh, "I might just have a way to get your answers. But someone else has to tell the story."

As my eyes fluttered, Baby emerged, speaking and behaving like a five-year-old, forced to tell truths he wanted to forget. He was reliving memory fragments, almost as if he were replaying inner videotapes. Everything in his mind seemed fresh and vivid. I can only guess when the events actually happened, perhaps over a period of time, maybe between ages one and four. From my recollection, corroborated by Dr. Smith, this was Baby's story. I recall Baby appearing only once (but Dr. Smith's notes suggest that I may have telescoped several sessions into one).

BABY *A time goes on h*

It's very dark. I'm not asleep. My hands cover my eyes. It makes it darker. But my hands make me feel warmer and safer. It's quiet now. Oh, no, I hear a squeak. No, not a squeak! Who's coming? No, no. Not the door opening. Oh, no, no light turned on. No light at all. Light on means happy. Dark is bad.

No, please don't pick me up. Please, please. I'm crying. He shouts at me. "You're bad!" Then I'm hit. My bottom hurts. My legs hurt. "You're a bad little boy! Such a bad little boy!" I'm hit again, again, again. Please stop. Don't hit me.

Then it's over. The door closes. I get into a little ball. My hands are over my eyes and mouth. Don't cry. Don't cry. It will happen again if I cry. Bad boy! Don't cry.

Now Dr. Smith comes over. I'm not scared of him. He hugs me. He won't hurt me. He doesn't have hurt in his eyes.

I sometimes make a mess. My diaper needs changing. I try not to cry. But then I cry. Sometimes it's okay. Sometimes not. I know when bad is coming. I get cleaned. But I hear it. "You're a bad boy. The very worst little boy." Then I feel something in my bottom. It's a finger. It hurts. I cry. Then something bigger than a finger. It hurts awful. I scream. Please stop. I cry again. I can't stop crying. "Bad boy! Bad boy! Bad boy!"

Dr. Smith holds me tight. He doesn't hurt me. I make myself small. Like a little ball. Nobody can hurt me now. "It's okay. It's okay," Dr. Smith says. "It's okay."

Another time now. I'm very bad. That's what I heard. "You're so bad. You know what you must do. Go get a branch. A sharp one with thorns." I go to the bush and break off a branch. "Okay, take your pants down." Oh, please don't. "It's your fault. You're bad!" *Slap, slap, slap.* Don't hit. Please don't. I'm bad, but don't hit. *Slap, slap, slap.* "You're bad. Don't tell anybody about this. Then it's going to be worse. Who is bad?" I'm bad! Don't hit anymore. Please. I'm bad.

Sometimes I try to hide. But I'm found. I'm bad! I scream out loud. But sometimes no one was mad. I'm bad. "No, you aren't, not if you take off your pants. See, now you're not bad. Now dance to the music. Jump up and down. Dance. Sing. Dance. Isn't this fun?" I'm not bad? "No, not today, you're not bad today."

"You are worst this time. A terrible boy. You must be burned." No! I screamed. No! I am picked up. Taken to the stove. There is a pot of boiling water. No! Please no! My hand. Don't pull my hand. No! My hand is taken close to the pot. It's hot like fire. Oh, please no! I scream, I cry. I try to get away. My hand is closer and closer to the pot. No! Then suddenly I'm put down. "Did you think you'd be hurt? Ha, ha, ha! Such a bad boy! So stupid! He thought he was going to be hurt."

I can't cry anymore. Dr. Smith holds me. No more crying left. I can feel the fire on my hand. Can't cry.

She said—"I'm a witch." She laughed and laughed. She ran around the room. A broom between her legs. "Ha, stupid little boy." She chased me. "I'm going to eat you." I'm crying. No! Please don't. I ran and hid. But I was found. "Don't be stupid. Are you scared? Just a joke. You really thought I was going to eat you? Ha, ha, ha. He's too stupid to know a joke."

As Dr. Smith held me, I laughed, too. A little laugh. It was a joke. I'm stupid. I thought it was real.

Once I found a little toy. It was a compass. I liked the black line. It stayed still when I turned around. Then it broke. The black line didn't work anymore. I heard the yelling. "You broke my compass! You're so bad! The worst this time!" I was dragged outside. There was the old icebox by the street, the one they replaced with the new electric refrigerator. I was pushed into the old icebox. The door slammed shut. *Thud.* The handle snapped shut. *Click.* I screamed. I cried. I hit the door. It was so dark. It was hot. I cried more. Help me. Please help me. There was no air. I couldn't breathe. I stopped crying. I went into a little ball. I tried to cry but I couldn't anymore. I was going to die. I knew it. Just before I couldn't breathe anymore, the door opened and I fell out. "You're bad! You're the worst boy in the world! Don't tell anyone about this! Otherwise back into the icebox. The next time, the door won't open."

IF TRUTH BE
TOLD ... THEN WHAT?

THIRTEEN

ROBERT: "NOW WE KNOW.
SO I'M CURED?"

H IS STORY TOLD, BABY gave a final shudder and disappeared, never to
return to the outside again. I was left uncomfortably in Dr. Smith's
arms. I gave him a hug and he retreated to his chair. We sat across from each
other in stunned silence.

"Robert," he said finally, "is there more?"

"Yes," I replied quietly. "There's lots more—more incidents, more
details—but Baby told you the basic story. It must have happened dozens of
times over a considerable period of time, perhaps a couple of years or more."

"Are you okay? How do you feel?"

As I write this, more than a decade has passed since I learned about Baby.
How do I feel? I'm still answering the question. The answer changes almost
daily, but the question remains the same. Over the years, I've run the full emotional gamut from raw rage to grudging acceptance. I suppose today, as I replay

the awful truths in the *Baby Book,* the dominant emotions are "pity" (for the awful inner lives of abusers) and "forgiveness" (because that releases me from the terrible life of anger). But that's not what I felt right then, when Dr. Smith asked: "Are you okay?"

"You know what?" I said with clenched teeth. "I feel fucking furious. How can you do that to a little kid? Fucking a baby! And fucking me for a lifetime! Goddamned animals!"

Dr. Smith didn't say a word. He just let me pour it out.

"I'd like to take a broomstick full of splinters and shove it up their asses. And then . . . Oh shit. It's a joke. A fucking cosmic joke. I just remembered. They're dead. Those who did it are dead. Those who could have stopped it are dead. Everyone's dead."

"You're not dead."

"I might as well be dead. For fifty years, I've had this damned story bottled up inside. It's ripped apart my whole life. And they get away scot-free? Now I know the story and so what? There's not a damned thing I can do about it."

"Oh, yes, there is something you can do about it," Smith said softly. "You can finally start living your life." Smith paused and looked me in the eyes. "I'm proud of you, all of you. You did what most people cannot do. You stared the truth in the face. Without knowing what happened, we couldn't have gone much further."

I heard Dr. Smith, but I couldn't really connect with what he was saying. I knew he was being sincere and consoling. But his nice words seemed like a Band-Aid over a gaping wound. Realizing that my fury had no object—I could only scream at corpses—the anger drained away, leaving only emptiness.

Smith looked at me, trying to ferret out what was going on. "What are you feeling now?"

"To be honest, I'm feeling nothing. I feel numb, as if it all happened to someone else."

"Robert, that numbness is MPD kicking in again. You're a pro at hiding from memories, especially the worst memories of all. You know that, don't you?"

I nodded and went back to pondering. I felt another familiar emotion rising up. I couldn't suppress it, so I confessed. "Know what I'm feeling right now? I feel guilty. I feel like I did something very bad in telling you."

"Robert, that's why our work isn't done. You did something courageous tonight. You faced your hidden truth. And, finally finding that truth, you feel guilty and bad."

No one in the Castle, myself included, could cope fully with what we had just learned. We could not deny it. It explained so much. But we wanted desperately to run away from that knowledge. What happened to Baby was gruesome, but it was hard to keep replaying Baby's ordeal. Like doctors witnessing too many moaning patients, we sought emotional walls to let us go on. The Castle was filled with walls—walls to separate personalities, walls to hide from memories, walls to avoid unbearable pain.

I wanted time to think. Dr. Smith agreed that I could take a few weeks away from therapy, but he was always ready for emergency calls. I feared that the Castle would be thrown into frenzy—perhaps a time for introspection, or worse yet, maybe a time of retribution for revealing secrets. Instead, Baby's revelations brought the quietest internal phase since the diagnosis of MPD two years earlier. The stillness was uncanny. All personalities were aware of one another, but there was no activity, no arguments, no scheming. Total quiet enshrouded us—not just the gray Castle where we lived, but also the Black Castle on the Hill.

We were all mourning, but the grief was not solely about Baby. Of course I felt Baby's excruciating pain very deeply. And I was furious that my anger had no outlet. But Baby wasn't dead. Baby had just told his horrible story and had retreated back into the Castle. He was a victim, not a corpse.

It struck me that what we were really mourning was our loss of innocence.

For fifty years, each of us had been denying a fundamental truth. Now the awful truth was known. Deep down, each of us sensed that our lives, separately and collectively, would never be the same.

Each of us was asking the same question: What do I do now? For me, just as it was impossible to keep revisiting Baby's torture, it was equally impossible to think coherently about the future. I went through daily life robotically and my inner mind was a jumble of fragmented ideas.

In a lecture on modern China to a group of businesspeople, I found myself riveted on the Tiananmen massacre of 1989, teasing out unspoken parallels to my own story. The Chinese government "turned its guns on its own people and then blamed the victims for causing the massacre." Someday, I said, the truth about Tiananmen will be revealed in what the Chinese call a "reversal of verdict." But I wasn't sure that truth would "bring dancing in the streets." Maybe it would prompt a "quieter acknowledgment of a terrible event." Even after a reversal of verdict, I argued, "the Chinese would still be left with the ramshackle system of Communist government with its security police and propaganda machinery." "How," I wondered, "can you fully unlock all the economic and creative energy in China if it is still run by a government designed to make people believe lies?"

I realized it was quite a stretch to draw an analytical parallel between my MPD trauma and China's political trauma. But it felt good to be giving an outer lecture and an inner lecture on the same subject. A few weeks later, I gave another talk, at which the introducer summarized my résumé: "My goodness, this guy's done so many things I can't cover them all. Maybe he's got multiple personalities." After the shock wore off and I realized it was just a figure of speech, I recall it as the only amusing episode in the aftermath of Baby's tale.

In a more private frame of mind, I tried to find places of deeper refuge. What did I really value in life? What inspired me most? This was a troubling question because I was not a religious person. After I'd learned about Baby's horrors, it was more troubling—I was an agnostic trying to make sense of devastating knowledge. Where could I turn to shed light on this terrible tale?

What about terror and beauty in religion? My mind wandered back to age thirteen, when my father's parents took me to Europe. I loved Chartres cathedral outside Paris, with its towering vaults that seemed to lift you to an unreachable heaven. But in the museums, I was frightened by the awful tortures of the Christian saints portrayed in medieval and Renaissance paintings, breasts torn off of Saint Agnes and arrows shot through Saint Sebastian. Even as a child I'd wondered, Why is it so sad?

While I never found the answers in the content of Christianity, the glory of its art has sustained me through my life. I do recall being transfixed by Michelangelo's *Pietà*—a loving mother mourning the limp body of her son after his execution. She cradles his body, a last gesture of maternal love and deep grief, her left hand slightly raised as if to ask "Why?" To me, the image was utterly sad and utterly beautiful at the same time.

On that early trip to Europe, my eyes drifted often from the troubling figures to the edges of spectacular paintings. There, rising above the green landscape and brilliant blue sky, was white, translucent light. From an early age, I occasionally felt light like that when I met certain people who had an inner goodness of heart. I have sometimes wondered whether suffering childhood abuse has something to do with it. Perhaps an abused child develops an extrasensory perception, an ability to look beyond nice words and superficial personalities, a capacity to see inner character. It makes sense. In a world of sudden terrors, a child's life may depend on knowing what someone really has in mind. If you see light, it's safe; if there's darkness inside, watch out.

I felt the same deep inspiration from the great music of the Christian tradition. For me, the brilliance of Bach was not just in the musical sound and shape. Bach radiated the very same light as did the great Renaissance painters. It was a potent light, prompting you to follow its beam, whether to the world outside or to the world inside.

What did this have to do with discovering terrible child abuse? Perhaps these ruminations allowed me to think around the awful revelation, but not directly about it. I pondered the world of feelings, without feeling the feelings myself.

After two weeks, when I returned to Dr. Smith, I didn't know what to expect. I wasn't sure if it would be a celebration or a wake. Instead, Dr. Smith made only a brief reference to the momentous story of Baby. "Don't worry," he reassured me. "You've now confronted the trauma head-on. We've been there now. Both of us know what we must know. There were dozens of terrible episodes—every kind of sexual, physical, emotional abuse. We don't have to go back." He smiled at me. "So what's been going on in your head?"

I told him of deepened thoughts about music and art and seeing modern China in a different light. "But," I confessed, "I can't seem to react emotionally to Baby's story. I know it now. But I can't seem to feel it."

"Robert, you've spent a lifetime creating ways to avoid these memories. Suddenly the truth is known. You expect to embrace that truth overnight? Your mind has been fractured for fifty years. You probably never experienced a single unified emotion since you were an infant."

"But," I fretted, "I thought once I addressed this inner problem, big changes would happen. What about getting over MPD? When can I be sure what I want to do next after the Asia Society?"

Smith wrinkled his brow skeptically. "Have you been under some mistaken impression that this therapy is magic? That we find out about the trauma and *boom,* suddenly you are 'cured'?"

"No," I lied. I was indeed hoping for just that, an overnight cure.

"Good, I'm glad you didn't make that mistake. Because I never said any such thing. Yes, this is a big moment. Now you know what caused MPD. You have showed great courage in discovering what happened. But you aren't over

MPD by any means. Several personalities are still active. We need to fully understand what's happened. We need to put the pieces back together."

"Like Humpty-Dumpty?" I mused, trying to make light of my disappointment. "Can we put him together again?"

"Robert." Smith's cool voice deflected my humor. "We've got a lot of work to do. I hope you're up to it. Want to begin by seeing what we've learned so far?"

The psychiatrist correctly surmised that we had discovered the full array of personalities who lived in the gray Castle and the Black Castle. Baby, obviously, was the biggest story of all. We now knew about the severe traumas that occurred in my early childhood while my father was away. We had found "the root cause of MPD." We also knew that my success imperative had very early roots as well, going all the way back to my father's return from the war. Smith cast it as a "tale of two families"—a prominent cosmopolitan family and a modest family with rural roots—prompting all sorts of jealousies and resentments.

Smith confirmed that Baby's memory was crystal clear on the fact that the abusers were *not* my parents. And from other reports inside the Castle, Smith reasoned, it was also obvious that the abuse did not come from my father's side of the family. But he also underscored the fact that since the abusers were long dead, it made neither moral sense nor psychological sense to dwell on them or identify them to others.

Our vow to hide the abusers' identity was easier said than done. To be honest, when rage reigns in the Castle, it has been hard to keep quiet. But over time, I have found that withholding the abusers' names, and refusing to stay in an angry state, actually helps the healing process. The trick is to accept that past, never forgetting it, but then finding a way to move beyond it. "Forgiven, but not forgotten" is actually the only way to proceed with therapy and with life.

Smith began a little summary. "So your two role models, your father and your paternal grandfather, set the achievement bar very high. And your mother certainly was the chief cheerleader. Thus Baby had an impossible task. How do you cope with knowing you are the 'worst boy in the world' when your job is to become the greatest possible success?"

"Why didn't I just collapse under the weight of it all?"

"That might have happened. But sometimes kids are incredibly resilient. You refused to give up. You were a fighter. Given that, splitting up inside was really the only solution, psychologically speaking."

Smith guessed that Bobby emerged very early in the process as the logical successor to Baby; after all, someone had to be the child who took the abuse and who bought into the "bad boy" line. Smith also surmised that Robbey materialized early on as well; someone had to fulfill the family's high expectations.

"And the Castle," I wondered, "when did it take shape?"

"Probably at the same time. A castle is a perfectly logical way for a child to organize a battleground. You couldn't put Bobby and Robbey in the same room, could you? All boys are fascinated by castles. You just took it one step further and embedded a castle in your head."

"And from then on," I said, "it was just a story of struggles between personalities? Couldn't it have been a bit more peaceful?"

"Peaceful? MPD is all about squabbles and struggles. It's often a power contest. Robbey was in charge until his grade school methods didn't stand up to college demands. Then Bob took over, with Robbey as his unknown sidekick, until he burned out after thirty years of leadership. And then, after bickering with Bob for all that time, you, Robert, became dominant. But you brought something entirely new. For the first time, Robert, you reversed the process of constant fracturing into new personalities."

Smith paused and began counting on his fingers. "Let's see, you represent a three-way merger—Robert, Bob, Robbey. And what about Young Bob? I would guess that he's inside you as well. In fact, come to think of it"—Smith counted again—"maybe you are a seven-sided merger."

"Seven-sided merger? What are you talking about?"

"I'm going to guess that we may not be seeing the Librarian and Baby again. It's quite possible that both are now merged into you. And what about the clock guy—Lawrence? I'll bet he came along with Robbey. That's seven, right? Robert, Bob, Robbey, Young Bob, Librarian, Lawrence, and Baby! Yep, seven! Not bad at all—a major step toward integration. Congratulations!" Dr. Smith gave a little smile, perhaps to salute himself as well as to encourage me.

I didn't feel in a celebratory mood at all. I suddenly felt a heavy, uncomfortable weight in my chest. A seven-sided merger was a troubling new thought, and I didn't want to discuss it. So I changed the subject. "Know what really baffles me? It's Tommy and the Witch. Why does it require two of them to torment Bobby?"

"Wait a second. You've got to fully understand the beginning of your dissociation. It involves Baby, Bobby, and Robbey. This is tricky stuff. Okay, now we know about the abuse to Baby. Baby seems to have hung around long enough to absorb more pain than any thousand children should endure. Baby was an innocent victim—that is, until abuse took his innocence. The very moment he felt pain and was told 'you're bad!' he began screaming— 'I'm bad'—in the hope that the abuse would stop. But abusers need more than that. They need victims who buy into the abuse, victims who really mean it when they say 'I'm bad.' The 'bad-boy' self-image had to be perpetuated with a new personality—'Bobby the bad.' That was the very first split in your head, the first moment of extreme dissociation. And, of course, there was also great pressure to succeed, giving rise to the second split—'Robbey the good.'"

I knew that Dr. Smith was trying to help me understand my disorder in good analytical fashion, but it was all giving me a severe headache. I could feel forces bubbling up: Bobby wanted to run away; Tommy and the Witch were very agitated. And as for me, I glanced at the clock, hoping it would prod Dr. Smith to finish his analysis as quickly as possible. "Okay," I said impatiently, "but why Tommy?"

"In MPD—indeed, in dissociation in general—it's not enough to know you are bad. You've got to keep the abuse happening, even when the original abusers may not be present. You're not alone. Self-abuse is a secret terror in American society. Lots of kids are hurting themselves. In your case, Tommy is there to make the self-hate take a physical form."

"It's still hard to think of it that way," I said, rubbing the rising pain in my forehead. "I know you see it as 'self-abuse,' but I still think of Tommy as just a bully in the Castle."

"Naturally, you still see things from a Castle perspective. Tommy's function is to keep the abuse active, now aimed at Bobby rather than Baby. Tommy is incapable of guilt. He believes he's entirely justified in his attacks."

"So why the Witch?"

"Robert, think about it. Where had you learned about witches?"

"Baby's story? He was frightened to death by someone pretending to be a witch. Is that it?"

"Of course. Baby didn't know it was all an act. Today, the Witch remains the voice of the abusers. She pounces on anything that goes wrong as proof that Bobby is bad. The hell of MPD is that it justifies the abuse internally. It's not enough to beat up Bobby. You need an inner source that rationalizes the abuse. That's your Witch. She authorizes punishments and Tommy carries them out. And then MPD continues the process to the end of life, or until it is stopped by therapy."

Smith paused for a second. "Think about it. The whole system was set up very early, probably between ages one and four, back during Baby's years. The terrible abuse gave rise to Bobby as naughty boy, Tommy as bully, and the Witch as apologist. Then the high expectations suddenly intervened, prompting the emergence of Robbey the student, then Bob the leader, and you, perhaps, 'Robert the idealist.' So it's all a vicious circle. You had to succeed.

Success had to cause some failure. Failure required punishment. Punishment proved you were bad. And then, to prove you were good, you had to succeed again."

"Damn." I shook my head. "When you describe it, it all makes a kind of weird sense."

"Sense? I guess so, in the way that a concentration camp makes sense. It was a closed system. It was escape-proof as long as no one found out the truth. Remember what was said to Baby: 'Don't you ever tell anyone. It will be much worse if you tell.' But, Robert, remember, the human mind is like a computer; nothing is ever totally forgotten. In this case, however, there was one terrible set of memories that had to be hidden away."

"So that's why Eyes cannot speak? And no one entered the Library?"

"Of course, but then you found out how to get Eyes to guide you to the truth. And you discovered how to get the essential information from the Librarian. You beat the system."

"Beat the system? Yes, I guess so." I tried to sound enthusiastic, partly to make Dr. Smith feel good at what was certainly a remarkable psychoanalytic achievement. "I'm grateful for knowing all this. Really I am. But the fact of the matter is . . . Well, I still don't feel very good. So we've got a fix on the past, but I can't figure out what to do next. I still feel guilty as hell."

"That's because even though you know why you have MPD, the old system is still ticking on. That's why you can't react right now. Most people might think that you'd be furious to learn the awful truth and then elated that you finally can address the real problem. That's because they don't have MPD. MPD exists to make you feel constantly bad, especially when you have reason to feel good."

I wanted to cry. I wanted to scream. I wanted to pummel someone with my fists. I wanted to grab my MPD and throw it out the window. I wanted to feel so mad that I could clear the air. I wanted to feel joy that, finally, at fifty, I knew what happened before I was five.

But all I could do was sit there and stare at Dr. Smith. "So, bottom line," I said finally, "how long before I can get things in new shape? How long before I'll be happy?"

Dr. Smith thought for a moment and then gave me a kindly-father look. "Well, we're clearly in a new phase of our work. I think we can crack back to visits once a week, twice if you really need it. How long before you can re-shape your life? That's a really long process. It really depends how much you can work toward real integration. There are still four major personalities—you, Bobby, Tommy, and the Witch."

"So we're really talking years, not months?"

"I think so. This doesn't mean you can't work at new professional op-tions. Your deal with Bob requires you to do several things, you know. Be-sides, you have to find the things which fit your own style."

"And how long before I'll be happy?"

Dr. Smith laughed. "Well, I suppose that's progress. That's what every one of my patients wants to know. I mean the non-MPD patients. Welcome to the real world. When will you be happy? That's a question for the rest of your life."

FOURTEEN

ROBERT: "NEW BROOM SWEEPS CLEAN."

As I look back on the early 1990s, after confronting Baby's terrible trauma, I wanted desperately to climb out of a deep chasm and bask in the sunlight. No matter Dr. Smith's warnings about a long struggle lying ahead, I could not shake my yearning for a quick cure. Damn it, after a lifetime of sinking into my hole, deeper and deeper, now I had grabbed this MPD thing by the horns. I felt that I deserved a new life infused with fresh activities and a nice dose of optimism. To be sure, I reasoned, I still had an active case of MPD, but now maybe I could keep it under control and turn to outside priorities.

I requested a meeting with the Asia Society board leadership and informed them I would be stepping down from the presidency in late 1992. The Bob part of me was touched that they pressured me to reconsider. But

I was politely adamant; after all, a fresh start was central to the merger deal I had negotiated with Bob.

Rumors abounded about what I might be doing next: University president? Foundation president? Ambassadorship? I found that it was really hard to make people believe me when I said that I had no plans. When a middle-aged head of an organization steps down, everyone assumes another leadership post. It's a game of coy secrecy. The tip-off for a really big assignment is to say: "I really don't know what I'm going to do." And in an election year, when a Democratic candidate like Bill Clinton has increasing opinion poll momentum, it's absolutely certain that a liberal specialist on Asia who "has no plans" is aiming for Washington or some embassy across the Pacific.

But I genuinely didn't have a clue about what I would do. Now, with Bob gone and, even more, with knowledge of the whole MPD story, it was inconceivable to take on a new leadership position. Coping with full awareness of MPD was a major responsibility in itself, especially dealing with the demanding personalities inside me: Bobby, Tommy, and the Witch. One thing I knew for sure: I was not Bob, and I had no desire to repeat his sad burnout. I began to think of a new strategy. Why not look for short-term consultancies in teaching, broadcast journalism, business advising, writing? Maybe I could rally the inner troops for short bursts of effort, but leave ample time for trying to move toward MPD integration?

The new once-a-week schedule of MPD meetings offered a respite from the total immersion therapy of the previous two years, yet I couldn't repress the obvious—my disorder remained serious. The inner personalities remained very active, prompting Dr. Smith to absorb a litany of concerns and complaints, sometimes intervening to smooth out disagreements. Though Robert, Bobby, Tommy, and the Witch each knew about the others' existence, our memory bank was still divided into four parts. And while Eyes had omniscience, she was still cloistered away in the Black Castle, not regularly accessible to the rest of us.

Worse yet, although the whole system was rife with chatter, none of us had an ability to overhear all conversations (the exception was Eyes who, of course, could not speak). Smith had to remember who could hear what from whom, who had said what to whom, and who needed to know what was said by whom. It is complicated enough in the gossip-ridden real world; just imagine what it's like when a psychiatrist has to comprehend the whole thing happening inside a single human being.

I remember feeling a bemused sympathy when Dr. Smith would have to say, "Tommy, is that you? Good, I thought so. It's just that Bobby sometimes has an angry look, too. Okay, I want you to know something. You know, Robert and Bobby sometimes have little talks. Well, Bobby wanted—no, I mean Robert wanted you to know something . . ." Dr. Smith was like a preoccupied mother, sometimes forgetting which child she was calling: "Quit that! Quit it, Johnny. Oh heavens, I mean Alice. Alice, you quit teasing Suzy right now!"

As of 1992, after two years of intensive therapy, the MPD internal structure of Robert B. Oxnam still featured the Castle and the Black Castle, and looked something like this:

Robert: the dominant personality, living in the central chamber of the Castle, now merged with Bob (whom he still thinks of residing on the outer walkway), Robbey (in the small study), the mysterious Lawrence (in the clock shop), Young Bob (on the outer wall), the Librarian, and Baby. No contact with the Witch or Tommy, and limited conversations with Bobby. Robert has the fullest knowledge of the Castle. He has absorbed the memories and abilities of those with whom he has merged. Robert is the only one who has heard the full story of Baby (by virtue of his merger with the Librarian).

Bobby: the abused child, but also the potential source of creativity, humor, and playfulness. Resides in the dungeon, whose door is locked by Robert. He is allowed short periods of exercise, but is kept under close scrutiny by Robert. Suffers infrequent but occasional devastating periods of punishment by Tommy.

Tommy: the inner source of anger. Resides in a strategically located garret with direct access to Bobby's dungeon and a door to the outside walkway. Usually inactive, but can suddenly inflict harsh punishments on Bobby (physical self-abuse) or exhibit sudden rage toward outsiders.

Witch: the voice of the original abusers. Lives in the Black Castle apart from the other three personalities. Intervenes at times of outer stress, authorizes Tommy to punish Bobby (self-abuse). Uncertain how much she knows about Baby's story or about how it was discovered. Possibly hiding a less malevolent personality underneath.

Eyes: the memory bank for the entire system. Eyes' recollections are "unfiltered memories," almost as if combining computerized notes with videotaped images. By contrast, the Librarian's records are "filtered memories," like an inner historian trying to make sense of key lifetime events. Robert's absorption of the Librarian is thus an event of considerable significance in terms of rewiring the Castle's memory structure. By contrast, Eyes remains at large, up for grabs in the merger process; she doesn't talk or act, but her factual knowledge is a potent tool.

By 1992, I felt that I was a survivor of the "perfect storm." Ironically, my Newfoundland voyage had taken me right through those waters where the disastrous episode occurred. What made the famous storm "perfect" from a weather forecaster's viewpoint were multiple lows intersecting to make for ungodly winds and waves. In my case, an intense psychiatric low intersected with a professional burnout to cause, I suppose, the "perfect" collapse.

After almost three years of intense therapy, I was utterly exhausted. The Castle's battery resources, designed for a single human being, were still driving four personalities. By the early 1990s, I knew why and how my MPD had started and evolved. But I didn't have a clue about how to put Humpty-Dumpty together again. Without independent financial resources, I needed new employment but was very unsure of future directions. I felt like a walking zombie in some 1930s Hollywood horror film.

Given my "therapy fatigue," I was relieved that Dr. Smith felt that once-a-week sessions would suffice. Since Dr. Smith's office was an hour's commute from my New York City apartment, a whole evening would be shot with a round-trip train ride and an hour-long meeting. I couldn't imagine doing that more than once every seven days. Besides, it was exhausting to go to a session where other personalities take over your body, spill their guts in short moments on the stage, and then drag us all home to review the wreckage. I needed both time and space to recoup my energies.

Above all, I felt a deep sense of guilt. If someone asked me to explain what living with MPD is like in three words, I would choose *self-doubt, self-hatred,* and *guilt.* I knew the origins of my MPD were surely "not my fault," but I fretted constantly about past episodes of unpredictable behavior and rage.

"Dr. Smith," I asked anxiously. "There's something I need to know. Am I a dangerous person? Please tell me the truth."

"You've done emotional damage to those closest to you, of course, but you're most dangerous to yourself. Inside, you have wrought terrible damage. And it remains a serious threat. It is extreme self-abuse. I don't just mean the terrible things that Tommy does to Bobby. Your whole internal system thrives on hate and guilt. Every one of you is caught up in a cycle that must be broken."

"Am I dangerous to people on the outside?"

"Not in the way you mean. You don't pose a physical or sexual threat to outsiders. But in the past, you were capable of emotional rage and occasional physical acts. There are fewer instances now, but you can still become extremely angry and cause deep emotional scars. As you've said yourself, your anger usually arises from some provocation, often a wrong accusation, but nothing justifies your overreaction. So you make yourself the problem. Tommy's vicious tongue is unleashed on an outsider, always away from any professional context. And what happens inside? The Witch revels in a moment that proves that the whole system is bad. She points the finger at Bobby. Tommy swoops down to torture Bobby. Bottom line, everybody feels like hell."

At that moment, and ever since, I have been racked with guilt about my history of outer-directed rage. How could I, of all people, become an emotional abuser? I knew firsthand the devastating impact of emotional abuse. In my own memory, the screamed invectives and shrieked accusations still hurt as much as, often even more than, the physical and sexual abuse.

I, Robert, was now far enough along in the therapy process to reconstruct vivid memories of earlier abuse—not just done to us, but also done by us. The Librarian was embedded in me, and her records were filled with truly awful moments of external rage. It was clear that the cruel link between the Witch and Tommy, causing frequent self-abuse within the Castle, had wrought considerable damage on the outside as well. Inside the

Castle, everyone, including me, had become skilled in blaming others. Now, as the repository for seven of the eleven personalities, I knew it was time to stop saying someone else was to blame. It was time to say, "I am responsible."

I understand today that abuse is a learned behavior, and that abused people are likely to abuse others. Yes, I know that abuse often tends to be handed down, generation by generation, in families who seem to specialize in genealogies of abuse. But I will not excuse my emotionally abusive behavior by citing such research that might imply "I had no choice." Maybe it might have been harder for me, but I did have a choice. I could have sought therapy earlier and really taken the advice to heart. Instead, I gave in to the temptation to indulge in abusive behavior, just as I gave in to the temptation to indulge in other addictive behaviors.

Abuse is perhaps the least-acknowledged illness. Other than the fact that I have suffered abuse and that I have been a serious emotional abuser, I cannot claim expertise in this field. But I do know that abuse denial is rampant in American society. Someone once said that "eighty percent of life is self-justification." When it comes to abuse, I think the percentage should be much higher. Watch out when people start protesting too much: "Oh, isn't that just awful! Can you imagine someone being like that!?" And watch out when some people describe the abuse they suffered in great detail, whether they do so in books or on television, and then claim they have never acted abusively toward others.

A new mantra—"MPD is an explanation, not an excuse"—played over and over in my head. And so I began the process of trying to make amends for past faults while endeavoring to rebuild my life. It was not made easier when those I had hurt failed to see that I was genuinely trying to right my wrongs and to create a more caring life. I chafed when I was typecast in an unchanging image and was told that I was just in "deep denial" or that I was simply a "selfish fucking bastard." At such times, throughout the 1990s, the Witch yelled, "You're bad! So bad!" Tommy would begin hitting Bobby's face, over and over. Crying in pain, Bobby finally screamed out: "I'm sorry. Please, I'm sorry. I'm bad. I'm so bad."

I found that I was not alone in feeling deep guilt. Rage and guilt abounded among other MPD patients I met at an ongoing seminar in New York City. Thank God, we have entered an era of self-help in which those afflicted with similar disorders can offer comfort and insight to one another. It may seem surprising that there are seminars devoted to so rare a disorder as MPD/DID, but given the population density, there are probably a thousand or more people with MPD living in the greater New York area alone.

The seminar might have been mistaken for a teachers' workshop, consisting of quite intelligent people in casual weekend dress. Many patients had not been diagnosed with a dissociative disorder until well into adulthood; until then, they had struggled through an early life of trying to hold together work life and family (with varying degrees of success) while endeavoring to explain away terrible anger and antisocial behaviors. I heard familiar descriptions of MPD therapy: wide arrays of inner personalities, impenetrable memory barriers and prolonged blank periods, various forms of "MPD architecture," deeply repressed childhood traumas. As patients shared stories, their underlying anger was often unmistakable. Some were now able to control it. Others could not, including one patient who confessed: "I just trashed my shrink's office!"

In the seminar, anger and guilt were close bedfellows. Everyone was familiar with the feeling of being inherently "bad": punished as "bad" children, acting as "bad" adults, assuming blame for "bad" events. Many had spent lifetimes of inner anguish coping with guilt. In one post-seminar private conversation, I found I shared a common MPD problem with two other patients. One of them described great progress when meeting with her therapist, but terrible times with family and friends who still viewed her as "the bad old me." The other lamented that some people reject MPD out of hand and adopt a "prove it to me" attitude: "Prove that you've got this disorder and that you're not just bad."

I added my own concern, mentioning stories of people who had feigned multiple personalities. Yes, it's true—some people fake MPD, perhaps to get attention. I had even heard this comment from a very naive woman: "Oh, you'll never get over MPD. All my friends with MPD know they'll never get over it." The other two patients just shook their heads sadly as if to say, "She has a circle of friends who are faking MPD? You can only pity those who are sicker than we are."

So, damn it all, if the inner guilt of MPD wasn't enough, I was discovering that MPD patients have to deal with an outer environment of skepticism and doubt. I tried to imagine asking cancer patients to prove that they were really ill and not just faking the pain. The problem is that MPD is not like cancer, where there is clear-cut, undeniable medical evidence. Only an experienced therapist can conclusively diagnose MPD and other dissociative disorders. Much of MPD therapy, including the emergence and evolution of "alters," occurs within the privileged "safe space" of a psychiatrist's office. By law and common sense, all outsiders, including family and friends, are excluded from this process.

After several years in therapy, I had zero doubt that I had MPD. I vowed that I would not waste time trying to "prove" my MPD to those who might doubt it. I felt nothing but profound sadness—even anger—for those who would feign this disorder, just as I would feel similar dismay over those who might pretend they were wheelchair patients.

I am well aware that "recovered memory" is a charged issue these days. It has caused many who have been accused of abuse, as well as some psychiatrists and lawyers, to raise serious objections to those who claim memory recovery. I have no doubt that some people may fake memory recovery—perhaps to get attention or revenge—thus giving rise to the term *recovered-memory abuse*.

Being neither therapists nor attorneys, those of us within the Castle complex can only tell our stories and let them speak for themselves. Our experience runs counter to those who dismiss all "recovered memories" or even disparage the entire profession of psychiatry. Without the process of recovering memory—most notably in Baby's story—we would still be shattered into eleven personalities. We owe much to the psychiatrists who specialize in this disorder, often treating limited-income patients, for trying to help what Dr. Smith estimates to be the thirty thousand Americans who suffer from MPD.

In the early 1990s, I met with a group of thirty therapists and psychiatrists dealing with dissociation at a special seminar held at the Cortland Medical Center in Westchester County, New York. Dr. Smith had asked me whether I would be willing to relate my experiences, hoping it would be useful both to the seminar's participants and to me. It was a remarkable two-hour session. My initial fears melted away as I found that talking to these people was a healing way to review my MPD history over the previous three years. And, from the warm responses I received during and after the session, I know the group found it a helpful way to relate my case to issues in their own private practices. Their questions probed deeply into my own experiences with different alters, my partial integration, my internal MPD organization, and the relationship between my outer life and MPD. I quickly saw that this was a very serious group of professionals devoted to understanding a rapidly evolving frontier area of psychiatric therapy. I was honored to be a part of it.

In private conversation after the meeting, one therapist asked me a question that has been with me ever since. "You know, you're among the few who have been quite prominent in spite of MPD. How does that make you feel?"

"Your question makes me feel guilty," I answered quickly, without much thought. "I think many MPD patients would have done similar things if they had faced my situation. Like them, I had an extreme childhood trauma. But unlike most of them, I also felt a huge pressure to be successful at a very early age. So, unconsciously, my system rewired itself. I feel my achievements may not have been *in spite of* MPD. Instead, they may be *because of* MPD."

FIFTEEN

ROBERT: "BACK FROM HELL.
NOW TO HEAVEN!"

EVER SINCE DR. SMITH first described MPD therapy, the search for the original trauma had seemed like digging for the mother lode. When we found it—when we actually confronted the truth in stark detail—surely the knowledge would herald the dawning of a new age.

As I look back many years later, this early-1990s optimism seems blissfully naive. It was like the hurricane's eye—some blue sky and sunshine—before the return of vicious wind and torrential rain. The brightest shaft of sunshine occurred not in professional life but rather in a new and enduring personal relationship.

My cluster of personal problems, especially the alcoholism and severe dissociation, had weighed heavily on my marriage. The outbursts of rage had also left deep scars within my family. After a brief attempt at reconciliation, my wife and I separated permanently in 1991 and divorced in 1993. I am deeply sorry for the pain that my problems inflicted on our relationship and on our children. At the same time, I am proud that both children have grown up to be very successful adults. I am also grateful that both have reached out to me in recent years in ways that have meant more than they will probably know. Both are very healthy and wonderful people, living proof that MPD is not caused by any genetic pattern whatsoever.

No doubt MPD therapy left me exhausted and feeling guilty. But I began to have other, more positive feelings. After all, I had a sense of accomplishment about sticking with a very difficult psychiatric process. The fighter inside me was not completely down for the count. I'd won some battles, but the war hung in the balance. Okay, I'd been to hell and back. Wasn't it time for at least a taste of heaven?

My angel came in the form of a woman named Vishakha Desai. From the moment Vishakha became director of the Asia Society's galleries, I was struck by her special abilities and style. I was astonished that, within a year, she remade the cultural programs of the Asia Society, organizing marvelous exhibitions in contemporary Asian art and Asian-American art. I envied her genius for cultivating an ever-widening network of friends and colleagues, donors, scholars and curators, museum directors, and Asian cultural leaders. To me, she seemed a benign version of an Indian typhoon, swirling across the national and global landscape, soon becoming president of the prestigious Association of American Museum Directors.

Vishakha and I hit it off professionally from the very beginning. I gave her free rein to reshape the cultural side of the Asia Society, and she responded by strongly supporting my program innovations in the United States and across the Pacific. Oh, how I wished this had been the environment I inherited back in the much harder times of the early 1980s. I remember once introducing Vishakha with unbridled enthusiasm: "It may be that my presidency of the Asia Society will be best remembered for hiring Vishakha Desai." Little did I know the real truth of my prediction. In 2004, Vishakha became the new president of the Asia Society, succeeding the long and successful presidency of Ambassador Nick Platt (1992–2004).

To top it off, Vishakha was a woman of great attractiveness and grace. As a child in India back in the 1950s, she had studied classical Indian dance and later performed professionally. Although she decided to leave a career in dance and pursue Asian art history, she kept the performer's sense of presence. When she talked, her long fingers offered eloquent punctuation to her main points. One member of the Asia Society's search committee said of Vishakha: "I really loved what she said, but I can't remember all of it. I was mesmerized by her hands."

I was mesmerized by more than Vishakha's hands, and blessedly, as it turned out, the feeling was mutual. Since I had made it clear I was leaving both the Asia Society and my wife, it might have seemed natural for Vishakha and me to pursue our romance openly. But both of us were concerned that our budding relationship might pose professional issues for the Asia Society; after all, I would still be her boss for a few months to come. So I quickly informed board chairman John Whitehead on a confidential basis. As always, John had a way of putting hearts at ease: "I see no problem at all. A romance on the job sounds like a great way to keep both of you focused on the Asia Society." And so, first in secret and then quite openly, Vishakha and I acknowledged that we were deeply in love.

Early in our private relationship, Vishakha confessed that while she had thrived in her professional career, she long had been plagued by what she called "the dilemma of the strong woman." An Indian astrologer, noting that Vishakha was a strong-willed "triple Taurus" (sun, moon, and Mercury all in Taurus), suggested that she acquire a yellow sapphire to soften her forceful rays. From my perspective, weakened as I was by serious inner problems, nothing could be better than strength in a romantic partner. Of course I covered my bets by buying her a yellow sapphire necklace as a gift, lest her strength become overwhelming.

Ironically, Vishakha also was attracted by an apparent "strength and togetherness" in my outer professional life. She confided to girlfriends that she had "finally met a man who had no evident emotional difficulties." Imagine her surprise when, early on, I told her my history of multiple personality disorder. But also imagine my surprise when, after listening intently, she responded with uncommon warmth and empathy.

"I never would have guessed it from your poise and professionalism at the office. Hmm, so instead of the most together man, I've got the most divided figure I've ever met. Well, what the hell, I love you, and that's that."

Shortly after I confided the truth about MPD to her, Vishakha witnessed many of the vagaries of my MPD. There was no question that we clicked professionally; she now knew about the strange alliance between Bob and Robbey, and she clearly respected their accomplishments. She also understood the complex merger that I, Robert, now represented, encompassing both Bob and Robbey. For all of these internal complexities, the core of our relationship was between Robert and Vishakha. It was I, Robert, who felt a magical sense when we talked at dinner, when we went to cultural events, when we chatted on hikes. We felt a sense of perfect simpatico. We had a warmth to our love which others found infectious.

But there was also an unstated imbalance which sustained us in the early years. Inside, I, as Robert, was exhausted and weak, trying to hold together a fragile cluster of divided personalities. Vishakha was strong and determined, quite willing to serve as the nurse to my vulnerabilities. She even had the strength to cope with occasional appearances of Tommy. Once I became quite irritated when Vishakha seemed less committed than I to maintaining the "secrecy" around our relationship. Tommy suddenly erupted from nowhere, screamed at her on the street, and threw a bag of food on the ground in disgust. Instead of the old "rage-apology" syndrome, Vishakha responded with firm understanding; she knew where the rage was coming from, but she made it clear that such behaviors were unacceptable. Her mature reaction had a taming effect on Tommy, whose explosions became a rare occurrence in our relationship.

The Witch hovered ominously over us just as she haunted the Castle. One night, Vishakha and I lingered over post-dinner coffee, talking about the challenges of MPD. She told me that she had never met the Witch and felt she should. I was horrified by her suggestion. Even worse, as she spoke, I began to feel a switch occurring inside and was powerless to prevent it. I saw Vishakha's eyes open wide as she steeled herself for what was ahead. She watched the gruesome transformation of my face and hands into the fierce, spiteful image of the Witch.

"Ah, it's the clever Vishakha. Trying to lure Robert away."

"You don't frighten me," Vishakha said, pretending to be calm. "I'd like to know you."

"You don't want to know me." I hissed at her. "And I don't like you at all."

"Why not?"

"Because you're sneaky. You try to make Robert happy. Don't you realize that it will end badly? This silly happiness will come to an end. Get away. Go away. I'm warning you."

"I don't agree. And I'm not going away."

"You'll see. Bad times are ahead. I'm warning you. And you know what else?"

"What?"

"I hate you. I'll always hate you."

As the Witch disappeared, I looked at Vishakha with pleading in my eyes. "I'm so sorry. I didn't want you to meet her. I just couldn't control her, not once you asked to see her."

Vishakha responded with unwavering clarity. "I'm glad I met her. It wasn't easy, but I'm glad I did it. Besides, I sense that she's not as scary as she might like us to think."

My God, I thought with relief. It was two strong women in a standoff.

The Black Witch versus the Yellow Sapphire. It was also a classic illustration of Vishakha's fortitude and her inherent capacity for finding potential goodness in the most unlikely places.

I didn't fully understand the wellsprings of Vishakha's character until I visited her family home in Ahmedabad, the capital of Gujarat in northwestern India. Vishakha was one of seven children of an extraordinary couple. Nirubhai ("Papa") Desai and his wife, known to all as "Ben" (which means "sister"), had been leading figures in the anti-British independence movement of the 1930s and 1940s. They were closely associated with Mahatma Gandhi, who, after he returned from South Africa, set up his headquarters in Ahmedabad. Nirubhai Desai, who had frequently been jailed for prolonged periods by the British, eventually became a leading journalist and a major voice for social and political reform. Ben was an activist as well, championing the women's movement before settling down to the rigors of raising a large family.

Papa and Ben, even in their late seventies when I first met them, were formidable figures. Papa was brilliant, widely read, highly opinionated, and passionate. Ben stayed more in the background, offering quiet hospitality, intervening when she had strong views. Until Papa's death from Parkinson's disease in late 1993, Papa and Ben were the perfect Indian couple. Papa's encyclopedic interests—ranging from music and art to mountaineering and fitness—rubbed off on his children. And Ben's steel will was visible in many of her offspring. Four of Vishakha's siblings (Swati, Anuradha, Abhijit, and Saptarshi) followed her lead and made the decision to leave India and live in the United States, while two (Chitra and Falgun) remained behind in Ahmedabad.

But it was Bobby, more than anyone else, who seemed at home in India. It wasn't a matter of letting Bobby out of confinement; instead, others seemed to reach in and pull him out. No one in Ahmedabad enjoyed the annual "Kite Day" more than Bobby, who found utter joy in the thousands of little kites flittering from rooftops against a brilliant blue sky. The whole city was engaged in joyous kite fights, punctuated by great cheers and groans when one kite string slashed through another. Bobby tried and tried, with no success, to cut down neighbors' kites with his own, and everyone found his cumbersome efforts very funny. He ate the plentiful Indian sweets until he could eat no more. At night, he played endlessly with the little Desai children; it didn't matter a bit that they spoke no English and he spoke no Gujarati. He somehow sensed that when they laughed with Bobkaka ("Uncle Bob"), they really meant Bobbykaka.

In October 1993, Vishakha and I were married in New York's Central Park. We reveled in our plans for the ceremony as we concocted, in the words of a good friend, a "five-handkerchief wedding." A gondola ferried us to the ceremony in a tent-covered area next to the boathouse at the edge of the lake; my blue suit was a quiet backdrop to Vishakha's strawberry-pink sari with gold threads shimmering in the early-afternoon sun. Vishakha and I read excerpts of poetry to each other—Rilke, Psalm I, the Chinese *Book of Songs,* Kabir, Pablo Neruda, the Chinese *Yue-fu,* and Philip Larkin—interspersed with classical guitar music played sublimely by Yasha Kofman. After each poem, we walked around a fire in traditional Indian fashion, seven times in all (the fire burned in a wonderful Grecian urn provided by our dear friend George Papamichael). At the end, the whole congregation read an Apache wedding song, and then Vishakha and I departed to the accompaniment of classical Indian musicians. We rode off in a white horse-drawn coach out of Central Park.

SIXTEEN

ROBERT: "MULTIPLE NEW JOBS
AS A CURE FOR MPD."

Now that Vishakha and I were married, I began a rather audacious professional quest. I resolved to hold the fort internally while finding a new panacea externally. While adamant that I was no new "Bob," I was riding high in the saddle, scanning the horizon for new opportunities, pretending my horse was fit and frisky. Somehow I thought that my newfound optimistic spirit would infuse the Castle.

The old academic mentality inside the Castle had led us to a serious miscalculation: if we just worked earnestly and honestly, we would pass the test with flying colors and graduate with honors. I did not realize that I had completed only what might be called "MPD 101"—diagnosing dissociation, identifying personalities, merging some alters, confronting the trauma. I missed the fact that "MPD 201"—absorbing the trauma, understanding the history,

| 179 |

nurturing further integrations, seeking new approaches to the outside world—might be even more challenging.

On the surface, things seemed to be taking a promising turn. It was Robert's chance for optimistic-looking new horizons in the wake of Bob's sad shipwreck. I wanted to forget about the darker forces inside. I was living in the sunlight of a new marriage and meaningful work. I began finding excuses to avoid my weekly trips to Dr. Smith's Scarsdale office. I wanted to avoid painful therapy and reminders that I still had a serious MPD problem. And when I did go to Scarsdale, I tried to stay in control and focus on professional options. When I framed a bemused question—"What should I do when I grow up?"—Smith's serious look reminded me that it wasn't funny in the context of MPD.

Only later did I realize I was still a troubled patient making a familiar error: "All I want to do is forget the past and pursue a happier future." Of course the inner past never stays neatly locked away; untreated nasty demons always have a way of nibbling away at that "happier future."

For me, the new era of happiness demanded some serious internal discipline. Robert had to exert firm control of the Castle. Bobby had to stay under lock and key; that seemed the only way to keep the Witch in check and prevent Tommy's rages. And so, after three years of intense MPD therapy (1990–1992), little MPD progress was made over the next three (1993–1995).

Vishakha asked repeatedly why I wasn't going to Smith. I answered, "It's utterly exhausting to face the other personalities fighting inside me. I just can't imagine looking for a new career while coping with inner warfare." MPD therapy dropped quickly from once a week to an occasional visit every month or two. Smith expressed concern, but reconciled himself to letting me find my own way; he said that he'd always be there for emergencies or to resume regular sessions whenever I wished.

Bobby was mad at me, even madder than he ever felt toward Bob. After all, Bob didn't even know about the Castle or Bobby or Tommy. So, after his initial hopefulness about the new merger, Bobby stewed away in his prison cell. I didn't dare let him out much, fearing he would mess up my chances for a new professional life. I spent less and less time focused on Bobby, except to keep him in check, and thus avoid provoking Tommy and the Witch.

To be honest, although I was fueled by a quest for "Robert's ideal job," the framework relied heavily on Bob's professional skills and Robbey's methodical back-office labors. My outer persona was more casual and less driven than Bob, but my inner self, the reflective "pre-dominant Robert," became less visible as I became absorbed in "dominant personality" life.

A year earlier, I could not have imagined taking a job in a profit-making institution. But my first foray led to the world of banking as senior adviser to a private investment organization for high-net-worth families. I accepted the banking consultancy, knowing it was really aimed at the Bob-and-Robbey team lodged deep inside me. Besides, now that I had left the Asia Society, I did need a regular source of income.

It felt quite strange walking into a plush wood-paneled corner office with a striking view of southern Manhattan. It was a world of expensive business suits, a shoe-shine boy who shined as you made phone calls, an almost un-limited corporate expense account, subscriptions to every research resource imaginable, a luncheon restaurant for staff, and a remarkably efficient secre-tary to handle all organizational and communications tasks.

Initially, the banking institution hoped I would bring new business from Asian accounts in spite of the fact that, as I told them, most affluent Asians managed their monies back at home. Their hope turned out to be un-founded, but they maintained the consultancy throughout the 1990s because I offered value in two other ways. First, I gave countless speeches on Asian business to clients and prospective clients throughout the United States, often at wealth-management conferences. Second, I organized Asian trips for several of the firm's leaders, serving as their informal lecturer and setting up meetings with key Asian leaders in business and government. As such, the institution benefited from what they called my "representational capacities." And for me, the job tapped my newly integrated MPD potential: Robert the teacher, Bob the public figure, and Robbey the researcher.

So, when it came to macroeconomic analysis in business settings, my three-in-one combination gave a lot of "value added" to discussions about possibilities in Asia and China. But the organization's special strengths—high-net-worth banking, asset management, and direct investments—never meshed easily with any of my internal personalities. From all accounts, I did my work well and with style, but no one inside me is a natural banker or businessman. The ideal business personality—passionate about structuring deals, willing to take significant financial risks, obsessed with fiscal details, motivated by making money—just can't be found in our Castle.

Okay, I wasn't cut out for business and banking. But what about teaching? After all, I, Robert, had always seen myself as a professor. I had two significant teaching opportunities in the 1990s: as an adjunct professor of Asian studies at Columbia University's graduate school and as a visiting Bernhard professor at Williams College.

On the surface, a teaching career seemed natural. But teaching took a heavy toll on life inside the Castle. I was in charge and set a high priority on my own meticulous reading, careful class preparation, strong teaching style, office-hour availability, and extensive comments in grading. It meant that the Robert–Bob–Robbey triangle was in full operation for fourteen hours a day or more. The old schoolboy grind was back, but now with a demanding professor watching over every move, day and night.

Why did I work so hard? I, Robert—unlike Bob—was a professor who had never taught; I was determined to teach properly, come hell or high water. Internally, it was hell I got. It had taken Bob thirty years to burn out as a scholar-turned-administrator. It required only a couple of years for Robert to burn out as a driven professor.

Bobby complained bitterly: "Work, work, work. Reading, lecturing, grading. Robert even graded forty papers in one night, typing comments for every student. Can you blame me for getting mad? Okay, so I did something bad again. I ate lots of food and got sick. Many days, I ate a dozen doughnuts in the morning. Then another dozen in the afternoon. And at night, I would eat a whole roast chicken, a big bag of potato chips, and a big carton of ice cream. I would get sick sometimes five times a day. I would even get sick when we stopped on the road."

By the winter of 1995, I lacked the energy to continue with a teaching career at all. Both Williams and Columbia, clearly pleased with the previous courses, had scheduled repeat "Professor Oxnam classes" for the spring semester of 1996. In January, shortly before the semester began, I called both institutions and abruptly opted out of my responsibilities. So once again, MPD left me feeling both exhausted and guilty.

The fault for this nosedive in my teaching career rested squarely with me. Both Bobby and I had several meetings with Dr. Smith during this period, and while we talked of exhaustion and frustration, we never mentioned the resurgence of bulimia. And, though Vishakha knew about bulimia as an earlier problem, I hid the severe relapse from her as well. In effect, I lied to everyone about the severity of my inner problems, especially to myself. After all, it was finally Robert's hour on the stage and I surely didn't want to bomb. *I'll deal with these problems later,* I said to myself, *as soon as I've found the right career.*

Bobby yearned to tell Dr. Smith how mad he was, but he was too scared: "I knew Robert wanted to look just perfect. If something went wrong, it would prove I was bad. If Robert got mad at me, everybody would know I was bad again. Then you know what would happen. You're right—the Witch and Tommy. So I just smiled and told my animal stories to Dr. Smith."

Also in the early 1990s, I did an interesting stint as "special correspondent" for *The MacNeil/Lehrer Newshour*, where I was asked to be the on-camera host as well as scriptwriter for a special series on China. The final product—ten programs, roughly twelve minutes each, on all aspects of China in the 1990s—offered vivid insights into China's economic takeoff, rural life, women and family planning, the People's Liberation Army, arts and culture, the question of human rights, and the legacy of the Tiananmen massacre.

Not evident in the television programs were the arduous difficulties we endured in shooting and production. Coping with the Chinese authorities was a challenge crafted in hell. I quickly learned that while Chinese officials often warmly receive scholars and educators (my previous roles), they are deeply suspicious of journalists (my *MacNeil/Lehrer* role). Before doing any shooting, we had to obtain official approval and agree to allow escorts to accompany us. On the way to an interview with an outspoken critic of China's atrocious environmental record, we were informed that "the interview could be dangerous" (our executive producer saw this as a direct physical threat and canceled the meeting). My hotel room was frequently searched by Chinese security personnel, and once I discovered computer disks removed from the room. One of the stolen disks contained my private "MPD Diary," with several hundred pages of my dissociation and therapy experiences. Although the disk was protected by a coded password, everyone in the Castle lived in fear that the Chinese would make my secret disorder known to PBS or, even worse, to the public.

My fears of personal exposure, the internal politics of our television team, and the perpetual scrutiny of the Chinese all took a heavy toll. Almost every night, I confided my worries in phone calls to Vishakha, who did her best to put my heart at ease, trying to help her freaked-out spouse keep a semblance of internal balance.

Conversations within the Castle were rising in pitch. "I prayed and prayed that nothing bad would happen," Bobby fretted, "but it did. Some of those TV people didn't like Robert. They thought he was too pushy. And I know that Robert thought they didn't know anything about China.

"It was kind of like a war. Robert tried to fight back. But he was losing the war. I could tell. He was caught between the TV people and the Chinese. So he ended up being seen as bad. Know what I mean? So I got sick a lot. But honest, I didn't do anything else."

Tommy didn't care what Bobby said. The truth was obvious to him. "It was Bobby's fault. So I screamed at him. Then I hit him on his head—very hard and many times. One time I burned his leg with matches."

And the Witch was right on the scene. "Robert, you're the big TV 'talent.' That's what they call you. Just keep doing it. Try to make nice. It doesn't matter. You're a loser, too. You're the new Bob."

Not surprisingly, although *MacNeil/Lehrer*'s *China in Transition* was deemed a success, I did not find a new slot in the world of television. On the surface, I was frustrated that the good work I had done as host/writer did not translate into longer-term work. But inside, I was relieved to be away from the terrible pressures of television production. I don't think the Castle could have survived much more of it.

Worse yet, I was beginning to think that I, Robert, was a total flop as the dominant personality within the Castle. I could float along as a part-time consultant in the business and banking world, but my heart was not in it. Teaching captured my heart and talents, but it devoured the personalities inside the Castle. The allure of a television career quickly faded when I saw the enormous toll it took on an MPD system. My pattern seemed ominously like that of Bob: outer success and inner failure. What the hell could I do right?

Aha, I thought, why not another novel? After all, *Cinnabar* was Bob's novel. So why not write Robert's novel? Besides, *Cinnabar* was written at an awful time, when Bob was falling apart, before he even knew about MPD. Dr. Smith once called *Cinnabar* "the greatest novel ever written by someone with MPD"—maybe the best review I received! But now I knew so much more about myself, and about novel writing.

And so *Ming* was born. Instead of a mystery thriller, *Ming* was a historical novel, set in the turbulent seventeenth century, at the very end of the Ming dynasty, as Manchus threatened to overrun China. *Ming* was indeed a better book than its predecessor. The two key characters moved the reader across the wide landscape of China into the competing worlds of Ming loyalists and Manchu conquerors, among the lives of Chinese elites and Jesuit missionaries. Longyan was an unusual hero: born with a learning disability into a scholarly family, disowned by his father, he became a brilliant general. His eventual lover, Meihua, was also a departure from the typical: a secretly literate woman in a society that frowned on female literacy.

While I thought that *Ming* was Robert's novel, Bobby had a very different take on the authorship of our fiction: "Who wrote the novels? All of us, and I really was involved a lot with *Ming*. I'm good at the stuff where you see inside other people. You know, like you sort of try to think like them."

Bobby was especially fascinated with Meihua, and tried to imagine how a literate young woman might cope with male-dominated imperial society. Shortly after *Ming* was published, I read a new scholarly book about women in late imperial China and was astonished to learn that Bobby's "guesses" about Meihua's life turned out to be historically accurate: many Chinese women were secretly literate; women did indeed invent a secret spoken language unintelligible to men; women did indeed play key roles in the Ming loyalist military struggles; and literate Chinese women did have high access to the late Ming court.

The good news was that *Ming,* unlike *Cinnabar,* was not the subject of negative criticism. The bad news was that *Ming* received almost no critical attention at all.

So I, Robert, was the second failed novelist inside our little Castle. What had I learned from my multiple abortive efforts to find a new career? Well, I wasn't destitute. I was still making enough money from business consulting to get by, and, of course, Vishakha had a thriving job and good income from the Asia Society. And she was endlessly supportive, providing an emotional counterweight to my mood swings.

My biggest lesson was that I couldn't consider a full-time job of any kind given the terrible MPD pressures inside. I would have to look for short-term work to which I could give my all for finite periods, then allow myself time to heal and recharge. It was a very painful lesson to learn. In effect, I was too sick to hold down a "real job."

One afternoon in the spring of 1995, I was startled by a phone call from a woman at the prestigious travel agency Abercrombie and Kent. "We have a VVIP trip to China, and we would like you to consider being the lecturer." Over the years, I have had many such calls, usually from people trying to get me to give a bunch of lectures in return for a free trip. The last thing I needed was yet another trip to China.

But the term *VVIP* intrigued me. I asked her: "Who are the 'Very Very Important Persons'?"

She answered: "Bill Gates and Warren Buffett."

The three-week Gates/Buffett trip to China was one of the most fascinating and demanding experiences of my life. It tapped virtually every resource within the Castle—releasing the positive energies of Robert and Bobby, and trying to restrain, sometimes with difficulty, the anger of Tommy and the Witch. I put my all my energy into the lectures—sharp outlines, clear points, ample humor, memorable facts—and they were well received. All the while, the entire Castle watched a remarkable spectacle as the world's two richest men visited the world's oldest continuous civilization.

For an inside-the-Castle view of the Gates/Buffett trip, Bobby's perspective is revealing: "I liked the games part. Guess what we played? A game called Truth and Bullshit—Chinese style! I'm not kidding. Robert was pretty good at it. And I liked the acting part.

"So what if those two guys are so rich? They're just like real people. Only funnier. One time Gates made a joke. He picked up a Chinese newspaper that had a picture of Gates and the Chinese president. He told Robert he knew what it said. Robert thought maybe Gates had studied Chinese. 'No,' Gates told him. It says 'Chinese President Meets World's Leading Computer Nerd.'

"And one time, we were all watching some musicians and dancers. But anyway, Buffett sees a guy hitting a big thin drum in his hand. Buffett whispers, 'That guy on the garbage-can lid is pretty good.'

"But sometimes things went wrong. Like when Gates made Robert mad at this birth-control clinic by asking questions about whether the Chinese were using that abortion thing to get rid of girl babies. Anyway, I thought it was somehow my fault. I was bad. That night Tommy hit me again and again. I couldn't cry because we were in a boat cabin with thin walls.

"The next day, Robert was so sick that he couldn't even go with the group. He felt dizzy and couldn't keep his balance. Doctors came and looked at Robert, but they couldn't find anything. He stayed in bed all day."

For all its tribulations and even its trials, the Gates/Buffett trip held a significant answer to my career dilemma. When Vishakha and I returned to New York, everyone wanted to talk about the well-reported trip. Nothing else in my background seemed to matter much except, "Aren't you the guy who went with Gates and Buffett to China?"

Slowly, it occurred to me that maybe this was the ideal solution to my dilemma. How could I continue MPD therapy and pursue meaningful work at the same time? Of course: Why not take business leaders on focused educational trips to China and other parts of Asia? While no one could match the incredible style of Bill and Melinda Gates or the grounded brilliance of Warren and Suzy Buffett, such trips would satisfy my desire to teach bright minds, my goal to find rewarding short-term assignments, and my need to make significant consulting income. Most importantly, such trips could capitalize on strengths in my MPD personality while minimizing the problems. In short, without knowing it, the geniuses of Bill Gates and Warren Buffett opened a new world for my inner Castle.

SEVENTEEN

BOBBY: "IT'S MY TURN. HERE'S BOTTLEMAN!"

I OFTEN FELT THAT MPD therapy was akin to fiddling with a LEGO set inside my skull. After years of work, we had finally found all the little LEGO blocks and started clicking them together in new ways. Now we had a durable Robert cluster of seven multicolored blocks. And next to us was another cluster—Bobby and his animals—tenuously linked to Robert's cluster by a single clicked tile (the key to his dungeon door). But the Witch and Tommy didn't fit into my LEGO system; instead, they hovered around the linked Robert and Bobby clusters, sometimes threatening the rickety structure with shrieking noise and violent hammer blows. Eyes did nothing but record the whole strange scene on her perpetually rolling video camera.

When things were quiet, the half decade after intensive MPD therapy (1992–1996) offered relative stability and often happiness. My marriage to Vishakha was a source of joy and energy; we never tired of each other's company. The quest for new jobs—investment banking, college teaching, television reporting, novel writing, and Asia lecturing—had provided income and productive outside involvement. Indeed, the Gates/Buffett trip had offered a new professional model of high-level business education in Asian countries.

But under the surface and inside the Castle, "Robert B. Oxnam" remained a fractured human being. Clearly, things had progressed from the Bob era, when, ignorant as we were about MPD and lubricated by alcohol, the whole system was rocked by sudden swings from smooth exterior to explosive interior, all masked by mysterious blank spots in Bob's memory. By contrast, now we were armed with knowledge about our disorder, partial integration of some personalities, growing internal communication, and some common memories. In terms of therapy, we had accomplished a great deal. But compared to a normal well-functioning human being, we remained way short of integration.

Looking back, I now realize that in my eagerness to be cured, I had created a fragile and volatile new structure. Instead of outer-directed rage, I sought to contain all personality conflicts within the Castle itself, turning outer explosions into inner implosions. It was a pressure cooker that, when overheated, let off steam in intense and frequent moments of self-abuse.

I wonder how this process looked on the outside. I suppose I projected a new kind of moodiness, going through short periods of focused high-energy around various projects interspersed with longer periods of quiet introspection. During those down-mood times, when no one was around, I could let the Castle battles rage in all their fury.

Of course, much as I tried, I could not hide all of these mood swings from Vishakha. Occasionally, in spite of my efforts to keep the lid on tight, the Witch and Tommy would erupt in her presence. I wish I could take back the angry, vitriolic comments that I made during those terrible episodes. Somewhere, Vishakha found the strength not only to forget and forgive, but also to transform herself into her nurse role. She knew precisely what was happening; she knew the personalities intimately and could speak with them directly. Usually, within a few hours, she brought the whole system back to a shaky stability. In this sense, she became the most effective therapist imaginable: knowledgeable, tough, resilient, and loving. It may sound odd, but over the years, my own battle with MPD has tended to enhance my partnership with Vishakha. Even in the rare rage-filled episodes, she knew that the anger was not coming from me, Robert. Instead, we were fighting demons together.

But little did we know, as 1997 rolled around, that the biggest challenge would come from another quarter, quite apart from Tommy and the Witch. The spotlight suddenly focused on the long-imprisoned Bobby.

BOBBY

The year 1997 was a really big year. For me it was, anyway. So many things happened that I can't remember half of them.

Oh, yes, one time was really awful. One night, right at the end of summer, I'm finally sleeping. Did you know sometimes I can't sleep? So I watch TV until very late. You might think I just watch crummy shows, like naked girls and cop chases and stuff. Well, I sometimes watch those. But I also watch good shows. I even watch the news. Honest I do. I'm not as dumb as you might think.

So let me tell you about this awful night. Well, maybe it was really early morning, like maybe six o'clock. I'm not really sure about the exact time. But I am sure that I had left the TV on. Suddenly I hear something on the TV. It's one of those news-bulletin things. You can always tell. No music, just somebody talking with a big voice. This guy is standing outside in

Paris—I know it's Paris right away because it has this big famous tower behind him. He says: "It's confirmed." That means it's really true. "Diana, former Princess of Wales, is dead. She was killed in a car crash last night, Paris time."

I jump up, wide-awake. Like I wasn't even asleep. "No," I cried out. "She can't be dead. Not Princess Di." I loved Princess Di. So for several days, I mainly sat by the TV set. I wished I could go to London. I would have taken flowers and stood in the street. I wanted to scream at that old ugly queen. And I wanted to clap for Diana's brother. When the funny guy sang that pretty song—you know, "Candle in the Wind"—I couldn't stop crying.

You probably don't understand about Lady Di. I mean, you might not know why I was so sad. You see, I think she was really like me. Inside, she thought she was bad. She did things like get sick after meals and stuff. And lots of people said she was bad.

But I know Princess Di was good. I can see people's hearts most of the time. I could see her heart when she was on TV. She was sort of shy, but she had a golden heart. I like people best who have golden hearts.

You know Princess Di died right in the middle of 1997. That was a real big year for me. It was like an Oreo year. I mean two parts, an early part and a late part, with something in the middle. Princess Di was the middle part. I don't mean it was like sugar in the middle. Not the dying part. But Princess Di was like sugar. I loved her. If she knew me, she might have loved me. I would have taken care of her and she would have taken care of me. And we both would have gotten out of prison. Well, she wasn't in a real prison. But I think her life was like a prison.

Let me tell you something. When Robert took over from Bob, I thought he might be nicer to me, maybe let me out more. I had been in the dungeon for a long time, you know. And unlike Bob, at least I knew Robert. He wasn't really my friend. He was kind of like a father. And I tried to be good so he might be nicer. But it didn't make any difference that he was on the outside.

He still kept me in prison. And he was too busy. So he didn't think about me too much.

Then, in 1997, I had a really good idea. I thought maybe I could help Robert with something. He's pretty serious, you know. He's even kind of boring. I don't mean he's dumb. But he doesn't tell jokes a lot. He doesn't even laugh much.

Okay, so here was my cool idea. After that Gates trip, he starts taking other trips, lecturing to those businesspeople. There's this organization where Robert takes businesspeople to Asia to learn about China and other countries. He gives really good lectures. I like the parts where he takes people through places like the Forbidden City. You know, that's where the emperors and all the ladies lived in China. He has great stories about the sex lives of emperors and eunuchs and stuff. Did you know that eunuchs, after they had their things cut off, kept it all in a bottle that they carried around? Know why? It's because the Chinese thought that you couldn't become worshiped as an ancestor unless, when you die, you have all your parts together. God, can you imagine carrying your parts around in a bottle all your life? Wouldn't it really be bad if, after hauling them around all the time, you left your bottle home the day you died?

Anyway, at night, a lot of these business guys drank a lot, so they just wanted to tell stories. I didn't drink anymore. That shows I'm pretty good, doesn't it? But I drank a lot of Diet Coke. These guys also gave out really good cigars. At night, I was like part of their club. I told lots of jokes and stories.

Sometimes I did funny things. Like one time, Robert told everybody to always give out name cards very carefully, holding the card facing the other person, always holding it with two hands. Robert said Chinese do that because it was like giving your whole self to the other person. But he didn't tell them that method was for older people. Younger Chinese don't do that anymore. Anyway, at dinner, our guys are doing it the way Robert told them.

But the young Chinese are flipping their cards all over the table. These Chinese are laughing at our guys.

So on the bus ride back to the hotel, people are making fun of Robert because his lecture seemed wrong. Robert wasn't feeling good and the laughing was hurting him. He tried to say something, but they were booing him. So I got up, pretending to talk like Robert. I took some of Robert's cards. "Oh, I forgot to tell you," I said, holding up a handful of business cards. "Here's the right way to make sure everybody gets your card." And I threw the cards all over the bus. Everybody laughed and laughed. Then they clapped. Robert felt much better. And so did everybody else.

So Robert started liking me a little more. He usually did the talking. But when he needed a joke, I was right there. The change between us was so quick no one could notice. And then, when the joke was done, Robert came back. Robert later told Dr. Smith it helped his "integration" thing. I don't know about that. But it sure was fun.

And when we got back, Robert started letting me out more. Sometimes it worked okay and sometimes it didn't. One place where it didn't work out okay was on the guitar. Now, you see, Robert really wanted to play the guitar, but he really sucks. He's got a great teacher, Yasha Kofman, and he's got really good guitars. He practices a lot, but he is terrible on rhythm. He thinks too much. It's really awful. And he won't let me touch his guitars. He thinks I'm just a kid.

I did something really bad one time. Robert is always trying new guitar strings. So one time, when he's putting on new strings, one breaks and makes a big scratch on a good Spanish guitar. He was very angry. So I figured maybe I could take away the scratch. When Robert wasn't there, I used a little varnish remover. At first it didn't do much. So I used a little more. Then it took off the varnish for a pretty big area. So what to do? I used more and removed the varnish from the whole top. But then it dripped and made a mess. So I removed the varnish from the sides and the back. It was really pretty. I liked how it looked. It was all nice clean wood, no varnish at all.

Robert was so mad. It turns out that the varnish is kind of important for good sound. I didn't know that. But Robert had to pay for a whole new job. Like eight hundred dollars for something called French polishing. So okay, it was a mistake. I'm sorry. But then he grounded me for a month. I was bad again.

But it wasn't my fault what happened to Robert's guitar playing. Some friends heard him playing one time and asked him to play a little concert. He was getting a little better and had a few decent pieces. But when he played for the group in their living room, he was so terrible that he wanted to cry. I know what happened to him. He was really scared, and then he sort of disappeared. I don't know who was playing. Maybe Robbey? But believe me, you wouldn't want to have been there. After that, Robert only played by himself. Then his right hand started to crumple up. Robert said it's called "focal distonia." No matter what he tried, his hand didn't work. So he finally quit and gave his guitars to that Juilliard School.

So that's all about Robert. What about me? You see, most of the time Robert used to keep me locked up. But except for the guitar-varnish thing, I had really helped Robert. So he let me out more. Besides, I know that Dr. Smith made Robert feel guilty about keeping me in the dungeon. I heard Dr. Smith tell Robert one time: "If you and Bobby can work things out a little more, it's going to help integration." I didn't know what that really meant. But I like this integration thing. It means I get out more.

Now want to know something weird? That whole year of 1997 was pretty quiet inside the Castle. I'm not sure why. Were the Witch and Tommy just waiting and watching? Robert had big theories about it. Like, maybe the Witch and Tommy were really acting only when the outside guy, Bob or Robert or whatever, did something. Know what? Robert thinks too much. It was really simple. I'm bad, you know, but I didn't act very bad that year. So if I'm not acting bad, it's hard for the Witch and Tommy to do anything.

Did I tell you about my deal with Robert? Anyway, it was maybe because I did some good things. Or was it that he felt sorry for me being so sad about Lady Di? Anyway, he starts talking about "a deal." We looked at a calendar. When he doesn't have to do big things like lectures and trips, I could go out most days. You see, we can't both be outside at the same time. You get that, don't you? When I want to write something, Robert would help me with e-mails and stuff.

So guess what? Back in the late 1990s, I started to write my story. Well, I told it to Robert and he wrote it for me. Want to know what I wrote? It's called "Bottleman." Here it is.

"Hi. My name is Bobby. You might think I'm stupid because I never learned to read and write. Robert does the writing for me. But I'm not stupid. Know what? You can learn lots if you watch TV late at night. You should try it. Try the History Channel if you want to know lots of old secrets. And Discovery Channel for animals, fish, tornadoes, and things. When bad things happen, like bombs and trials, watch CNN.

"Know what? I'm a cool Rollerblader. You ought to see me Rollerblade. I go to Central Park almost every day. Except when Robert has stupid meetings. You know the place called the mall and the bandshell? That's where you can find me most afternoons. Especially weekends, when a disc jockey plays loud music. It's great. Hundreds of good skaters all dancing with the music—kids and adults. Every race—blacks, Asians, Latinos, whites. We call it the Skaters' Circle.

"Know what else? I'm pretty easy to find. I'm this tall guy wearing a T-shirt and shorts and a baseball cap. My skates have dragons painted on them. Robert paid a guy to copy dragons from some Chinese vase at the Metropolitan Museum. But here's the best part. I can skate with bottles balanced on my head. Not just one bottle, but sometimes two bottles, and even three bottles. I can go forward, backward, heels, toes, spread-eagles. I can even balance bottles going through slalom cones. I use water bottles with flat tops. When I do my trick, the bottles almost never fall.

Bobby 13 year old

"Guess what my name is at the Park? I'm Bottleman! Lots of people take pictures of Bottleman. Sometimes they give me photos. Sometimes reporters write articles about the skaters and they always write about Bottleman. Sometimes TV people bring cameras. I've been on TV lots of times in New York and also in Germany, France, England, and Japan. I once was paid four hundred dollars for ten minutes of Bottleman—it's shown on KLM as airplanes come to New York. And one time TV people came from Taiwan. They took lots of pictures of me. And guess what? Robert talked to them in Chinese. They couldn't believe Bottleman spoke Chinese!

"Robert was a little embarrassed about Bottleman. Sometimes people he knew from business or teaching or the Asia Society saw me as Bottleman. Then the next day, Robert had to answer a tough question: Was that really you in the park on Sunday, skating around with bottles on your head? He never knew quite what to say.

"I thought those were dumb meetings anyway. 'Just tell them it's good for balance. It's true. Some famous lady ice-skater did it first. That's what I heard. It's a great way to learn balance.'

"So it got better for me and worse for Robert. One time a professor from Columbia looked at Bottleman with his mouth open. Then he and his wife just laughed at what they saw as crazy Robert. Another time, an older leader from the Asia Society saw Bottleman and just stared. Robert suddenly forced me to stop and run away. He said he felt like a monkey in the zoo. I loved it when Bottleman was on PBS—a special program called 'Wild New York'— but Robert hated it.

"Anyway, I'm a good Rollerblade teacher. I teach people for free. Lots of people. Everybody's scared at first. So I teach them my two most important things. Number one—how to balance—that's where the bottle comes in. Number two—remember to smile. If you're smiling, your body forgets to be afraid. Of course I teach lots of other things. I even teach advanced skaters. Youngest was a four-year-old girl. I taught her how to balance by carrying an imaginary tray with a pitcher of lemonade. Even now, she sometimes skates around pretending to serve lemonade. Oldest was an eighty-four-year-old lady. She was funny. Said she did parachuting last year and wanted to do Rollerblading this year. She asked me, 'Do you think my big boobs will get in the way?'

"Know what? I'm best teaching children. I make them do it right and have fun at the same time. They're too young to be scared if you make it fun. And some of them don't even know it's hard. Lots of them learn to skate with a bottle on their heads the very first day. It's amazing. They become so serious about it. Very soon they have perfect balance.

"I don't know if those children see me as an adult or as a kid. I don't think it really matters to them. Maybe they see me as old enough to be a teacher, but young enough to have fun with them. I'm not even sure how old I think I am. I've grown up, you know. I used to be about fourteen. Now I'm sort of like, maybe, eighteen. Maybe not.

"Know what makes me mad? It's when people ask me how old I am. I know what they're thinking. They're staring at someone who looks like . . . well, you know . . . like in his fifties. It makes me very mad. I hate being a young person who doesn't look young. I can skate just as well as the young ones. I can skate for long times. Like one day I skated eight hours nonstop. And I use hair dye so I look a little younger.

"It's not fair that I'm stuck in an old body. I've been in a stupid dungeon all my life. Now, finally, Robert lets me out. Thanks a lot. It's too late. I know I'm young. But that's not what people see. That's why I never look in the mirror.

"The skaters treat me like a younger person. Well, most of the time anyway. We're like a family. Lezley, Robin, Bob—they're the ones who run the Circle—I like them lots, but they aren't so young. And then I skate with a bunch of younger guys. There's another Robert guy—he's black, with big muscles; he can balance one bottle, and he calls me clown. Oh, yes, James, he's a super skater and the nicest guy. And then the disc jockeys—like Jay, who does it a lot of the time, but I like the English lady best, she's called Miss Behavior, but I don't think that's her real name. And sometimes I race with the other guys—like Egal, he's from Israel, and Richard, he skates funny but he's nice.

"Dr. Smith sometimes asks me about how old I am. Well, I told him. I'm sort of someplace between fourteen and eighteen. It all depends—on the day, on the place. You know what I mean?"

Okay, that's what I "wrote" back then (I really sort of said it and then Robert wrote it for me). Anyway, I held back one part of the story. Now Robert wants me to talk about girls. I don't want to. Please—I give Robert my "deer-eyes" look—but he doesn't give in. Okay, I'll do it, if I have to.

Well, it's true, I don't just do Bottleman. I also like to do skate dancing. I have my own style. Not really disco. More like ice-skating. I dance with lots of girls. Some of them are really good skaters. Others I teach to dance. I think they like dancing with me because I do it different. I think girls like slow, smooth dancing. That's nice because it's sort of like, well, you know, hugging.

Robert wants me to talk about Bridgit. Bridgit was like twenty-five. She used to be an ice-skater in France. We skated great together. It made lots of people smile. I got to know her better and told her my story. She was an artist and made a great picture of Nester the Desert Mouse.

Then, well, you know what happened. Vishakha was away for a long time. And I went to Bridgit's apartment. I told her about Robert and Vishakha and the marriage. But she said it didn't matter. So, well, we lived together for about ten days. It was really nice. But then she said it did matter about Vishakha. Bridgit wanted me to live with her. I didn't know what to do. Eventually, I knew I couldn't live with her. So it was over. I was very sad. And so was she.

Now you've got to know something. This was really a big deal for Robert. And Vishakha? She was in Australia. But she found out since Robert wasn't home to get her calls. Robert told her something about how this wouldn't hurt the marriage. But he said this was important for me, Bobby. And Robert told Vishakha the truth—Bobby, that's me, didn't want to wreck the marriage. Robert said he had hoped it would blow over without Vishakha ever finding out. Well, it was too late for that.

Okay, this got real complicated. I talked a lot with Vishakha when she got back. So did Robert. I wasn't going to feel bad about this whole thing. That was the old Bobby, but the new Bobby wasn't going to feel bad. I said that the marriage was between Robert and Vishakha, not Bobby and Vishakha. I always liked Vishakha and I was happy for Robert. But I wasn't married to Vishakha. She was like a nice aunt. She liked my—what did she call it?—playfulness. But, like Robert, she didn't seem to think I could do music. She said she loved both me and Robert. I thought she wanted one person—a lot of Robert and a little bit of me. I told her that I wasn't going to leave to be with Bridgit. But—I told Vishakha—at least Bridgit seemed to love me as Bobby, not part Bobby and somebody else.

See, I told you this was a mess. It gives me a headache just talking about it. I think it would have been a mess without MPD. But, God, it was really a bigger mess with me and Bridgit and Vishakha and Robert. Like the whole world was involved. Robert was at least smart enough not to throw me back in the dungeon. He knew that would have caused the Witch and Tommy to be involved. I would have said "I'm bad," and then Tommy would have beat me and the Witch would have laughed and Robert would have been sad and Vishakha would have seen the Witch again.

Actually, Bridgit solved it all by trying too hard. She even had a meeting with Vishakha where she said she wanted me to live with her. Then Vishakha said to both me and Robert: "If that's what you want, I love you too much to stand in the way." I thought that was really cool. You know, like strong.

So we have this meeting with Dr. Smith. Dr. Smith talked to me like a real person. He tells me about single women in New York. They are looking for fun, but they really want this relationship thing. So it was fun, at first, then it got complicated.

But know what? When Bridgit found out I wasn't going to end the marriage, she broke it off right away. I was sad for a while, but then I got okay. Robert and Vishakha were okay, too. Every once in a while, Vishakha asked about seeing Bridgit at the park. I told the truth: "not for a long time."

Vishakha seemed okay on the outside. But I knew she was wondering. She was wondering about MPD—if this integration thing happens, will there be another partner? I didn't blame her. She was smart. It was the right question.

Actually, I think the Bridgit thing ended up being pretty good for both of us. Over time, I became much more caring about Vishakha and her feelings. We are lots closer today than we were before Bridgit. I try to find ways to help her and not to hurt her. Time changes things, you know. We almost never talk about Bridgit, but I think Vishakha is much more sure that I am not going to walk away. She's right, but it's partly because she treats me differently today.

Vishakha and I are kind of bonded in a new way. She can always spot me—and that's sort of tough, you know, because she has to watch for me, Bobby, even when she's talking to Robert. She's really good at seeing me inside when Robert's outside. "That's you, Bobby," she says, "isn't it? Bobby, come out now. I know it's you." And suddenly there I am, giggling like I was found in a game of hide-and-seek.

And I also can see Vishakha's feelings even when she's not really aware of those feelings. I call her "Nanubua"—it means Aunt Nanu, picked up from what her Indian nieces and nephews call her—but now I feel lots closer to her than it sounds. Sometimes I have to be a little pushy—"Nanubua," I say, "don't say 'No, I'm not feeling upset,' because I know you are feeling upset down inside." She almost always smiles and says, "How do you always know what I'm feeling? How do you know my feelings even when I don't recognize them?" I give her my little grin, the one with a cocked head and eyes wide open; it says, "It's me, Bobby. I'm an expert in hearts and feelings." She knows I care lots about her heart and feelings.

But all that new bonding—is it sort of like love?—came later. Back then, in late 1997, I was caught up with my own feelings. I was really sad. Robert now says 1997 was Bobby's year. But when the snow came and I put my Rollerblades away, it didn't feel like Bobby's year. Princess Di was dead and I felt dead.

I, Robert, was left feeling deeply saddened and deeply guilty about the Bridgit business. I knew how much it hurt Vishakha, and it happened partly because I was too weak to stop it. Just as I overlooked Tommy's abuse of Bobby earlier, I also pretended not to know that Bobby was off on a romantic adventure. I guess I thought that it would be a short-lived fling, and since Vishakha was away, it might not be discovered. In the daytime hours, I tried to make sure that I called Vishakha in Australia, but I couldn't be in the apartment during the evenings when Bobby was out roaming. And that's just when Vishakha made several unanswered phone calls. Anyway, since I could have kept Bobby locked up, I must bear the responsibility for letting him out.

See, I told you I wasn't cut out to be the dominant figure—I couldn't decide whether to be his father or his friend. After it happened, much as I hoped that it would blow over, I knew that the memory would be an open wound for some time to come. I do know that both Bobby and I are blessed with Vishakha's forgiveness.

ESCAPING THE CASTLE TO A SUNLIT MEADOW

EIGHTEEN

BOBBY: "I DID IT. WE'RE OUT.
NOW WE ARE THREE."

THE BRIDGIT AFFAIR, SO devastating when it occurred, prompted one remarkable change in our MPD life. Bobby had always lived in the world of intense feelings and impulsive actions. He had always bounced between very frightened and very happy, nothing in between. He was never a thinker. In the winter of 1997–1998, however, Bobby fell into a wholly new mood. In the wake of the affair, Bobby became quiet and reflective. He returned to his dungeon voluntarily and sat in stillness, day after day. Even when we made occasional visits to Dr. Smith, Bobby seldom showed his face.

BOBBY

My head was in a funny place. It was in between happy and scared. In the old days, except when Tommy was hurting me, I used to try to be happy. I played with my animals, I made jokes, I went Rollerblading. All kinds of stuff.

But after Bridgit, I was just sad. Okay, I didn't mean to hurt anybody. But it did hurt Vishakha and Robert. And it did hurt me.

So I started thinking a lot. Could I figure something out that might make things better? Not just for me, but for everyone? Then one day, I had my best idea ever.

ROBERT

I assumed that Bobby was enduring his first real case of the blues. If I had known what he was really thinking about, I surely would have intervened. Dangerous thoughts were swirling in his mind. Having found the whole structure of his life intolerable, he began seeking radical alternatives.

Never in a thousand years could I have imagined the outcome of his thinking. It was so dangerous that it could have created an MPD civil war, but it was so brilliant that it transformed us all. He implemented his extraordinary plan one night in January 1998. I had no inkling of the change until I got up the following morning.

Every morning when I awoke, it always was the same. Before my eyes could adjust, the Castle seemed captured in a mist. I always shivered in the cold drafts and felt rather creaky and old. The oil lamps were out and the dead fireplace logs gave off a musty charcoal smell. Coming awake in the Castle always made me pull the comforter tighter and wish I could sleep forever.

But why was today so different? Why was I wide-awake right away? Why was there so much light?

Suddenly it hit me with a jolt: I was no longer inside the Castle. Instead, I was in bright sunshine, blue sky, and puffy clouds. I was seated on a grassy meadow looking down across a wind-rippled, dark blue lake. There, on the other shore, was our Castle as I had never seen it before, from the outside looking in. The Castle's gray walls were mottled with sunlight, its towers poked into the sky, and its flags fluttered colorfully in the breeze. Behind me was a forest-covered mountain opening to a treeless, craggy ridgeline.

How could I possibly be outside the Castle after a lifetime of dark confinement? I looked to my right and immediately saw the explanation: Bobby sat quietly on the grass, admiring the view, a smug smile on his face.

BOBBY

"Like it? We've escaped. We're out of the Castle."

Robert looked really funny. He was like a fish. His mouth was open and moving, but nothing was coming out. "But what . . . ? But how . . . ?"

I know laughing wasn't a good thing to do. But I just couldn't stop laughing. Robert was just sitting there with a dumb look. I know he was desperate to find something normal. Maybe he could scold me for something. "My God, Bobby," Robert said, "what have you done? What about Tommy? Didn't he try to stop you?"

He was right to think about Tommy. Of course I had to go out of the Castle through Tommy's room. I couldn't have walked by Robert's chair. He would have awakened and wrecked the whole plan.

"Tommy?" I said with a smile. "Tommy's less of a worry now. I made a deal with Tommy. Now he's part of me. He gets out of that terrible little room in the Castle. And it's my job to deal with his anger. He wasn't sad at all. He just agreed. With Tommy on my side, there was no one to stop my plan."

"No one?! What about you-know-who?"

I pointed across the lake. "Take a look."

Robert made another mouth-and-eyes-open fishy look. He could see our Castle on the rocky mountain. No fog or clouds around it. But there was no Black Castle at all. It was totally gone.

"But where is you-know-who?"

I pointed to my left and Robert's eyes followed. He saw a beautiful woman with black hair. She was sitting without moving at all. Her eyes were sort of half-open. She had one of those quiet smiles. She wore a dark blue robe that came over her head. She looked like something out of a painting.

"Who's she?" Robert whispered.

"She's Wanda. She's the woman inside the Witch."

"But how . . . ?"

"That's the best part of my plan." I was so happy with this part. I just rocked back and forth and laughed. "Know how I sometimes see lights in people? You know, I see the light coming from golden hearts. Well, I thought I saw a light in the Witch. So I took a chance. I had a meeting with the Witch. We made a deal."

"What deal?"

"I told the Witch about seeing a light inside her. She was angry and made lots of awful noises. But I just stared at her. The light was still there, even brighter. Finally, she turned into Wanda. Eyes is now part of her. Oh, by the way, Wanda speaks only to us, not on the outside. She has the power to help things go well. But if things don't, she can always become the Witch again."

Robert looked back at Wanda. She smiled at him. Not a sexy smile. Don't worry about that. It was like a religious smile. Then she went back to that deep sitting thing. I thought she looked like Mary, you know, the mother of Jesus. Anyway, I knew that it was hard for Robert to imagine that she was the Witch.

"See her puppy?" I said. "That's Ragamuffin. He's my favorite. I gave him to Wanda. They love each other." I pointed over my shoulder. "My other animals? They're free, too. They're running all over the Meadow. They're so happy."

"But, Bobby," Robert asked, "up here, outside the Castle, who's the dominant personality?"

I looked Robert right in the eyes. "That's the deal. In the Castle, someone was always in charge. Up here, we're all equal."

NINETEEN

DIVIDED WE STAND

A T NIGHT, AS I looked down from our new mountain Meadow perch, it was hard to imagine a more beautiful setting. The moonlight etched silhouettes against the cool blue-black sky and a gentle breeze puffed clear, soft air. The Castle, once a battleground for contentious souls, rested calmly on its massive rocky outcrop. The Castle stood as a solemn reminder of another age, a museum of ancient personal history. Wanda, Bobby, and I, along with a scattering of animals, sat in utter stillness like small black boulders on a gray expanse. The silence was broken only by the soft cycle of our breathing merged with the wind's whisper.

Maybe I should have been angry with Bobby for his crazy plot to whisk us out of the Castle and plop us on the Meadow. He might have told me in advance. But, to be honest, he was right that I would have done my best to thwart the plan. Just imagine a wild scheme that flew directly in the face of

Tommy and the Witch. Well, damn it all, it worked. I guess you can't argue with success. Even so, I was left baffled by the Great Escape, as we came to call it—how could Bobby have transformed everything on his own? No outside guidance? No inside accomplices?

When I asked Dr. Smith, he was clearly surprised at the escape and the new mergers. But from his encouraging comments and pleased demeanor we knew that he strongly approved of the new Meadow framework as a key step toward his goal of "integration." We felt that Dr. Smith saw the Meadow as an MPD middle ground between the very-fractured Castle and perhaps a very-together "Summit."

I suppose I should have been outraged at my loss of dominant-personality status. But, to be honest, I was never much of a status seeker, inside or outside the Castle. Frankly, it was a relief not to have all the burdens of leadership resting on my shoulders. I had never aspired to be number one.

But we had just escaped the Castle and I was worried that no one was in charge. How could the three of us share power and responsibility? Would a newly empowered Bobby charge off in all directions without control? How could I trust a beautiful woman who might suddenly become a rancorous witch? And what was in it for me? Was I just the formerly dominant old guy, now irrelevant to life on the Meadow?

I heard a little bell-like sound, like the high-pitched *ping* one hears in a Buddhist temple. Although it was unlike the vibrations that announced Bobby's incoming messages, I knew someone wanted to intervene. I glanced at Wanda.

Wanda had a soft smile, but her eyes conveyed a sense of penetrating directness. "Don't worry so much"—that was her message—"just breathe. When you have thoughts, just let them go. Just say, 'Thinking.' Say it to yourself. 'Thinking.' Concentrate on your breathing. Nice, slow, easy."

Wanda's words were soothing and demanding at the same time. I felt I had no choice but to obey. My eyes fell toward the grass. My breath seeped in and out like a slow bellows, pushed gently by an eternal rhythm. I was rooted to the ground. Wanda knew exactly what was going on in my head. Can I really trust her? Is this Meadow only a brief resting place? What's going to happen on the outside?

Ping. The bell sounded, but there was no message. It was a gentle reminder: "Your mind is drifting. Focus and let go." I'd practiced the basics of meditation with a good Buddhist teacher, Bill McKeever, at a retreat center in northern Vermont. It was a painful experience—hours on end of rigid sitting, interspersed with a little walking meditation. But at the end, I told McKeever: "When I was meditating, it felt like all the personalities were lining up."

Ping. This time Wanda's command was clear-cut. "Stop thinking. Just breathe. Exhale, it's like 'expire.' Every outbreath is like death. Every inbreath is like rebirth. Until we finally die with our last breath. Then we truly 'expire.' But in Buddhism, it's not the end. It's an endless cycle, birth-death-rebirth, next lives receiving the karma of previous lives. Like candles, lighting a new candle before the old one is extinguished."

Bobby was a little angry that Wanda was doing all this talking with me. Why wasn't she giving him more attention? After all, Bobby thought, hadn't he gotten us all out of the Castle? And didn't he give Wanda his favorite animal, Ragamuffin?

"Don't be sad, Bobby," Wanda said softly with her eyes. "I know what you're thinking."

"You do?"

"Yes. That's because Eyes is part of me now. I can see inside of you and Robert. Know what I see now?"

"What?"

"I see both an opportunity and a danger. The opportunity is for you and Robert to work together. Can you imagine what you could do together? Remember last year in China? Wasn't that fun? You could do lots more like that. But the danger is that you'll go your separate ways. You especially, Bobby."

"It's because I'm bad, isn't it?"

"Bobby, I want this clear. You aren't bad. You're old enough now to know why you used to think you were bad. But it's just not true. Is that clear?"

"Yes, I guess so."

"Okay. Do you know what responsibility is?"

"I think so. It's when you can do lots of things. But like, you pick good things to do. Not bad things."

"Exactly. So you're not bad, but you could still do bad things. I want you to show responsibility to do good things. Understand the difference?"

"Uh-huh."

"It doesn't mean you can't have fun. It doesn't mean you have to do just what Robert tells you. It does mean you and Robert have to work together more. Okay?"

"Okay."

As time went on, Wanda's presence on the Meadow had a significant effect on both Bobby and me. I was astonished that someone who had emerged from the fearsome Witch could offer such peace and insight. I knew Bobby felt a little chastened that Wanda, who had countenanced his escape from the Castle and his new equality, would seek to teach him self-discipline. But Wanda offered stability to both of us, like the third leg in a three-legged stool.

Now that we were reduced to three personalities—all in the open on the Meadow rather than constrained by Castle architecture—the flow of communication among us was far easier and more frequent. But our actual process of communication is hard to explain to people not afflicted with MPD. Of course we did not actually visualize one another, but still relied on the old Castle instant-mail approach. Yet now our give-and-take was much more refined, almost as if each of our inner computers could convey a wide array of human feelings. Such nuanced overtones infused most of our Meadow conversations. To make this affective environment intelligible, I have resorted to physical descriptions, as if the three alters were actually real outside people—saying, for instance, "Wanda stared at me, so deeply that I knew I had no choice but to listen."

Thinking back to the late 1990s, I now recognize that we were not only on new ground outside the Castle, but also that each of us had evolved considerably since our escape. Wanda, of course, was the polar opposite of the Witch. But the fact that the Witch was now part of Wanda reminded us of awful past memories and possible future crises. She was our living example of "forgiven but not forgotten." And Bobby, for all his adolescent instincts, seemed a bit older than when he was under constant lock and key.

As for me, I do know that as far as my outer roles were concerned, Wanda and Bobby prompted a greater sense of openness in me. I felt there was a richer array of colors in my emotional palette. Instead of saying "I think," I was more tempted to say "I feel." And in speeches, I could "feel" a real connection between me and audiences and an awareness of how various individuals were reacting as I spoke.

As the "Meadow years" flowed across the late 1990s and into the new millennium, several activities seemed to involve all three of us. On certain occasions, it even seemed appropriate to use the pronoun *we,* as in "we decided to do this" or "we agreed about that." At the same time, all three of us—Wanda, Robert, and Bobby—were clear that these were moments of partial integration. Much of the time, we pursued quite separate, sometimes conflicting paths. The malady of MPD still hung over us. Nevertheless, it seemed apparent that the lush Meadow was a far better landscape for pondering integration than was the dank old Castle.

In 1998, for instance, I, Robert, accepted board membership in the Rockefeller Brothers Fund. The RBF was rare in nurturing a board that genuinely encouraged active trustee participation. In welcoming me, Robert—whom everyone still called Bob—the RBF had no idea that Wanda and Bobby also came along for the ride.

Of the three of us, I was the main outside figure on the RBF board and loved the fact that the RBF welcomed both academic thinking and practical experience. That rich mixture of thought and action characterized RBF leadership—former chairperson Abby O'Neill, former president Colin Campbell, current chairman Steven Rockefeller, and current president Stephen Heintz. It was like the best possible consulting job, albeit without pay, where I could focus my attention on specific meetings, make extensive comments, but then have lots of free time for other pursuits and coping with MPD. I was able not only to offer Asia-related insights to the RBF, but also to add perspectives on those places where values and pragmatic programs intersected. On a personal level, my close friendship with Stephen Heintz, with his brilliant combination of humanism and pragmatism, emboldened me to share my MPD tale with him. Not only were his insights caring and remarkable, but also Stephen and his wife, Lise Stone, have become true heart buddies with Vishakha and me.

Wanda never talked at all, but she looked for the spirit, what Bobby calls "light," inside people. Everyone knows the Rockefellers are rich, but many in the Rockefeller family and nonfamily members of the board also have philanthropic light. Wanda was delighted that they were so serious about giving money away for good causes: protecting the environment; helping minority teachers; solving security problems; improving democracy; working in South Africa, the Balkans, South China, and New York City. At meetings, Wanda just watched and listened. Then she pushed me to talk when we saw "light"—by this, I mean consensus points that are responsive to people's feelings. She revered Steven Rockefeller, who is a Buddhist and a professor of religion.

And Bobby? Let him tell it: "I got Robert to tell jokes and make people laugh. Sometimes people were too serious. Blah, blah, blah. Once I got Robert to say that some words sounded too big. How could any organization be 'for the welfare of all people'? That was a mistake to say because it turns out that was a quote from the original old man Rockefeller. Oops! Some stared like I'd taken down my pants. So I made a joke for Robert to tell: 'If we were in Japan, I'd have to commit ritual suicide.' Everybody laughed. If people laugh, then they're probably not going to be mad."

In 1999, I became chairman of OPUS 118, a program for the teaching of string instruments to inner-city elementary students in East Harlem. The program was started by an inspired teacher, Roberta Guaspari, who fought against great odds to keep her violin program afloat. When her salary was cut in 1990, Roberta was joined by a wonderfully determined photographer, Dorothea von Haeften ("Dodo" for short) to fight for reinstatement. In turn, Dodo enlisted her husband, Arnold Steinhardt (first violinist of the Guarneri String Quartet), who managed to involve such notables as Isaac Stern and Itzhak Perlman for a benefit concert at Carnegie Hall. Dodo's "Fiddlefest," as it was called, was a gigantic success, garnering enough money for Roberta's salary and enormous publicity for the program. The valiant story of Roberta Guaspari was captured in an Academy Award–nominated documentary film, *Small Wonders* (1995), and in a feature film, *Music of the Heart* (1999), starring Meryl Streep.

Bobby loved OPUS 118: "Those kids were amazing. I mean, like six to ten years old, and they play at the White House and at Knicks games. And I cried a lot at the movie. You know, not bad tears, but like movie tears." Wanda agreed, describing OPUS as a "light in the inner city."

But I, Robert, was frustrated that after the excitement over the movie was over, it was hard to take the OPUS model to other cities. Where could we find millions of dollars to bring string-instrument teaching to urban kids around the United States? But in spite of such headaches, one incredible benefit of OPUS was my becoming friends with Dorothea von Haeften and Arnold Steinhardt.

"Know what I liked best about the movie?" Bobby chirped in, referring to the Streep film. "It was the part where all the kids were nervous before they played at Carnegie Hall. Just before they walk onstage, Meryl Streep says, 'Oh, one more thing. Remember, play from here.' And she taps her heart."

TWENTY

MAKING MUSIC ON THE MEADOW

L EST ONE THINK THAT peaceful collaboration reigned on our Meadow, separatism and struggle were still major features of post-Castle life. Music was again a major battleground for Robert and Bobby. The guitar, which abruptly departed our lives in late 1997, was replaced by the cello in 1998 as the new weapon of choice.

I had always loved the sound of the cello, and was a huge fan of Yo-Yo Ma. Soon I had a good cello and bows, a fine teacher named Ted Mook, a wonderful duet partner named Lynne Rutkin, and a violin-flute-cello trio coached by Yvonne Hicks. So I was raring to go with a new musical passion.

The good news was that the cello, with bowing rather than plucking, did not tax my near-crippled right hand. I worked on basics religiously—scales, arpeggios, exercises—trying not to get ahead of myself technically. Within the first year, I felt I was making good progress. I could play my way through the first three of Bach's six challenging cello suites as well as some works by Vivaldi, Saint-Saëns, and Schumann. I embraced the ethos of the cello; when I first held my old cello and bow each day, I felt transported to another era, to old concert halls when classical music was everything and where stages were lit with oil lamps and candles. The cello, unlike the guitar, seemed to fit my body. It was easy to imagine playing well, hugging an instrument as it projected its beautiful voice.

The bad news was that I was better at imagining good cello playing than doing it. From an MPD perspective, the biggest change from guitar to cello was that I now actively sought Bobby's participation. It seemed like such a good idea. I thought we might tap Bobby's creativity and youth to enhance the music making. And I felt it might be a good way to interact now that neither of us was the dominant personality.

In practice, however, the Bobby–Robert duet team on a single cello was a nightmare. While we were "equal" in the Meadow, we were not "integrated" on the cello. I suppose it would have been simpler if I, Robert, had done the left-hand fingering while Bobby did the right-hand bowing. Instead, it was two completely different beginning students struggling over who was playing the instrument at any given time. Each student had different strengths and problems. Worse still, each of us thought he was better than the other. If MPD personalities argued in standard human dialogue rather than internal, nonverbalized communications, it would have been a screaming match.

"Why can't you have fun while you're playing the cello?" Bobby asked snidely. "Think of it like Rollerblading. Balance. Relax. Smile."

"I'm not against the fun part," I replied with parental exasperation. "But you can't just make up the rhythm as you go along. You can't just pretend you're hitting the right notes."

"You don't do the rhythm right, either. You're counting in your head. All the time. Then you lose your place."

"Bobby, you don't even read the music at all. You just try to memorize it. And you get it wrong."

"Well, so what? At least I don't make those stupid faces. Groan, Robert's trying to make it all sound good. You think you look like Yo-Yo Ma playing the cello? You look like Yo-Yo Ma sitting on the potty!"

After his abortive effort to "fix" the scratch on my guitar, Bobby was exceptionally careful about the cello and bows. He went to instrument and bow shops, watched master craftsmen like a devoted apprentice, and learned an enormous amount about the world of strings. He could converse with professional musicians about bridge adjustments, bow balance, and different kinds of horsehair. Bobby also had a million ideas for teaching the cello, and often drove our duet partner Lynne Rutkin wild when he would try to impose his latest idea on her. And when she didn't appear to listen, he would sometimes become outraged, as his Tommy side was offended. In retrospect, Lynne was remarkably understanding in tolerating frequent musical lapses and occasional emotional excesses.

The lesson was clear: playing music well demands an integrated approach in which all components come together—at the same time and on time. In my head, I knew that rhythm is the absolute foundation of music. As Isaac Stern has said, "We all have rhythm in our bodies. Just listen to the regularity of the human heart." Bobby clearly had rhythm when he Rollerbladed to all kinds of music from classical to rock. But Bobby's innate rhythm never synchronized fully with my reading of musical scores. When we tried to play with chamber-group partners, the crazy-quilt stitching unraveled. Robert was Robert, and Bobby was Bobby, and when it came to music, seldom did the twain meet.

Rollerblading was still Bobby's primary passion after we departed the Castle. During the week, he skated at least two hours a day; on weekends, it was four hours a day or more. Although he still liked skating with women, he was more careful after the Bridgit episode. But he never gave up his self-image of a single, young man. And as for me, I eventually found Bobby's bottle trick less embarrassing; I think most folks just saw it as the antics of an older, slightly wacko fellow enjoying offbeat exercise. When nonskating professional acquaintances came by, Bobby put down the bottles and disappeared, allowing me to engage comfortably in conversation. Following Bobby's suggestion, I would tell them: "The bottle balancing was invented by a famous figure skater. It's a marvelous teaching method and besides, it's fun."

Skating aside, Bobby continued to resist the growing pressure to become integrated with me. The champions of integration were Vishakha and Dr. Smith.

"Bobby," said Dr. Smith, "why can't you see that life could be even better if you linked up with Robert?"

"Sure. Lots better. Robert gets my energy and fun. And I get to be in my late fifties. I get forty years older in one day."

"But otherwise," Dr. Smith said, "the two of you are often at odds. No one wins."

"Okay," Bobby said to Dr. Smith. "I'll integrate! But only if Robert integrates into me. We can be called Bobby and we'll be, like, in our early twenties. Now that's cool. I get old-man abilities. You know, like experience, reading, and writing. See if Robert's willing to do that."

"You see," I said to Dr. Smith, "Bobby's absolutely hopeless. He knows we can't change outer age, but he just won't give up. He becomes more stubborn each day."

"I love everything about Bobby," Dr. Smith replied. "But I know integration is the right path. It would be good for all concerned. Without it, both of you will be frustrated. And I'm not sure what we do next."

"Right now," I replied, "it's an absolute dead end. Bobby believes in separate but equal. I suppose it's not right to say we're totally separate. I guess it's something like 'collaborative multiplicity.' Bobby won't budge an inch beyond that. He'll work together when it suits him. He stays apart the rest of the time."

"Whatever your term," Dr. Smith said sternly, "I still call it multiple personality disorder."

In March 2000, I joined Vishakha for her monthlong Rockefeller Foundation fellowship at Bellagio on Lake Como in northern Italy. The Villa Serbelloni, where we stayed, dates to the twelfth century and its gardens and wooden paths extend across hundreds of acres atop a rocky little mountain. You can almost hear the courtiers, the noble ladies, the monks, and the soldiers as you walk around the villa grounds and down the narrow cobbled streets of the town. Bellagio was a place for high art and music, for political gossip and intrigues, for violent battles. And just across the lake, as the Italian guides pointed out, was the little town where Mussolini was murdered.

But Bellagio had a special meaning for Robert, Bobby, and Wanda. We could not believe our eyes as we arrived at the villa and absorbed the view. Bellagio seemed to replicate our inner MPD architecture and landscape. The villa was very much like a medieval castle sitting on a large, rocky hill. At the bottom of the hill was a wide windswept lake of blue, rippled water. Across the way, rising from the lake, was a wall of steep mountains rising to a long ridgeline that linked their summits. In the midst of the mountain forests, directly opposite the Villa Serbelloni, was a large meadow. By day, warm sunshine brought a sparkle to the mountains, the meadow, the lake, and the castle. By night, the moon etched a mountain landscape painting in deep hues of blue and black.

The eerie magic of Bellagio touched each of us, like an ancient wizard's wand, defining our sharply separate natures, suggesting ways we might join hands. Wanda felt she had been a nun in a past life, someplace in Italy. When she heard the Bellagio cathedral bell toll each hour, she felt she had heard the bell before, so very long ago, marking the passage not of hours, but of years. She remembered wanting a life of peace but living in a time of war. Her faith had worn thin. Why such suffering, pain, sickness, death? Why are all condemned at birth to live a cycle of sin, confession, and more sin? Why is happiness possible only after death?

Speaking for myself, I was so glad I came to Bellagio as "Robert the spouse" rather than as a Rockefeller fellow, as originally planned. It was a perfect vacation with a cultural spin. During the day, I practiced cello in my *estudio*, a fifteenth-century guardhouse with incredible acoustics. When she wasn't working on her book, Vishakha and I walked the streets of medieval Bellagio, shopped in the larger town of Como, sipped cappuccinos by the lake. In the evenings, we ate pasta, chatted with the other Rockefeller fellows, and listened to lectures followed by Aleksandra Vrebalov's lyrical piano playing. Bobby was very attracted to Aleksandra—a Serbian composer and, at age twenty-nine, the youngest of the fellows.

"Attracted?" Bobby blurted out. "I fell in love with her. She looked like Meryl Streep. She wrote amazing music. I liked some of it. But what I liked she said was 'too approachable.' I thought that meant it's 'too easy to like.' That didn't make sense to me. She even wrote a piece for cello and piano. It wasn't hard, but I screwed it up. She didn't mind. Know what? She even talked like Meryl Streep. You know, in *Sophie's Choice.* I saw Aleksandra's study, where she wrote music. She smiled nice. She let me call her Sasha. But she seemed sad deep down. Robert said that's because she's from Yugoslavia."

Okay, it's true. Bobby did fall head over heels in love with Aleksandra. But it's also true that Vishakha and Aleksandra developed an enduring friendship. Clearly, there was a real spark between Bobby and Aleksandra, but both were careful not to let anything develop beyond friendship. I no longer had the power to constrain Bobby's life. To his credit, he did absolutely nothing that would suggest a physical relationship. Nevertheless, this raised a deeper unresolved issue. I was in Bellagio as Vishakha's spouse, but Bobby's heart again went in a very different direction. Within the MPD structure, Bobby had a corner on the market for passionate instincts.

Bobby was right about me: both in music and in life, I lived in my head. Vishakha and I shared many things—values, opinions, tastes, ideas, experiences, feelings—but the kind of passion Bobby experienced was not among them. It was my fault, not hers. But I didn't know how to cope with it. Nor with Bobby.

"I was so sad to leave Bellagio," Bobby said mournfully. "I cried in the car on the way to the airport. I was so happy in Bellagio. I had a good idea. Since Vishakha and Sasha were friends, why didn't she come live with us? That way everybody could be happy. But Sasha thought I was crazy. Besides, she said there was an 'age difference.' Funny, I thought of Sasha as much older than me, rather than me being older than her."

Wanda, who observed everything but stayed out of the fray, learned something else from Bobby in Bellagio. She became fascinated by the way that Bobby saw "lights" in certain people. He had seen Wanda, for example, inside the Witch. He also saw Aleksandra as linked to a supernatural creative force by a "beam of light." After a lot of meditation, Wanda found she could glimpse lights as well. Even before she saw the works of a remarkable painter, another Rockefeller fellow named David Ivie, she envisioned multiple shafts of focused light, like a lantern shining out of knotholes in a hollow log. Amazingly, David's works feature beams of light, often illuminating parts of paintings, creating a spiritual, otherworldly feeling. As for Vishakha's light, Wanda saw it in different terms. She envisioned Vishakha as a lighthouse keeper who was able to focus her high-intensity beacon to help many people, but who often found it hard to keep the candle in her bedroom from going out.

In just two weeks, Bellagio had brought remarkable clarity to our MPD. It had been exactly ten years since Tommy first burst forth in Dr. Smith's office, prompting the MPD diagnosis. Therapy had revealed a great deal—eleven personalities, two castles, terrible childhood trauma. And therapy had been productive—several internal mergers, escape from the Castle, only three personalities remaining, each combining skills and memories of earlier alters. Memory barriers had weakened, so that all three—Wanda, Robert, Bobby—knew what the others were doing, although not always what the others were thinking (except for Wanda, who had omniscience). In the outer professional world, all three had found that cautious collaboration yielded better success than total separation.

In one sense, perhaps we had achieved the dream of every psychiatrist. After all, we had probed deeply into our life history, faced troubling traumas, curbed difficult patterns and addictions, identified our inner selves and outer roles, and found ways to carry out a productive collaboration. Isn't that what any psychiatric patient is supposed to do?

Even though we were not fully integrated into a single personality, there were significant benefits to the "collaborative multiplicity" we had worked out among ourselves. MPD therapy had given us an uncommon awareness of our inner psyche. Unlike many "normal" people, we were acutely aware of what was happening inside us, whether in castles or meadows. Individual personalities could concentrate on honing separate skills and insights to a very high degree. Normal people might even envy the focused clarity of this MPD system. I, Robert, could concentrate, attention undistracted, on areas of reading, analyzing, talking, and writing. Bobby could give boundless energy to athletics, humor, imagination, and teaching. Wanda could direct her soul to other challenging pursuits—meditating to seek inner awareness, mediating on the Meadow to keep Bobby and me in line on the outside, and probing into the hearts of others. And, when one of us was occupying "outer time," the other two could be working on separate "inner channels."

By the time of the Bellagio sojourn, each of us had come to look upon our MPD world as normal. Surprising as it may seem to normal, integrated people, each of us had reasons to resist full integration. Bobby, of course, was deeply determined to keep his youth, his energy, and his personal freedom. Wanda worried that total integration might undercut her internal incisiveness and outer perceptiveness. To be honest, even I worried that complete integration might dampen the drive I brought to my consulting work and writing. In short, each of us feared losing that creative spark that had defined us as separate personalities. And each of us fretted that integration might be intolerably boring. MPD is many things, but it is seldom boring.

But all of us had to admit the chilling downsides of partial integration. The Bellagio experience starkly clarified the dilemma of a single body with three personalities, sometimes collaborating but never truly integrating. Simply put, "we" could not act consistently as "I" in the world of human relationships. Consistency is as fundamental to human life as rhythm is to music. Without consistency, it is impossible to be a good parent, a good friend, a good professional, a good mate.

Vishakha often said, "I love all of you." But she yearned for that "all of you" to achieve some sort of integrated harmony even if, as she said, "an integrated you might seek another alternative." Sadly, none of us has ever been able to reciprocate such love in a full sense.

Maybe, each of us thought, we could find our love through music. Couldn't we find it by channeling our energies into one instrument and one composer's music? But the tragic truth became apparent. We could each love the cello separately, but we could not play it lovingly collectively. The fact of the matter is that while we had learned to accommodate one another, often in ways that created outer success, we had not learned to love one another in ways that created inner cohesion and consistency. Without integration, we could only pine for human love and musical love; love itself would remain beyond our separate grasps.

So by the end of the 1990s, our landscape had changed to the beautiful Meadow, allowing us to develop a new perspective, in every sense of the word, on the Castle that had encased us for a half century. But for all we had accomplished, we were stuck halfway up a mountain, unable and unwilling to join hands and pull ourselves to the top. We knew that we could accomplish good works in the human world, but we doubted that we could ever learn to be fully human in the process.

SECTION SIX

BEYOND CASTLES
AND MEADOWS

TWENTY-ONE

THE PAINS OF COLLABORATIVE MULTIPLICITY

I SUPPOSE ALL THREE of us survivors—Wanda, Bobby, and me—really wanted to start a new chapter in our lives called "Living Happily Ever After." After all, each of us had sufficient reason to say "enough's enough." And we were finding some contentment in the ups and downs of life on the Meadow.

But the years right after the start of the new millennium brought more hurt than happiness. At the risk of being melodramatic, it seemed as if some diabolical force had decided to test us all. "Ha," said the devil. "So you've made some peace in your internal world. Big deal. Now wait and see what I have in store for you."

Although Bobby and I were blissfully unaware of any impending problems, Wanda had some darker premonitions stemming from her Buddhist beliefs. Buddhism, she believed, began with the notion of accepting pain as an unavoidable part of life. Pain, she argued, can become our best teacher.

Wanda's Buddhism and modern psychiatry are in total agreement: the root cause of pain must be identified, and the individual (or personalities, in the case of MPD) must "own" that pain. MPD exists for the opposite reason: in order to avoid traumatic memories, the child says "I'm bad" and splits apart rather than acknowledge what really happened.

Wanda showed me that the ultimate confrontation is between who we really are and our egos. The ego is always looking for gratification, seeking to avoid pain, and trying to control everything around us. Buddhists see meditation—concentrating the mind with a focus on breathing and letting go of our thoughts, images, and feelings—as a good way to release us from the thrall of our egos, allowing us to cope with pain, physical and psychic, in the process.

Imagine how much worse this ego business becomes when you have eleven of them. And imagine, even after whittling this number down to three (each of a pretty good size), how tricky it is to concentrate on "not thinking" during meditation.

Surprisingly, given his jumpy nature, Bobby listened attentively to Wanda. Forgoing his usual squirming and wiggling, he sat in rapt attention. "I like listening to Wanda, even when I don't understand what she's saying," he said. "I think she's heart smart. Sometimes, a few days after she says something, I suddenly get it."

And what about me? To be honest, during my dominant-personality years (1991–1997), I was both overly idealistic in my expectations and overly cantankerous when my expectations weren't realized. I just figured that once I'd confronted the hell of MPD and therapy, real life would be a bed of roses without thorns. But in the Meadow—listening to Wanda and watching Bobby mature—I received a dose of realism and resiliency. I stopped trying to find the perfect job and, occasionally, was able to cope with the fact that disappointment is part of life.

So, as the outside world entered the new millennium, our inside world was learning some good lessons, finding some space where our three ego spheres could overlap. But as it turned out, the new era proved, in terms both of our inside world and of the outside world at large, that we had all been blissfully naive.

On the sunny morning of September 11, 2001, I was writing away at my desk, window open to enjoy the fresh air, when I heard a plane screaming above Manhattan. Since I was five miles away, I never heard the crash, but I was informed of the tragic news by a phone call from Vishakha's brother in Cincinnati. I switched on the TV just as the second plane exploded into the World Trade Center.

At that moment, our three parts may have reflected the inner reactions of many other Americans: Robert, who kept repeating a mantra, "Oh God, I don't believe this;" Wanda, who immediately reacted that "the world will never be the same;" and Bobby, who just cried inconsolably.

While we tried to cope with a shattered outer world, our fragile inner structure was also rocked by some difficult challenges. Encouraged by friends who believed I was ready to tell this story, and with Bobby and Wanda at my side, I started to write a book. But the early drafts felt stilted and strangely disembodied. I, Robert, now know that I was a major part of the problem: I was an overly dominant narrator, often stifling the voices of the other personalities. It was intensely disappointing to realize that while we had made real strides with MPD therapy, we weren't together enough to find the right voices to tell our story. We decided not to proceed toward publication.

Then we were hit with a bombshell: in spite of firm promises about confidentiality, someone leaked the story of my book project. An online magazine made it public with my name ("Robert Oxnam, China scholar and president emeritus of the Asia Society"), my disorder ("living with multiple personalities"), and enough details to make it stick ("Oxnam suffered from up to 13 personalities, but has been able to manage them, honing them down to about three. One of them is an inline skater named 'Bottleman' or 'Bottleboy' ").

We were suddenly in the worst of all possible worlds. News of our secret story was out. And now there was no forthcoming book to put the story into an understandable context. It was a juicy rumor without explanation—it spread rapidly by word of mouth, over the Internet, and by a brief reference in a New York tabloid. Surprisingly, I had only three direct phone calls in the aftermath, but I know that hundreds of my colleagues heard the story. I could no longer go anywhere without wondering who had heard the gossip. I quickly told the whole story to the leaderships of key organizations with whom I had active affiliations—including the Asia Society and the Rockefeller Brothers Fund. All were extremely supportive, expressing hopes that I would feel ready to publish the book someday.

A few days after the press leak, I attended a reception at the Asia Society galleries on Park Avenue. When I introduced myself to a circle of people, one young man said: "Oh, you're Robert Oxnam. You're the guy with multiple personalities." From that moment, I knew that life under the cloud of an unexplained rumor was going to be hell. I might as well be wearing a "Hi, I've Got Multiple Personality Disorder" button on my lapel at social functions.

The decision to suspend writing, and the press leak, rendered all three of us devastated hermits. I spent countless hours holed up in my apartment, leaving only for a very few professional meetings. Bobby kept skating, but mechanically without his usual zest. Wanda simply said nothing. She seemed to meditate day and night. Although Vishakha sought to help, I retreated even from her. I put everything related to the book away. My computer gathered dust, swept away only by occasional rounds of e-mails.

Bill McKeever, my Buddhist friend, was one of the few who kept close contact during those dark days. He told me later that he "really feared I would not make it." He felt that "I had almost given up on life" and that all he "saw was gray when he looked at my face."

At Christmastime, just when I was certain we had reached the depths of living hell, I found it could get worse. I was informed that my MPD had become a serious issue with my ongoing consultancy at an association of business leaders. For twenty years, in the words of one leader of the organization, I had been the "superstar lecturer" in their international business-education program. I had led their much-heralded trips to Asia, invariably winning the highest marks in the rigorous evaluations of participants. In turn, I felt that these Asian business-education trips were among the best professional experiences in my life. In fact, they were important trips for all three inner personalities—Robert, Bobby, and Wanda—who were able to achieve a rare level of collaboration on these voyages.

Suddenly, prompted by a single complaint that my MPD might render me dangerous to the organization, the mood changed dramatically. Certain leaders began viewing me with suspicion, seeking to contain what they saw as "the MPD issue." Although many figures remained very supportive, it was clear that a minority was poisoning the well. Pestered by veiled accusations and new restrictions, I was spending more and more time defending myself, leaving me less and less energy to perform my real work.

Deeply hurt by this experience, I was on the brink of cutting ties to an organization that had been very important to me. But just before making my decision formal, I took an hour's walk in Central Park. Suddenly I felt a surging resolve to give it one last shot. I had given my all to these people for years, with very positive results, and now they were treating me like a pariah. Enough was enough.

I decided to stand up for myself. I told the organization's leadership that I had sought legal advice, and had determined that I had grounds for a major defamation-of-character suit. It was my decision to terminate all association with the organization and to pursue legal action unless they met several requirements. The effect was immediate and remarkable. They agreed to all conditions in a clear and conciliatory letter.

When I told Dr. Smith about this turn of events, he was elated. "I'm so proud of you," he said. "That was exactly the right thing to do. I wish I had your balls."

Although I was a little taken aback by Smith's uncharacteristic foray into vulgar slang, a deeper question jumped to mind. Whose balls were they? Who had made the tough decision to confront the organization with an un-compromising proposal? Who had turned a terrible defense into a winning offense?

Oh, my God. We hadn't had time for a "committee decision." Indeed, the action I had taken wasn't based on a decision reached by *any* of the three of us—not by Robert, Bobby, or Wanda. It wasn't a "we" decision. Was this possible? It was an "I" decision! It was the first "integrated decision" in any-body's memory.

All three of us were amazed that we could resolve a horrible dilemma with a single mind. It was our biggest step in MPD therapy since we escaped from the Castle three years earlier. None of us was under the illusion that we had suddenly fully integrated. But now we knew that temporary integration was possible, under the right circumstances, and with remarkable results. I coined a new phrase: "situational integration."

Almost instantaneously, like a reconciliation between feuding lovers, my relationship with the organization became better than ever. For the three of us on the Meadow, our victory had the same impact—bonding and respect—like triumphant veterans of some foreign war. Wanda's observation about pain be-ing the best teacher certainly had ample illustration. And since I was responsi-ble for outside negotiations, I was feeling pretty good about my leadership skills. At least, I proved that I could get beyond the idealism/disappointment cycle and deal with vexing real-world issues.

"What are you talking about?!" Bobby sent me an outraged message. "Are you claiming credit for the decision to get tough? It was my idea! I wanted to tell those guys off in words you've never heard from me. Only Wanda told me not to. She said it was 'beneath us.' So I said we've got to hit them right on the nose. Tell them we're not going take it. Let them know about the lawyer. And that's what worked. They were just being big bullies. Then they became little puppies."

Stung by Bobby's comment, I looked to Wanda for support. *Ping!* "Bobby's right," she said. "It was his idea. He gets the credit. And, Robert, watch out, your ego is your worst enemy."

This episode made it clear that memory barriers, whether from ego or MPD, still impeded my recall of some events. For instance, what really happened in the Great Escape of 1998? I, Robert, have told you the story exactly as I recall it. But the question has gnawed at me; the escape from the Castle seemed too simple, too neat. No matter how hard I tried, I was unable to recollect any more nuanced details.

Not until years later did the solution to this puzzle come to light. The secret revolves around a gifted Italian woman named Agnese Barolo (she is also known as Agnese Rizvi, since she is married to the brilliant and affable scholar Gowher Rizvi, now at Harvard University). Agnese has a successful career in what might be called "life consulting" for organizations and individuals, including such activities as looking for body signals through Indian chakras, exploring past lives, and guiding meditations. She describes her work as focused on the present and future, as opposed to psychiatrists, whom she sees as working primarily with the present and past.

When I first met Agnese in Asia Society circles in the early 1990s, I had two very different reactions. On the one hand, I knew immediately that she had an unusual ability to see inside me and to envision my future problems and opportunities. Off in a corner at a cocktail party one evening, she calmly described forces competing within me, detailing many of my personalities with uncanny accuracy. I was so riveted by her quiet voice that I ignored all the other guests for two hours, listening to her describe my future as filled with "darkness and then light."

On the other hand, even though Bobby was utterly fascinated by Agnese, the Bob and Robbey parts of me viewed her with slightly jaundiced eyes. None of us doubted her ability to peer deeply inside other people—after all, our own Castle complex, and our MPD therapy, were filled with such experiences and abilities. But Agnese's work seemed so New Age, so unconventional, that it made my part of my Castle anxious. And Agnese had this curious way of saying startling things; for instance, I will never forget her conversation stopper at a dinner party one night when she observed: "So many problems in life are caused by overly tight sphincters. Americans, in particular, have tight anuses."

Maybe because I myself was so uptight, so to speak, I resisted her suggestion to come to her home-office in Pelham, just north of New York City. I also worried what Dr. Smith might think. Would he worry that Agnese might be tinkering with my unpredictable psychiatric disorder at a fragile moment? But after several friends said, "Agnese is working wonders for me—you should see her," I finally took the plunge and visited Agnese without informing Dr. Smith. I said to myself: *Dr. Smith is my psychiatrist; Agnese Barolo is just offering supplemental insights.* Later, when I confessed to Dr. Smith about seeing Agnese, I was quite surprised that he seemed unperturbed. Similarly, when I explained Dr. Smith's role to Agnese, I was heartened to hear her say, "It sounds like you have a great guy."

All worries vanished over the course of ten or fifteen visits to Agnese. She was very warm, professional, and helpful. With soft music in the background, she showed me proper body positions and breathing techniques, guided me through meditations involving journeys through inner woodlands and dark pools, and prodded me to recall past-life experiences (producing some unusual, often quite credible results). I emerged from these rigorous sessions feeling more centered and hopeful, and considered them a nice completeffect to my occasional visits to Dr. Smith. But there was one curious aftereffect of my sessions with Agnese: I often had heavy, dull headaches, similar to those I'd had when I began MPD therapy, signifying that, unbeknownst to me, other personalities had been active.

Then, for six years, Agnese was away from New York, first in India and then in Boston, and we had almost no contact. Finally, after she had returned to Pelham and reestablished her practice, we had a grand reunion on Thanksgiving weekend—Agnese, Gowher, Vishakha, and me. Agnese was delighted to hear of my forthcoming book, but was perplexed that I still seemed so surprised about the escape from the Castle.

"Robert," she said, taking me aside, "you don't remember that I met others inside your Castle—the Witch, Bobby, Tommy? You don't remember the long talks I had with Bobby about how he might reach out to Tommy? And you don't recall that when I met the Witch, Bobby saw an image of a Madonna-like woman in a soft robe?"

I stared at her, dumbfounded. I did not remember any of these events, except a vague recollection of the Madonna-like woman. Agnese's startling comment brought back the familiar headache. Not only had Agnese's conversations with my inner personalities been kept out of my memory at the time they occurred, but Bobby hadn't revealed anything about them even when I was writing this book. I had been deliberately kept in the dark.

Later, with a chastening tone in my request, I gave Bobby a chance to clarify what had happened. "You kept the whole Agnese thing secret from Dr. Smith," Bobby retorted. "Why wasn't it right to keep our talks with Agnese secret from you?" Since I didn't have any good answer for Bobby's reasonable question, I just sat back and listened.

"Okay, here's what happened," Bobby continued. "I always liked Agnese a lot and I think she trusted me. Remember how you and Bob used to fight, and then you formed an alliance? Well, Agnese got me to see that maybe, just maybe, Tommy wasn't as bad as I thought. Agnese pushed me to try to think of Tommy as a friend rather than an enemy. But, of course, that meant that the Witch would have to stop giving orders for Tommy to hurt me.

"Now here's where Agnese did something amazing. She talked right to the Witch. Agnese sounded both tough and gentle at the same time. She wouldn't let the Witch be mean. And somehow, Tommy and I were allowed to overhear. The two of us couldn't believe what was happening. The Witch wasn't being scary. She was quietly listening to Agnese. And then, staring at the Witch, I saw a big white light, and suddenly I had this picture of a pretty woman on a hill, right in my head. I wanted so bad to make that dream come true."

Hearing Bobby's account, I just shook my head in astonishment and admiration. It was headline MPD news: GREAT ESCAPE CONSPIRACY REVEALED. Instead of acting as a dangerous radical in carrying out his scheme, Bobby had shown himself to be quite rational, at least in MPD terms. Bobby put the pieces together, following patterns already suggested in Agnese's sessions. Bobby's initiative was both intellectually creative and psychologically healthy: linking with Tommy and activating the Witch's transformation into Wanda. Bobby's decision to escape to the Meadow was simply brilliant: he had fashioned fresh architecture for a new era—a beautiful outdoor setting without walls, but one that never allowed us to lose sight of the old Castle.

Without training in dissociative psychiatry, Agnese had coaxed us to a new stage of integration. Because of her gentle nurturing of my MPD personalities, she had facilitated the realization that I had never imagined. She had paved the way to a creative psychological coup d'état and opened a fresh chapter in our MPD history. I had this image of Agnese Barolo roaming across eighteenth-century northern Italy—a famous soothsayer and healer accompanied by her beloved stray animals, known to all as the "midwife of the mind."

TWENTY-TWO

VALUES: "WHAT THE HELL
DO WE BELIEVE IN?"

D R. SMITH OFTEN SAID: "When MPD alters merge, whether a partial or full integration, no one 'dies.' Instead their attributes become part of a new composite personality. But that is not true of values. Before real integration can occur, there must be some sort of blending of values. If not, the integration will fail."

His observation, central to nurturing us from the shocking discovery of eleven-personality MPD to quasi-harmonious tripartite cooperation, left us with two unanswered questions. Could we find a shared core of values to guide feelings and actions? And should we follow Smith's advice and push for full integration, essentially merging Robert, Bobby, and Wanda into a single personality?

These questions fluttered through our Meadow conversations for several years after the start of the millennium, especially when we pondered whether to get back to writing a book. The chatter was often most intense during down times and in between my lecturing and consulting responsibilities—quiet moments on airplanes, late nights when we couldn't sleep, walks back home after Bobby had been Bottleman. Sometimes one of us would essentially think out loud, meaning that the other two were listening. Sometimes two of us would have a chat while the other was just eavesdropping. Over time, we made progress, not only in honing our own views, but also in groping toward a more coherent set of answers that spoke to all of us.

In this quest for common values, all of us sensed profound changes inside. Perhaps because we were speaking about a single topic, searching for a coherent conclusion, our deliberations seemed more organized. That was remarkably new in an MPD system that had always been as fragmented and fractious in its conversations as in its personalities. And there was something else—a certain blurring of our conversational styles: Bobby seemed somewhat older and wiser; Wanda appeared more engaged and less authoritative; Robert felt more assertive but less didactic. We all wondered: Did our discussions suggest rising potential for a single, integrated personality?

"About this 'values' thing," Bobby blurted out one day. "I don't like the word. Sounds like Robert blabbing away in the classroom. How about this: 'What the hell do we believe in?' Isn't that better, huh?"

Bobby didn't wait for us to answer, but began a stream of messages. "Now here's the problem. It's not that the three of us don't believe in things. But the question is: What do *we* believe in?" So Bobby explained that he had a big problem: "Whatever Wanda says to make me feel good, deep down I still think I'm bad. I suppose I'll always feel that way. But okay, supposing I really want to act good. What is 'good'?"

Bobby continued: "I think that little children and little animals sometimes are smarter than adults. Know why? They can see good and bad hearts right away. Good hearts give love and food and hugs. Bad hearts give hits and hurts." Bobby said he thought that most people lost this ability as they became older. But he saw a ray of hope: A few adults are stronger inside. They don't give up their good hearts.

"Maybe," Bobby reflected, "it's because I'm still a kid. Maybe it's even because I've been hurt a lot. Anyway, I know right away, almost always, about who has a good heart. It's this light thing. A few people have strong inner lights. But most people have 'lights-out.' 'Lights-on' not only means a good heart; it also means really caring about other people's hearts.

"Now here's the main thing. Good is when people, no matter what their age, struggle to keep their lights alive. Good is when they help others with dim lights to make those lights brighter. Most of all, good is when they try to link up with other people who have good hearts.

"Okay, last idea. I think of the world as a huge mountain. But it's very dark and cloudy and smoky. You've got to climb the mountain. But it's all covered up and it's so hard to see. Even if you have a good light, it's not enough. You've got to find other people with lights. And when you get enough lights, then you can climb and not fall off. It's scary. You're not sure what's at the top. But with all the lights, you might get there. And even if you don't get there, you might help people on the way."

Wanda and I stared at Bobby in stunned silence. Wanda exuded a soft maternal glow, like a teacher who had just been surpassed by her student. "Bobby, I'm so proud of you. That's it! That's the right way to think."

At that moment, I felt an electric energy between Wanda and Bobby, something more potent than either possessed alone. As the energy subsided, Wanda became pensive. "How about the three of us? We seem pretty happy with how our lights play off one another. So aren't we worried that integration would make for duller light and a more boring life?

"Of course we know we're losing some things by staying separate. We're on a meadow, but we're not at the top of the mountain. Rather than climbing,

I've got a more modest goal. Can't we move a little closer to one another without losing separate identities?"

Wanda explained that she believed in "engaged Buddhism," that pursuing a disciplined, meditative life was not done for its own sake, but in order to achieve outside action. "That's exactly what Bobby is saying with his notion of lights coming together on a mountain—seeing the best in ourselves and trying to link with the best in others."

After listening to Bobby and Wanda, what could I add? I had to admit to being pretty eclectic about values. "I'm not a doctrinaire anything. I'm against fundamentalism—whether Christian Bible-banging or Islamic jihad. I'm more of a mixture of Wanda-style Buddhism and social gospel Christianity.

"When it comes to putting values into action," I asserted, "I don't think we should sell ourselves short." In spite of MPD and in spite of all my carping, there had been a lot of value-driven action, even in Bob's day. I've got to admit that he transformed the Asia Society into a major bridge between Americans and Asians. "And what about the last decade since I became dominant, and the last few years since we've shared power? There has been a strong dose of values in everything we've done—teaching about U.S.–Asia relations, fiction writing about China, TV programs and business education concerning China, music teaching in the inner city.

"The problem is not the absence of values," I reflected. "The problem is how and where those values are applied." In recent years, we have been in an experimental period, trying to come closer to MPD integration on the inside, trying to find new outlets for our more integrated values on the outside. I used to be obsessed with finding a new career path with a "cause" embedded in it. After turning sixty, I mellowed a lot. Now I tell folks that I'm "post-résumé"—taking on projects that really speak to my heart rather than to my career.

I agreed with Wanda. We were on a good path. We were outside the Castle, on the Meadow, almost like a family. Wanda seemed more and more like a wise sister and Bobby like a rapidly maturing son. On good days, we made some decisions, big and small, without having vexing meetings first. On bad days, we were still living divided lives, caught in our own thoughts and moods.

Our most sustained collaborative endeavor was teaching brilliant graduate students at China's Beijing University (Beida, for short) in the spring semesters of 2003–2004. We gave a seminar course on U.S.–Asia relations in the school of international studies. At the outset, it wasn't an easy experience, but over the two years, it evolved into one of the most rewarding things we have done. I think that's because what I originally saw as a "Robert job" evolved into a "Wanda, Bobby, Robert job."

Perhaps the best proof of our combined strength came when we were lodged in the spectacular Packard Pavilion, a renovated palace perched on Nameless Lake (Weiming Hu), with its meandering estuaries, tiny pavilions, and large pagoda. The school of international studies' faculty went overboard in arranging meetings and lectures to assist with my research for my planned book on the future of America and China. All of us—Wanda, Bobby, and Robert—were involved in the new course structure, featuring lots of class discussion, short lectures, and guest speakers.

But beyond the classroom, too, each of us was transformed during the two years we were at Beida. Bobby came center stage in all sorts of remarkably constructive ways while never losing his impish character. In 2003, very self-conscious about speaking Chinese, I generally resorted to English. In 2004, Bobby shocked the previous year's students and faculty, and even surprised the new batch of graduate students, by speaking Chinese constantly.

Let Bobby tell it. "In 2003, Robert lectured too much, discussed too little, and tried to control everything all by himself. It was boring. So in 2004, I just went for it. I let the Chinese fly, flowing right through Robert. You see, I'm the one who's pretty good at Chinese. When I didn't know a word, I got

Robert to look it up in the dictionary. I spoke Chinese all day long for over two months. I even invented a trick. When I got mad at Robert, like when he worked too hard and didn't let me play, I just turned off the Chinese. Then, when he was nicer, and desperate to speak again, I just turned the Chinese back on."

But Bobby had another surprise in store. I had returned to guitar practice in 2002, taking lessons with a marvelous guitar artist, David Leisner, who had found a radical way to deal with my focal distonia problem. But Bobby was impatient with our slow progress (painstakingly trying to use the thumb and three fingers) and took the shortcut of playing classical pieces with just his thumb and forefinger. As he'd done with the Chinese language, Bobby found musical fluency at Beida.

"I took a funny portable classical guitar along which can only be heard on earphones or speakers. So I got some cheap speakers and started playing outside the Packard Pavilion, where hundreds of tourists came on weekends. At first, I played so lightly that few could hear. Then lots of people stopped to listen. I played louder. They clapped. I played like I never have before. I wasn't worried. It was just fun. Then I stopped and talked with the crowd in Chinese, telling them about my guitar music. I started showing kids how to play—even little ones could do the right-hand rhythms while I did the left hand. Soon hundreds of people wanted to take pictures of me with their kids or friends.

"It became a Beida happening. I realized it was more about saying things with music than getting everything right. People asked for advice on teaching kids music. I ended up with lots of music friends, even some professional-type musicians who played with me or sang with me. It was really cool.

"I cried the day I left Beida in May 2004. It was like I had come alive, really alive, for the first time. I got a good-bye note from a student I didn't even know—she said she was crying, too, because when she listened to my guitar, it reminded her of her family and boyfriend who were far away."

As for me, Robert, the 2004 Beida seminar was the best teaching experience of my life. From the first day, the three of us inside created a sort of quiet fire that lit up the students. In turn, the students, all of them, were brilliant in their remarks and writing, but even more, they were remarkably forthcoming in expressing feelings about China, America, and the rest of Asia. As a result, we were together all the time, in small groups over dinner, in individual meetings, in excursions to various shrines and hiking areas around Beijing. It was more like a family than a class—totally radical in the hierarchical Confucian teacher–student relationship and, though I didn't talk about it, totally novel in my previously strictly divided MPD experience.

Odd as it might seem, I came to realize that our inner MPD structure offered me an unusual advantage as a teacher. Once multiple personalities are able to interact internally, it is easier for them to operate empathetically in a multicultural context. While one of us was talking, the other two were listening and watching, making it easier to sense feelings. When discussing international issues, I was surprised that I could instinctively sense not only American reactions but also Chinese reactions.

In short, this old professor learned far more by listening to his own students than they learned by listening to his lectures. And since this professor just happened to have multiple personalities, he found that Bobby and Wanda were often more perceptive about "Chinese thinking" than he was. As a result, my MPD side and my Asia side came together in a splendid moment at Beijing University.

The rewards were not just academic but also personal. Several of my most talented students now speak of me as their "American father." Gao Jun, now studying in Japan, and his girlfriend, Edith "Curly" Wang, consider themselves my Chinese son and Chinese daughter. Liu Hua (now at Washington University, St. Louis) and Yao Yuan (pursuing studies in Japan) are also part of my growing Chinese extended family. Chen Jing, my 2004 teaching assistant, also suggested a father/daughter relationship. I told Chen Jing about my

MPD story and she responded with sincere understanding (it was the first time I had ever dared broach the subject with a Chinese person). In turn, she shared her family history and sought my support for her dream of studying in the United States and becoming a professor of international relations back in China. (She is now a doctoral candidate at Princeton University.) I always melt when she says good-bye on the phone, using the Chinese word for father. "*Zaijian, baba.* Bye bye, *baba.*"

Vishakha came to Beida in early May 2004 for two weeks, on her first trip abroad as president-elect of the Asia Society. One day, as my students and I were visiting temple sites to the west of Beijing, we concocted a new Chinese name for Vishakha—"Ding Wenjia" (丁文嘉)—combining a distinguished surname with the appropriate personal name, meaning Culture and Joy. The students embraced her and loved her seminar on India in U.S.–Asia relations. On Vishakha's birthday, May 1, the students organized a fantastic party at our apartment that was a total surprise. Surprise parties are not in the Chinese tradition, but all the students got into the spirit, ordering a wonderful cake, a huge bouquet of flowers, and offering gifts from faculty and themselves.

And what of Wanda? She was our spiritual center at Beida, the one who brought the Meadow's peace and light to Beida. She nudged me when I became too absorbed in the classroom experience or a little too self-critical when my lectures at other universities or research institutes didn't go as well as expected. She smiled proudly at the emergence of a new Chinese-speaking and guitar-playing Bobby, but also tried to check his sometimes excessive exuberance and his often excessive demands on time.

Beyond China, we also became aware of how we were interacting differently with our Indian family. Each of us had embraced the Desai family, both in India and the United States. But it used to be a disaggregated embrace: Robert talked to older folks, Wanda communicated about spiritual matters with Ben, and Bobby spent joyous hours with the kids. Now, without really thinking about it, all of us became happily involved in family life. That meant a whole new set of linkages to the young adults in the Desai clan— Vishrut and Reema in New York and Anokhi and Antara in Baltimore—who have come to the United States for education and jobs. We bonded in lots of ways—from fun, to advice, to learning, to fretting—and all that required the active input of all three of us.

It is in these family ties, more than anywhere else, that the easy interaction of Robert, Wanda, Bobby has come to seem most natural. I suppose, if we watched a videotape of family gatherings, we could spot the flow of my inner personalities emerging on the outside. But we are too absorbed in going to real movies and chattering away over meals to waste our time doing MPD analysis.

So the whole state of mind is changing inside us. I think that makes all of us more relaxed and more productive at the same time. We're finding that this sense of openness allows a very different, more receptive outlook on the outside world.

Against this hopeful backdrop, it is sometimes tempting to forget that we have multiple personality disorder. The early summer of 2004 offered a chilling reminder that the disorder could still erupt in a flash with potentially disastrous consequences.

Bobby, in the wake of his joyous experience at Beida, returned to New York in a very dark mood. After having been something of a celebrity and a guru in Beijing, he found little allure in an occasional skating session at Central Park. He wandered aimlessly around the apartment, babbling Chinese and wishing he could be back at Weiming Hu. He would cry out, "I want to go home. Beida was my home. It was the only time I was really happy. I could have died happy there."

Finding it impossible to console Bobby, I continued researching my China book, when I learned that my mother had suffered a stroke and passed away at a Connecticut hospital. Although her health had deteriorated in recent years, her death was unexpected and sent shock waves through her loved ones. I soon became enmeshed in preparations for her memorial service. My mother's death—severing the last link to our childhood—was a deeply jarring MPD moment. I tried diligently, and unsuccessfully, to keep the MPD system from fracturing under the stress.

With few activities and little outside attention, Bobby became more and more depressed. Knowing that alcohol was off-limits, he drank large quantities of caffeine in the forms of coffee and Diet Coke—keeping him, as well as Wanda and me, up half the night. The wee hours were always Bobby's time to watch television and play the guitar; he prized the very insomnia which exhausted me.

One evening at dinner, Vishakha noticed how much Diet Coke was being consumed and asked: "Do you really want to have another glass? It will keep you from sleeping." She said it to be helpful, in a somewhat maternal tone of voice. She never intended it to be a fuse that lit a bomb.

Suddenly I, Robert, disappeared and there was Bobby. "It's none of your business!" he shouted. "When I was in Beijing, I didn't have anyone telling me what to do."

And then Bobby disappeared, and for the first time in years, Tommy reemerged with hissing sounds and clawlike fists. Grabbing the large plastic Diet Coke bottle, he threw it against the apartment window, breaking the glass and splattering the liquid all over the kitchen. Tommy then began hitting Bobby—Tommy's fists smashing into Bobby's head. Finally, he shot a threatening glare at Vishakha and quickly faded away.

"Oh no, Nanubua," Bobby cried, hurt more by Tommy's outburst than the barrage of blows. "I was mad, but I had no idea that Tommy could still do that. I tried to stop it, but Tommy just came out of nowhere. I'm so sorry, Nanubua. I'm bad! I wanted to die in Beijing. It's my fault."

Vishakha did her best to maintain her composure. She came over to console Bobby. Just then, Bobby's face transformed into a contorted, fierce image with piercing eyes. "Just what I wanted," cackled the Witch. "Bobby's bad again. He must be punished—"

Two voices shouted a command to the Witch at the same time: "*No! This cannot happen!*" One voice, sharp and clear, belonged to Vishakha. The other, equally forceful, loud on the inside but inaudible to Vishakha, came from Wanda.

In the face of such pressure, the Witch tightened her eyes, stared hard, and disappeared just as Tommy had done. The typhoon had passed as quickly as it arrived. Only Bobby's whimper could be heard. "Nanubua, I didn't mean it. Really I didn't. I'm so sorry. I'm bad. I'm always bad." And then Bobby also retreated from view.

All that was left was a broken window, a terrible mess in the kitchen, and the silence that follows a catastrophe. Vishakha and I hugged each other and I uttered my words of apology. She shook her head as if to say that she knew that the damage had come from other sources. Both of us knew what the episode meant: no matter how much therapy and how much integration, MPD would continue to hang over our heads like a sword of Damocles. Our only solace was that four of us had interceded quickly: Bobby, Wanda, Robert, and Vishakha.

But the healing process always takes time. Vishakha was the quickest to heal among us; within an hour, she was telling me, Robert, "It happened. Let it go." But I knew it would take days, perhaps even weeks, for the aftershocks to pass. It was a terrible setback, a total MPD fracturing that we had not experienced for a long time. Wanda and I retreated to the quiet of our own separate thoughts.

None of us gave much thought to Bobby, who roamed about the apartment, muttering in Chinese, "I'm bad," over and over again. Nobody noticed the afternoon when he opened a bottle of sleeping pills and downed a couple of dozen. Apparently, he immediately changed his mind and tried to purge his stomach in well-practiced bulimic fashion, but his effort was only partially successful. It wasn't until five hours later that Vishakha, having made several unanswered phone calls, rushed back to the apartment and found me lying unconscious on the floor. The first thing I remember was seeing Vishakha and a psychiatric nurse talking to me in the hospital. Somehow we had escaped self-inflicted death.

The following morning, still groggy but partly recovered, I sought to apologize to Vishakha for such a stupid act. The suicide attempt, the first since we had entered therapy fifteen years earlier, left me totally shocked. And I felt responsible—I had been too self-absorbed to notice the rapid deterioration in Bobby's condition. I should have connected with Bobby. I should have scheduled an appointment with Dr. Smith. I should have warned Vishakha of impending danger. I not only felt guilty, but also exceptionally selfish.

Immediately I did what I should have done weeks earlier: I set up an emergency session with Dr. Smith. He understood the situation and was enormously consoling. All of us—Robert, Bobby, and Wanda—pledged that we would never let something like this happen again. Instead, we would learn from the experience, heed the warning signals, and intercede before it was too late.

Instead of chastising us, which is what we expected and thought we deserved, Dr. Smith surprised us. "I know you won't do it again—none of you," he said quietly. "You have too much at stake. Not just your own lives, but also that of Vishakha. Imagine the devastating impact on her. And we would have lost all of you—right after your incredible China discoveries. You're on the brink of a new chapter. All of that—and all of your hard work—would have gone in an instant."

Dr. Smith stopped, as if to keep his composure. "Yesterday, bad as it was, may have been necessary. Now you know what you won't do. And now you can explore what you can do. It may come as a surprise, but I'm proud of you. You—all of you—have turned an important corner."

I watched with astonishment as the highly professional Dr. Smith started to cry. He removed his glasses and accepted my offer of a Kleenex tissue.

No—we won't do it again. We owe it to ourselves, to Vishakha, to Dr. Smith, and to all those we love.

Wanda and I watched Bobby carefully in the aftermath of the suicide attempt. For weeks, he was quiet and sullen. Then, by late summer, his mood became more buoyant. He returned to his guitar playing and Rollerblading. One night, he sent an inner message to us: "I'm sorry. I really didn't think what I was doing. If I killed myself, I know it would have killed all of us. I really won't do it again. Besides, I saw death and it taught me something. Life is tough, but interesting. Death is easy, and possibly boring."

Wanda and I exhaled with relief. Bobby was back, seemingly strengthened by the awful experience. Ironically, as autumn came to the outside world, a bright summer sun finally broke through the clouds over our Meadow. Across the lake, the Castle rested quietly on the hill, a reminder of a past that no longer enchained us. Somewhere above our heads, the great Mountain reached a summit, a long climb that no longer obsessed us. We were no longer eleven, but neither were we one. We were three and we were learning to like who we were, separately and together.

I thought about Bobby's favorite T-shirt, with the message on the front: *Ten percent of life is what happens to you. Ninety percent is how you react to it.* While that philosophy properly emphasizes the ninety percent, it also makes the ten percent all the more valuable. It puts you in the right state of mind for understanding those wonderful apparent accidents that make life worth living. Let me tell you of one such happy accident that changed all of our lives.

What do you do on Christmas Eve in New York if you're not Christian, but rather an eclectic collection of souls—Buddhist (Wanda), humanitarian (me), "light" cult (Bobby), Hindu (Vishakha, at least originally), and Jain (our niece Reema)? This sounds like the start of a bad Internet joke, doesn't it?

Vishakha, of course, had the answer—she looked at the *New York Times* for the best classical music in town and picked All Souls Unitarian Church on Lexington Avenue because it was featuring a Bach oratorio. It was a cold, clear night and All Souls Church looked very pristine in its classic whiteness, with its elegant lines and very tall spire. The Bach performance was fantastic, both the singers and the instrumentalists, just what we wanted.

Now here's the accident part. I looked at the nice little program and discovered, to my consternation, that this wasn't just a musical offering, but a real religious service as well. Trying to overcome my instinctive disappointment, I explained the various parts of a Christian worship service to Reema. Instead of a sermon, the program listed *Homily by Reverend Forrest Church*. Oh, my God, I thought, a homily is sure to be stuffy and dull . . . and can you imagine a preacher who calls himself Church? Only later did I find out that the reverend's real name is Forrest Church, and he is the son of the famous U.S. senator Frank Church.

Reverend Church, looking rather resplendent in his crimson Harvard doctoral gown and grayish white beard, announced that this was his "twenty-seventh Christmas homily." Reverend Church suddenly let fly with the most fiery words I've ever heard from a pulpit. Noting that America was now under Code Orange for a possible terrorist attack, he suggested that what we really needed was an "angel attack." Like the shepherds who were "sore afraid," we should be terrified to our very souls by these angels, who would force us to rethink what we were doing in the world. We should reject fundamentalism of any kind, whether Christian or Muslim, on the grounds that those beliefs "exclude some rather than include all" in their definition of religion. We should recognize that "organized religion has been a greater cause of evil in the world than any other force in history." He welcomed us to come back to All Souls Church (now I understood the name) and told us that the experience would always be "Bible optional."

The preacher's words went through our Meadow like the angel attack he described—a "flash of white phosphorescence." No need for a meeting this time. We all instinctively agreed with Bobby: "fucking fantastic." We restrained the desire to jump up on a pew and clap. When the recessional passed us, I gave Reverend Church a big thumbs-up. He smiled and gave me a warm little punch on the shoulder for thanks. Afterward, I shook his hand at the church portal and said, "Finally, after a lifetime of waiting, I've been to a really great Christmas service."

The next day, I sent Reverend Forrest Church an e-mail telling him a little about my work and asking for a meeting. To make a long story short, we became instant best friends, bonding through lunches, e-mails, dinners with both of our spouses (his wife, Carolyn, is just as remarkable as he is, being a prominent person in the investment world and very active in women's causes). We read each other's books. He is much more prolific than I am, with over twenty titles to his name. *The American Creed* is a must-read.

After we had shared our personal stories, I finally summoned the courage to tell Forrest my MPD story. His response comforted me immediately—nothing judgmental at all, instead an instant sense that "my story" related strongly to "his story." It was Forrest who was adamant that my book be published, "not as your psychological autobiography" but rather as the "autobiographies of your MPD personalities." His comments had the tone of loving insistence—it felt like a "divine command" from someone who didn't talk much about divinity.

When an accident of those proportions occurs, you know there are no real accidents, just people who are receptive and people who aren't. The real truth is that Forrest Church embraced not only me but also all the personalities in the Castle and Black Castle. By gently urging me, Robert, to get out of the way, he gave all of us identities and voices.

Sometimes the most memorable nights on the Meadow were the darkest ones. This particular memorable night featured a black moonless sky with flickering stars and the glowing swath of the Milky Way. It was the kind of night when the three of us huddled together and realized how deeply we were bonded, not just to one another, but to life itself. For the time being, we would remain separate personalities, but we were linked by a common soul.

"It was that night," I recalled to Vishakha, "that we decided to write the book. That night, the three of us—Wanda, Bobby, and me—said that we loved each other. And we agreed about something else—each of us loves you deeply."

"I'm proud of you," she said gently, tears in her eyes. "You're all taking a giant step. It's about truth, light, and love. I love you, too. All of you."

UNDERSTANDING DID THERAPY:
THE CASE OF ROBERT B. OXNAM

by Jeffery Smith, M.D.

I HAD BEEN WORKING with Bob for six months when Tommy first appeared. From previous experience, I knew immediately that the dramatic change in the person in front of me was the kind that happens only with multiple personality. I reflected on the coincidence that Bob, who had consulted me for help with alcoholism, had found someone who had experience with multiple personality as well. Many, if not most, patients are misdiagnosed for years.*

I did not consider myself an expert like Richard Kluft, who had treated

---

*"Bob" was the name of the first person who came to see me. As I became aware of the true complexity of who he was, and the uncertainty of who he would become, it seemed natural and comfortable to stick with the original name.

many DID patients, but, in fact, for the previous several years, I had been deeply immersed in work with my first multiple. She had come into my life in 1977. At that time, *Sybil* had been published, but there was practically no professional literature on the treatment of DID. I had heard of the condition, but had never seen a case, even of simple dissociation. As we worked together, my patient and I learned about healing traumatic wounds. We confronted the most terrible things that could be done to a child. We learned of the survival role of each of her personalities, and how they came to be. We had to learn to deal with multiple agendas, often in conflict, sometimes violently opposed to the therapy itself. In many ways, this patient helped me mature as a therapist and a person. She taught me that multiples have a special "radar" for looking into the emotions of others, including their therapist. This made perfect sense, as her very life had depended on her ability to read her abusers' emotions. Even if I had wanted to be artificial with her (which I didn't), she would have seen through any pretense immediately. As it was, whenever I was afraid or resentful, it would be spotted. I learned that the only way I could help her was by being honest and being myself. I also learned that my humanness, even the weakness that I felt most ashamed of, was ultimately forgivable.

So when Bob's multiplicity came to light, I knew I wanted to work with him. I was afraid that he might prefer to be treated by someone more experienced than myself, but I felt I needed to make the offer anyway. I was pleased that he decided to stay. While MPD is a serious condition and the therapy arduous, the results are typically good. Perhaps this positive outlook is an indication of how successful multiplicity is in protecting the individual from even more extensive trauma damage. The good prognosis is also due to the fact that the acts of acknowledgment and acceptance that lead to healing, though extreme, are all within the range of human possibility.

OVERVIEW OF MULTIPLE PERSONALITY

Multiple personality should not be controversial, nor should it be the subject of sensationalism. It is simply an effective and natural way for a child to cope with inhuman degrees of abuse. Multiple personality is made up of ordinary parts of human experience, rendered extreme by circumstance.

Having started working with multiples when the official diagnosis was *multiple personality disorder,* I tend to prefer that term. It is more direct than the current *dissociative identity disorder,* which may be more precise a term, but seems too abstract. Perhaps best of all, just *multiple personality* is a descriptive term rather than an official one and puts us on strong literary ground. Out of habit, both Bob and I tend to revert to the acronym MPD, even though it is outdated. Please forgive us.

There are different levels of abuse. First, there is the everyday kind that we talk about freely. People manipulate, scream, make threats, hit, control, frighten, bully, and intimidate. Being hurt in these ways is a terrible experience. It is much worse for children, especially when they do not have someone to validate their pain and help them heal. Such experiences may harden us and leave scars, but they are an unfortunate part of what one might call "ordinary" life.

Next, there is the level of abuse that appears in the news. With horror, we learn that children are subjected to sudden violence, rape, and torture. Still, these are "ordinary" crimes.

Then, there is a degree of abuse that most of us would rather not know about. This is the kind that extends over years, or involves those closest to the victims. Reports are scarce. There have been a few trials where, typically, the accused perpetrators look respectable in comparison to the victims. We see flyers with smiling faces of children who are missing. We hear about child pornography, but we are not privy to personal experiences of the children being forced or manipulated into participation. We hear about children who have been molested, then killed, but we avoid imagining the hours before their wish to die came true. These are examples of the kind of inhumanity that we conspire to cover up. It is naturally human to ignore or gloss over the most extreme degrees of helplessness and pain. In my work, I have found that I sometimes shy away from hearing about terrible experiences. Having helped my patients arrive at a willingness to reexperience their pain, I have had to remind myself of the importance of my staying present, as well.

Just as children manage to forget, society has a long history of denying abuse. According to Ernest Jones's biography, when Freud first announced that the cause of hysteria was sexual trauma, he received an "icy reception" from his Viennese colleagues. Soon after, he ceased talking about trauma. Psychoanalysis, likewise, entered into a dark age of ignorance. During my training, in the early seventies, the standard textbook of psychiatry, Freedman and Kaplan, stated that incest was a "rare" occurrence. Soon thereafter, the women's movement brought the truth back for a brief appearance in our collective consciousness. Sadly, the combination of lawsuits and managed care have again encouraged the covering up of reality.

In my view, the controversies surrounding multiple personality have the same source as the disorder itself: the very human wish to avoid acknowledging overwhelming helplessness and pain. A movement has grown up about "false memories," but how is it that we can read about dreadful things happening to children almost daily, and then be told that adult recall of the same kinds of experiences is deluded? Skeptics have tried to argue that multiple personality does not exist, based on the false logic that if one case is questionable, all others must be, too.

Multiple personality begins with dissociation. When we note that adult victims of disaster seem to be in a "daze," we are referring to a degree of dissociation. There is a dis-association of feeling from fact. Trauma survivors will often remember the moment they dissociated. For example, a child who was being molested focused on a spot on the ceiling. Soon she began to experience herself looking down dispassionately from the ceiling as if the girl below were someone else.

Where there is complete amnesia, the dis-association is more extensive, involving memory as well as feeling. If we think of dissociative amnesia as a kind of circuit breaker for emotional trauma, then we can ask, what makes a particular trauma severe enough to trigger loss of memory? The first and most important factor, in my view, is aloneness, the lack of a safe person with whom to share the event. The need for human connection, especially in times of stress, begins very early in life. Before we are old enough to walk, we make use of empathic connections to soften the impact of frightening and painful events. Simply the hope of reuniting with another may be enough to shield us from the full impact of trauma. Prisoners go to great lengths to write on scraps of paper or tap on walls in the hopes of communicating their experience. Even a slim chance of someone knowing strengthens our ability to cope and avoid emotional damage.

A six-year-old girl in the process of being abused by her drunken stepfather was able to keep from being overwhelmed by hoping that her mother would soon return. When her mother did come back, the girl quickly realized that her mother was no more able to stand up to her abuser than she was. Suddenly aware that her hope had been illusory, she did something no six-year-old should do. She ran out of the house alone into the night. Years later, the only thing she remembered was the image of headlights shining in her eyes. Aloneness makes traumatic events much more damaging and dissociation much more likely. It is not clear to what degree the ability to dissociate is inborn, and to what degree it is a skill learned under conditions of trauma. Whatever the balance between the two, when events overwhelm emotional defenses, the damage is less when it can be encapsulated by dissociation.

Trauma survivors who are not able to dissociate often sustain greater damage than those who are able to split. The harm to self-esteem and to the sense of safety affects their entire being. By contrast, multiples often have parts that are entirely spared the effects of trauma. There may be joyful and innocent children existing side by side with those personalities that have been most damaged. Young Bob, full of sensitivity, enthusiasm, and innocence, was spared in this way. In addition, it often appears that remaining frozen at a certain age in childhood is a way to maintain innocence. Like Bobby, alters may remain children until the safety afforded by treatment creates conditions that allow them to resume growth and maturation.

The term *multiple personality* does refer to the most striking feature of the disorder, but it also misplaces the emphasis. The key to making sense of dissociative identity disorder is to look not at the personalities but at the memory barriers between them. We could describe a house in two ways, either as a collection of rooms or as a collection of walls. Both are true, but one cannot construct a house out of rooms. Only walls can be constructed, and rooms are the result. When we first confront multiple personality, we see dramatically different personalities before our eyes. We see rooms, and it is easy to forget that their existence is really a consequence of there being walls—that is, dissociative memory barriers resulting from trauma.

As memory barriers become fixed and are maintained over time, the personalities on opposite sides develop separate histories, values, allegiances, possessions, and relationships. All of us have different sides to ourselves. Multiples are not unique in this way. The difference is that "singletons," as multiples sometimes call the rest of us, have a shared consciousness and memory. We, too, have different facets or parts of themselves, but our sense of our own identity is unitary.

The differences in nonmultiples' behavior from one circumstance to another are often greater than we think. A multiple patient called to leave a message and was surprised when I picked up the phone personally. My voice was not the one she expected. "Oh, you are your secretary," she said. Indeed, my businesslike voice and personality were very different from the me she knew, and the difference was shocking. She came to describe me as "sloshing around" within myself, as opposed to the sharp switches that she experienced. Thus, having different parts is not the exclusive province of multiples, but having amnestic or memory barriers between parts of the self is.

A consequence of memory barriers is the development of sharply distinct personalities that diversify even more over time and are capable of vying for control over the body they inhabit. Given these dramatic differences, and the tendency of alters to emphasize their differences, it is no surprise that both patient and outsider tend to focus on the personalities rather than the barriers that separate them. By moving our focus back to the barriers, we can see that the condition is a natural consequence of the common human capacity for dissociation in the face of trauma.

HOW PREVALENT IS DID?

The Sidran Foundation Web site (www.sidran.org, an excellent starting point for further information) states that the incidence of DID is as high as 1 percent of the population. Bob gives a figure of one in ten thousand. He is quoting my estimate, derived from the following informal calculation.

The area my practice serves has a population of about one million. In almost thirty years of practice, I have seen between two and three thousand patients overall. Among these, I have made first-time diagnoses of DID in four people, excluding those referred because of my interest in dissociation. After I began working with Bob and expressing my interest in DID among colleagues, I began to hear about other cases. I cofounded a study group for therapists with an interest in dissociation, which hosted local conferences. This put me in a position to hear about many of the known cases in our area. From this geographic area, I have personally met about twenty multiples. If we extrapolate to include cases undiagnosed or outside my professional circle, it is easy to imagine a total of five times that number, or one hundred. This works out to one in ten thousand.

My estimate is, in all likelihood, conservative, but I feel comfortable in saying that it is not exaggerated. This number highlights another important aspect of the epidemiology of DID. We know that abuse of children is common, but the figure of one in ten thousand emphasizes that DID arises in families where the level and kinds of abuse are in the extreme category.

WORKING WITH BOB

Before Tommy appeared, I now realize there were clues to Bob's disorder. There were the episodes of explosive rage in which Tommy would briefly take over. These were dramatically "disjunctive"—meaning that there was an abrupt jump in style and behavior. But flying into a rage can also happen in the absence of dissociation. Bob caught my attention when he described how, if asked about work while on his boat, he would become agitated. I noted this but did not actually think of DID. In Bob's case, the diagnosis would have been especially difficult to make because of his particular "architecture." With the exception of the Tommy episodes, I had not observed any switches. Bob was always present on the stage, but sometimes he was animated by Bobby and sometimes by Robbey. He took on their characteristics without actually switching.

Once Tommy had appeared in the office, the diagnosis was clear. From then on, the switching that would happen in sessions was much more classic in appearance. After a few minutes, Bob would seem to run out of things to say. I would ask if there was anyone else who wanted to speak. Bob's eyes would begin to blink. Suddenly his voice would change, his face would look different, and his body would take on a different style of movement. A new conversation would begin with the one who had appeared. I soon developed relationships with distinct "ones of him."

There had been talk in professional circles about hypnosis and "calling out" alters. These techniques seemed entirely too "pushy" to me. First, given the complexity of the system and the vast amount that I did not know about its inner workings, it would have seemed entirely presumptuous to assume that I knew best what needed to be done next. Sometimes I had an idea of what the agenda should be, and sometimes I knew there was resistance to confronting some issue, but overall, it is characteristic of the treatment of multiples that the therapist must tolerate a great deal of ambiguity and not knowing. Second, hypnosis seemed controlling and manipulative, and multiples have already had enough of this type of experience for a lifetime. It seemed to place the doctor too much in charge. My experience of treatment is much more as a partnership in which the patient brings knowledge about his or her inner life and I contribute my understanding of people and my personal reactions. Together, we pool our information and work on healing.

So, in the collaborative style that had worked for me before, I listened, asked questions, and learned about Bob's alters. I thought of some, like Bobby and Young Bob, as manifesting the true needs and wishes of the system. On the other hand, major components of Tommy and the Witch represented internalized attitudes and values from the abusers. I had learned from my earlier experience that even if alters seemed very negative in their outlook, they had originally come into being for the purpose of survival. Pointing out how they had had to "identify with the aggressor" in order to protect the whole could lead to positive alliances even with those personalities who seemed most opposed to the therapy.

One of the most poignant moments in the treatment was a meeting with Tommy sometime after our first encounter. I knew that I had to build a relationship with him for the therapy to succeed. He was physically larger than me, and since our session was held in my private office, there was no one I could summon in case of trouble. On the other hand, I had learned to have great trust in the system. As in political life, when one part of a multiple seems to take over control, the other parts form a silent majority. Just when the minority seems ready to do something irrevocably destructive, the majority reasserts itself to save the day. So as I braced myself for the meeting with Tommy, I was armed with genuine interest and confidence that he, too, was basically there for the purpose of survival. I felt reasonably safe, but knew our meeting could get out of control if events unfolded too fast.

In order to slow things down, I had previously made a wistful announcement that "sometime" I would like to speak with Tommy. I wanted to leave the timing vague so that the system, not the therapist, would choose the moment. That would be far safer than if I forced the issue. Suddenly Tommy was there, snarling and showing his tortured face. His growls were menacing, but the fact that he had appeared was an indication that he was interested in dialogue. I had a feeling that no one had ever listened to him before. Though he would not want to trust me, even Tommy might be touched by someone genuinely interested in him. I persisted in my questions. As I did so, he began to show another side of himself. Beneath the gruff exterior, there was a soul who was indeed doing his best to help the system survive. He was dutifully following orders, but he, too, had a feeling side. Even in our brief encounter, as his vulnerability showed, I felt a strong connection. I found myself feeling a great warmth for Tommy, perhaps because he had been so misunderstood and isolated. Soon he disappeared and Bob returned.

Robbey was more of a problem for me. I had learned that the cardinal rule of DID treatment was to avoid what I call "alterocentrism," forming an alliance with one alter against others. Each personality had his or her own agenda, and would try to pull me into schemes for eliminating or thwarting the others. My patient was the whole Bob, and it was important to reinforce this, even when dealing with one part at a time. I had become accustomed to this dual perspective, relating to each as an individual but not forgetting the whole. However, Robbey's compulsive, rather joyless, detail-oriented style was not mine at all. Between Robbey and Bobby, I had a more natural affinity for the latter's playfulness. Of course Robbey picked up my bias. He chided me for preferring his rival. Like a parent at Christmas, it was my duty to treat each equally and not have favorites. But I knew Robbey was right. I did my lame best to recognize the critical importance of his lists and notes, his memorization and his amazing precision. However, I could not cover up my feeling and had to admit that I did have trouble with his style. Somehow I was forgiven for my feelings, and we managed to have a productive relationship.

Early in the treatment, I could see that one of the most important themes was the imprisonment of Bobby. He was the source of creative energy and joy. My patient would remain exhausted and burned out as long as Bobby's spirit was held down. I could see that the forces working against this were ultimately the internalized attitudes and values of Bob's abusers. Thus, the ongoing theme of the treatment was for him to become freed from the powerful negativity that he had absorbed. The way to do this would be to uncover the truth of what had happened to him. As knowledge of his history unfolded, it would become more clear where the negativity came from. He might have to struggle with it, because such attitudes do not change easily, but there was already a powerful drive to heal and become free.

In the course of clarifying Bob's history, I knew we would first encounter resistance to recall. Having once forgotten, the alters that carried the knowledge would be reluctant to reexperience the trauma, even though this was the only way to heal the wounds. We were going to have to traverse this process of uncovering and healing before we would finally be able to tackle the negativity.

In the meantime, there was a life to live. Bob was having a great deal of trouble at work. He would constantly complain of being exhausted. The tug-of-war between Robbey and Bobby was wearing him out. I tried to help Robbey and Bobby reconcile their differences enough to allow some energy to flow to Bob. This working together was the beginning of another crucial therapeutic process, that of helping the alters to come to respect and later love one another. Only then would their need to remain separate begin to lessen.

TWO THERAPEUTIC GOALS AND TWO HEALING PROCESSES

Let me digress to clarify how I see DID treatment in general. If we boil treatment down to its elements, there are just two therapeutic goals. The first is to process and detoxify the buried memories of trauma and the second is to help the long-separated parts come to know, respect, and ultimately love one another. As these are accomplished, continuing to remain multiple will no longer be a necessity but a choice. The work might focus on trauma at one time and on the relationships between parts at another, but the therapist must keep both goals in mind at all times.

In working toward these goals, we make use of two distinct healing mechanisms. These two are often mistaken for one, which I believe is one of the reasons for continuing confusion about how psychotherapy works. In fact, the two mechanisms have their origins at different points in child development, take a very different time course, and demand different emphasis from the therapist. The first is the mechanism by which painful experiences are detoxified. For reasons which will become clear, I will refer to this by its original name, *catharsis*. The second is the process by which negative values, attitudes, and attachments derived from abusers are modified. I will refer to this healing mechanism as *internalization*. Both mechanisms may be involved in any phase of the therapeutic work.

CATHARSIS

In 1893, based initially on work with Anna O. (who probably had DID), Freud and Breuer published an astonishing discovery: "We found to our great surprise at first, that each individual hysterical symptom immediately and permanently disappeared when we had succeeded in bringing clearly to light the memory of the event by which it was provoked and in arousing its accompanying affect."* This healing mechanism allows for the processing of emotions so that memories of traumatic events no longer evoke the intense distress that originally caused them to be repressed. Note Freud and Breuer's emphasis on both remembering and feeling.

This cathartic healing applies to current trauma as well as to old, remembered trauma. When we experience a distressing moment in everyday life, our first recourse is to share it with someone we trust. As we reexperience the feelings, the other person understands empathically and almost immediately we begin to feel better. Modern behavioral treatments for trauma such as Exposure Therapy and EMDR (Eye Movement Desensitization and Reprocessing) emphasize the same elements as Freud's catharsis: the telling of events and the activation of emotions.

While there is general agreement on the need to remember and to feel, a third and crucial element has systematically been neglected. Regardless of the school of thought, essentially all therapeutic paradigms include a therapist witness. It is obvious to laypeople that one needs an emotionally attuned witness, yet most academic accounts, including Freud's, ignore or underplay this part of the cathartic experience.

Empathy is so important that I have come to use it as an indicator of when

---

*Sigmund Freud and Josef Breuer, *Preliminary Communications, The Standard Edition,* Vol. 2 (London, Hogarth Press, 1893), p. 6.

healing is taking place. If I do not feel the other person's pain, then there must be some block in myself, or something missing in the patient's account that is keeping me from an emotional understanding. It is important to say here that empathy does not mean putting on a solicitous attitude. It is something that happens spontaneously when one human being comes in contact with the details of another's experience. It is also important to note that empathy does not mean a perfect understanding. It is as close as one person can come to understanding another. Thus, in my view, three elements—remembering, feeling, and an empathic context—are the required ingredients for cathartic healing.

In Bob's case, the work with memories revolved mainly around the experiences of Baby and took place over the course of a few weeks. I heard the full range and breadth of terror that was inflicted. During those sessions, my role was much the same as it would have been if I had been present during the immediate aftermath of the events. He shared the experience and I listened and witnessed. Academic accounts of trauma work sometimes focus on the development of a coherent narrative of the events and the working out of issues of responsibility and blame, but in my view, these are part of the other task of therapy, the modification of negative internalized attitudes and values. In the Baby sessions, little discussion or intellectual work was needed, only sharing in an empathic context.

Since the subject of how therapy works has been a prime focus of my professional work and teaching, let me go just a little further to point out that the emotional processing in catharsis follows a pattern that first appears in the infant at about nine months. Starting at that early age, brain development allows children to engage in what Daniel Stern calls "affective attunement."* They begin making use of an emotional connection with mother to soften and manage painful emotions. For example, when a toddler falls, he or she will first make

*Daniel Stern, *The Interpersonal World of the Infant* (US, Basic Books), p. 173.

eye contact with the mother. This happens even before crying begins, and the look on mother's face largely determines whether the child will cry in pain or simply go on playing. This empathic affect regulation continues to be an important part of the ability to cope with adversity. It is this early form of affect regulation that later provides the basis for catharsis in psychotherapy.

Work with trauma patients shows dramatically that catharsis alone is not enough for treatment to be successful. A predictable part of the experience of trauma is the internalization of negative attitudes and values. These do not change easily, and even sharing them with an understanding other hardly makes a dent. These unhealthy values and attitudes take much longer to change, and require great persistence on the part of both patient and therapist. In fact, the dramatic differences between the cathartic healing of painful memories and the laborious modification of internalized negative attitudes are of such magnitude that they suggest that the two are entirely different psychological processes.

INTERNALIZATION

Internalization is both the mechanism by which trauma causes negative attitudes, values, and attachments to become part of the self, and the means by which they can later be replaced by positive ones. Often, as in Bob's case, negative internalizations can hinder the uncovering of traumatic memories. Some alters may feel that it is their duty to keep the past secret. This is an example of a value that has become deeply embedded in the makeup of that alter. Alters may also embody the attitude that they are not deserving of help or healing. Treatment may have to overcome these internalized barriers before memories can come to light and the patient healed. In addition, conflicting and incompatible attitudes and values may play a major role in keeping alters from accepting one another. Finally, for multiples as well as other trauma survivors, internalized negative attitudes must change for the patient to be able to accept a happier and more successful life.

A full account of how internalizations are laid down and later modified is beyond the scope of this essay, but I will present a brief synopsis.*

Briefly, my work has led me to believe that the trigger for all internalizations is the experience of potential aloneness. At moments when we are feeling vulnerable in our connections with others, we are most susceptible to internalizing attitudes, values, and attachments. In the case of trauma, these vulnerable moments are precisely the ones that occur when we are most at the mercy of the abuser. It is not surprising, then, that the negative attitudes that trauma patients internalize are closely reflective of those overtly expressed by the abusers or embodied in their actions. The Stockholm syndrome and the mechanism of "identification with the aggressor" seem to refer to the same phenomenon. In addition, in my view, the same mechanism applies to the way we acquire values in childhood, and later to the way more positive values are internalized in therapy.

In childhood, Allan Schore and others have described how at about eighteen months, maturation of the frontal lobes of the cerebral cortex begins to permit essentially permanent internalization of values, attitudes, and attachments.[†] This is an important advance. The younger toddler can manage painful feelings by making empathic contact with mother, but has little ability to restrain his or her behavior. However empathic she may be, mother's patience begins to wear thin as all the pots and pans in the cabinet are spread out on the kitchen floor. Increasingly, the only way to prevent a painful disruption of the mother–child bond is for the child to develop the ability to keep behavior within an internalized template of what is acceptable. These templates are the precursors of values and attitudes. At the same

---

*Jeffery Smith, "Reexamining Therapeutic Action Through the Lens of Trauma," *Journal of the American Academy of Psychoanalysis and Dynamic Psychiatry*, 32 (Winter 2004), pp. 613–31.

[†]Allan N. Schore, *Affect Regulation and the Origin of the Self* (Hillsdale, NJ, Lawrence Erlbaum Associates, 1994).

time, the maturation of the brain allows the child to begin to feel shame when he or she fails to adhere to these incipient codes of acceptable action.

Note that just as in the case of trauma, the situation in which early internalizations take place is one that poses a potential threat to the mother–child bond. Again, I believe it is at moments of vulnerability that the parents' values and attitudes are internalized. Toilet training gives us an example. As the child continues to remain in diapers, there is increasingly a challenge, if not a threat, to the parent–child connection. Conversely, the child's internalization of the parents' positive feeling about cleanliness strengthens the connection. This internalized value becomes a permanent part of the self. As adults, even when it is involuntary, we feel shame for failing to adhere to these early childhood values.

How, then, can negative attitudes and values, internalized at moments of trauma, be replaced in therapy? I believe that the process is the same as the one that led to their acquisition. Old values and attitudes are not removed, but layered over with new, healthy ones. Therapists may be shocked at the notion that we, ourselves, might be the source of new values and attitudes. We feel strongly that it is not our role to impose our personal values on our patients. On the other hand, to our patients, we cannot help but represent the value of health over sickness, and like it or not, what is transmitted often goes beyond this basic attitude. Work with trauma patients has shown that an actively positive stance is helpful, if not required, to counteract the patient's feelings of low self-worth.

What, then, about the subtle sense of vulnerability to loss of connection that triggers internalization? Indeed, it has been observed that if the therapy is too cozy, if we are too closely bonded with the patient, then change does not take place. I would suggest that the moments when the patient internalizes more positive values and attitudes are those that occur when there is a feeling of vulnerability. The patient senses an "expectancy" on the part of the therapist. In working with Bob, the expectancy often came in the form of silence or a smile that conveyed the message that "I know this is hard, but you can handle it." Interestingly, the stance of expectancy that fosters change in values and attitudes is subtly different from the empathic closeness that is best at moments of catharsis. As a therapist, one can be both empathic and expectant at the same time, but catharsis calls for an emphasis on the former and internalization on the latter.

Fortunately, in most instances, even with trauma, there are positive attitudes and values that have been internalized early in life, before the negative ones. In treatment, these positive values can be reawakened rather than having to be created. This makes the task much easier. On the other hand, unlike catharsis, which seems to yield permanent healing, internalization only layers positive values over the negative ones. It remains possible, under adverse cir-cumstances, for the old negativity to be retriggered and to take over. In order to cement the positive values and maintain the gains, it is important that life become more satisfying and lead to a healthy stream of positive experiences.

It is important to note that internalization works differently with multi-ples than it does with others. What is internalized belongs to one alter, not to the whole. When negative values are internalized, because of the nature of the abuse, they are often extreme. Some alters become the embodiments of destructive and self-negating attitudes so that others can be spared. This nat-urally leads to tensions among alters, rather than ambivalence within oneself, as is the case with other trauma survivors. In fact, it is the healing of these tensions that constitutes the major therapeutic goal along with the healing of painful experiences. Thus, internalization is the key therapeutic process in promoting the goal of bringing alters together, while catharsis is the process most closely allied to working with traumatic memories. At the same time, as I have pointed out, each healing process has a place in both therapeutic tasks.

In Bob's case, it was the Witch who held much of the negativity. Other alters, such as Tommy and Bobby, had to follow her orders but did not fully embody the negation of self. For the Witch to become Wanda and eventually join with Robert and Bobby, something drastic had to change in her values and attitudes.

When I first met the Witch, she was hostile and angry, but my curiosity did elicit something very important. I found out that she was driven by a need for fairness. She was outraged at what she saw as unfair treatment to Bob's abusers. Thus, I found that underneath her negativity, there was a sense of justice that was even stronger. As a champion of justice and fairness, she could begin to evolve into the spiritual Wanda of today. As her sense of fairness was understood and respected, she was able, with amazing ease, to revert to a deeper layer at which she revealed a positive attitude toward life. However, as happened several times, certain circumstances, especially humiliation, were able to trigger the return of the Witch, ready to denigrate and punish.

INTEGRATION

At the beginning of his DID treatment, Bob was interested in moving rapidly toward integration. Now, with an appreciation of the role of incompatible attitudes and values in keeping alters apart, we can see how both catharsis and healthy internalization had to take place before integration could become a possibility. Of course there was resistance. As often happens, rather than change their attitudes, alters prefer to eliminate the one with whom they disagree. In this case, I have to explain what I call the "law of conservation of persons"—that is, the belief that no part of the self can be eliminated. If we take a less "alterocentric" view, it is obvious that memories, feelings, capacities, experiences, and attachments belonging to any part also belong to the whole and therefore cannot be eliminated.

As alters move toward integration, the dissociative barriers soften a little at a time. For example, an alter who starts with no knowledge of another alter gradually comes to know about the latter's existence. Next, he or she may begin to hear the other's voice inside his or her head. This leads somehow to knowing what the other is feeling and, finally, to experiencing this as if it were his or her own feeling, too. This sharing of knowledge and feeling is known as *co-consciousness*.

When integration happens, there is considerable individual variability in the way it does so. Those times when I have been present, the experience has been quietly dramatic. During treatment of another DID patient, at one moment I was saying a sad good-bye to someone I had grown close to. Within seconds, she was gone, but her characteristic sense of humor and some aspects of her voice and facial expressions were uncannily superimposed on another personality that had not manifested such traits before. In Bob's case, one integration took place at the end of a session as he was on his way from the chair to the door. He simply told me that it had happened. Later integrations took place privately.

Perhaps it would be better to make a distinction between *fusion* and *integration*. It is possible for alters to fuse into one, but just as in corporate mergers, there needs to be a lot of processing of "cultural differences." While memories, skills, and knowledge can easily be pooled, differing values do not easily coexist. For nonmultiples, dealing with internal conflict is part of life. We have mixed feelings about many things. Much of the work of psychotherapy has to do with working out unconscious conflicts of values. When DID patients deal with conflict, it is experienced as a conflict between alters. The jockeying that goes on among alters is, in effect, the equivalent of singletons' struggle with internal conflicts. As DID patients approach integration, they are shocked to find themselves inheritors of internal conflict. They are often taken by surprise since they have little experience in dealing with such conflict. As is evident in Bob's story, much of the real work of integration is the gradual working out of conflicting and contradictory values and attitudes.

When therapists are too enthusiastic about integration, patients tend to become suspicious of their motives. The decision of whether to integrate is best left to the patient. Eventually, as in Bob's case, the disadvantages of remaining separate begin to weigh heavily. I remain curious to see whether his current triumvirate of co-conscious alters will move toward a final integration or remain as distinct as they are today.

GROWING

Growth and maturation may not be the explicit focus of DID treatment, but they are often a result. Alters who are frozen in time begin to grow through stages of development. As stated above, the central theme of Bob's recovery was the integration of Bobby's joy and energy into the whole self. In order for that to happen, Bobby himself had to undergo a process of maturation. As the intensive therapy ended and I began to see Bob less often, at each meeting, I was interested to see how Bobby had grown. Each time, I would ask Bobby how old he felt. He went through clearly recognizable phases from early adolescence to adulthood, shaped by his experiences and the need to adapt to the realities of his world.

Often the growth was accompanied by great pain, as it is in nonmultiple life. I suppose I was annoyingly "shrinklike" in smiling knowingly when Bobby was up against something painful that I knew was going to make him grow. While he hoped he could find a way around a situation, I would be wanting him to face it head-on. Each time he did face the situation directly, he came out the stronger for it. Some of the situations were terrible, as when the plans for his book were leaked. I hoped that he would not lose his idealism and internalize a new negativity.

How it is that some alters, such as Young Bob and Baby, can be integrated without growing, while others must grow before integration can take place, is not clear to me. This is one of the reasons why I believe therapists must guide with a light touch. There is so much that we cannot anticipate or know in advance. The same is true when we are dealing with the question of which alter might become the "final" one. Therapists may be tempted to assume that a single dominant alter will eventually subsume the others. Such assumptions often turn out to be wrong. When Bob's multiplicity first appeared, neither Robert nor Wanda was anywhere to be seen. Multiples seem to have their own blueprint for healing, and one of the main contributions a therapist can make is to recognize and value the patient's inner direction.

WHAT THE REST OF US CAN LEARN FROM THE DID EXPERIENCE

There are three important ways that all of us can learn from the experience of multiple personality. The first is that we all "slosh around" in our own beings more than we realize. We think of ourselves as one when we are arguably a collection of different facets. The second lesson of multiple personality is that dissociation is a much more common experience than we generally realize. The third is that emotional growth is not just for the young. It can be resumed where it was left off regardless of the amount of time that may have passed.

With the availability of such new techniques as brain scans that show the immediate effects of mental activity, the field of neurophysiology is a source of much excitement. One current area of active research is the difference between *explicit memory* and *implicit memory*. Explicit memory is processed for storage in a structure known as the hippocampus, while implicit memory is more diffusely spread out in the brain. Simply stated, *explicit* refers to that which is in the foreground of our consciousness and accessible to language, while *implicit* refers to the background, or context, and is nonverbal.

Thus, when my patient pointed out that I was "my secretary," I was taken by surprise. Once she had pointed it out, though, it was obvious, but before that, the knowledge was implicit, or background, information. It had not occurred to me that I was "different" when I answered the phone. On the other hand, when I was in session with my patient, I was "tuned in" to her world. It was not artificial, or even voluntary, that my voice, manner, and inner feeling were drastically different. Her world called out a different facet of myself. When she brought this to my attention, my awareness of my own states moved from background to foreground, from implicit to explicit. As awareness shifted from background to foreground, I could do more with it. I could attach words and "think" about what the words represented. This experience has left me much more conscious of the variability of facets in what I used to think of as a unitary self. I have learned much more than I would otherwise have known about how different facets of my personality correspond to different desires and goals that are more loosely "integrated" than I might have thought.

This distinction is important in understanding how we slosh around within ourselves. Explicitly, those of us who are not multiple think of ourselves as "a" person. We identify that person with a name and personal characteristics. This single identity is in the foreground. However, in the background, the reality is more complex. There may be many sets of feelings or feeling states, perhaps associated with different situations and surroundings. These different facets of ourselves may be incompatible, even contradictory. Since they are not in our foreground consciousness, we tend to gloss over the degree of incongruity. Much of the time, the differentness remains in the background, unrecognized.

Multiples and nonmultiples can benefit equally from addressing internal conflicts and contradictions. This is one of the major goals of any psychotherapy. Contradictions in values and desires often cause significant problems. For resolution, one value must win out over another, or a compromise must be found. Young Bob's innocence and idealism were in conflict with Robert's pragmatism and Bobby's desire to do what felt good. As I said, nonmultiples experience the same thing as internal conflict. Just as Bob was unaware of his multiplicity, our assumed unity of self tends to make us unaware of our contradictions until some outward factor forces acknowledgment.

Whether for multiple personality or for the dysfunctional patterns that afflict so many, a main purpose of psychotherapy is to bring these contradictions into explicit consciousness in order to facilitate their resolution.

A second lesson to be learned from Bob's experience is that dissociation is more common than we tend to think. Dr. Herbert Spiegel of Columbia University once said in a lecture on hypnosis, "I would hope my surgeon is in a trance." What he meant was that doing surgery requires a level of concentration that shuts out all distractions. For all of us, it is common to focus so intently on something that we lose awareness of our surroundings. Athletes, for example, often do not notice an injury until after a competition. This probably represents a form of dissociation. We are not surprised when we hear that an individual was "in a daze" following the death of a loved one, but we tend not to connect this phenomenon with its mechanism—dissociation. Posttraumatic stress disorder has become a household word, but people who use the term are often unaware that key symptoms of the disorder involve dissociation. Indeed, the American Psychiatric Association DSM-IV criteria for the diagnosis include "inability to recall an important aspect of the trauma," a feeling of "detachment or estrangement from others," and a "restricted range of affect."

A third lesson comes from the courage to change that Bob showed. His resumption of unfinished growth and development, left off in childhood, is dramatic but not exceptional. It is common to say that you "can't teach an old dog new tricks," but my experience has been different. Difficulty in undergoing change is not a function of age. Rather, I have come to believe that we actively resist change, in large part through myths we create about who we are. We doggedly hold on to behavior patterns and attitudes that keep us stuck. When change must happen, age does not turn out to be the barrier one might think it is. When he first came to see me for treatment, Bob presented as a successful executive, burned out in his job and drinking too much. He could have soldiered on in his unhappiness, as so many do, but forces from within seemed to propel him toward change. First, he was successful in confronting alcoholism. His hard work in recovery led to the unmasking of his multiplicity. At that point, Bob was not afraid to take on a process of change without knowing where it would lead.

For the rest of us, like Bob, fear of changing the concept we hold of our own identity may be the biggest blockage to growth and healing. "Oh, that's me, I always . . ." is easy to say, but is often fundamental to maintaining behavior patterns and attitudes that cover up contradictions and prevent them from being resolved. Bob's journey should remind us that we can always ask why and that there is no cutoff date for exploring the amazing hidden reaches of our own being.